VIRTUE

Readings in Moral Theology No. 16

Previous volumes in this series

VIRTUE

Readings in Moral Theology No. 16

Edited by
Charles E. Curran
and
Lisa A. Fullam

PAULIST PRESS
New York • Mahwah, NJ

Cover design by Lynn Else

Library of Congress Cataloging-in-Publication Data

Virtue / edited by Charles E. Curran and Lisa A. Fullam.
    p. cm. — (Readings in moral theology ; no. 16)
  ISBN 978-0-8091-4685-7 (alk. paper)
  1. Virtue. 2. Ethics. I. Curran, Charles E. II. Fullam, Lisa.
  BV4630.V58 2011
  241′.4—dc22

                                                          2010046151

Published by Paulist Press
997 Macarthur Boulevard
Mahwah, New Jersey 07430

www.paulistpress.com

Printed and bound in the
United States of America

Contents

PART THREE:
SPECIFIC VIRTUES

Acknowledgments

We are most grateful to the following authors and publishers for the permission to reprint the articles in this volume. Romanus Cessario, *The Moral Virtues and Theological Ethics*, 2d ed. (Notre Dame, IN: University of Notre Dame Press, 2008), 76–79. © 2008 by the University of Notre Dame. Reprinted with permission. Stanley Hauerwas and Charles Pinches, *Christians Among the Virtues: Theological Conversations with Ancient and Modern Ethics* (Notre Dame, IN: University of Notre Dame Press, 1997), 149–65. © 1997 by the University of Notre Dame. Reprinted with permission. Brad J. Kallenberg, "The Master Argument of MacIntyre's *After Virtue*," in Nancey Murphy, Brad J. Kallenberg, and Mark Thiessen Nation, eds., *Virtues and Practices in the Christian Tradition: Christian Ethics After MacIntyre* (Notre Dame, IN: University of Notre Dame Press, 1997), 7–29. © 1997 by Trinity Press International. Reprinted in 2003 by the University of Notre Dame Press. Reprinted with permission. Stephen J. Pope, "Overview of the Ethics of Thomas Aquinas," in Stephen J. Pope, ed., *The Ethics of Aquinas*, 37–46. © 2002 by Georgetown University Press. Reprinted with permission. www.press.georgetown.edu. Charles E. Curran, *The Catholic Moral Tradition Today: A Synthesis*, 111–30 plus endnote pages. © 1999 by Georgetown University Press. Reprinted with permission. www.press. georgetown.edu. William F. May, "The Virtues in a Professional Setting," *Annual of the Society of Christian Ethics* (1984): 71–91, published by the Society of Christian Ethics and reprinted with permission. Jean Porter, "Moral Language and the Language of Grace: The Fundamental Option and the Virtue of Charity," *Philosophy & Theology* 10 (1997): 169–98. Reprinted with permission. Louke van Wensveen, *Dirty Virtues: The Emergence of Ecological Virtue Ethics* (Amherst, NY: Humanity Books, 2000), 115–29. © 2000 by Louke van Wensveen. Used with permission of the author and publisher. James F. Keenan, "Virtue Ethics and Sexual Ethics," *Louvain Studies* 30, no. 3 (2005): 180–97. Reprinted with permission. Anne Patrick, "Narrative and the Social Dynamics of Virtue," in *Changing Values and Virtues*, ed. Dietmar Mieth and Jacques Pohier, *Concilium* 191 (Edinburgh: T. & T. Clark, 1987), 69–80. Reprinted with permission. Paul J. Wadell, *Happiness and the Christian Moral Life: An Introduction to Christian Ethics* (Lanham, MD: Rowan & Littlefield, 2008), 219–36. Reprinted with permission. Lisa A. Fullam, *The Virtue of Humility. A Thomistic Apologetic* (Lewiston, NY: The Edwin Mellen Press, 2009), 135–73. Reprinted with permission.

Foreword

This volume on virtue is the sixteenth volume in the series *Readings in Moral Theology* from Paulist Press. Richard A. McCormick and Charles E. Curran began editing this series in 1979, and the series has continued after McCormick's death in February 2000. Lisa A. Fullam, who specializes in virtue ethics, has joined Curran as the coeditor of this volume.

This series brings together previously published articles dealing with a common theme. Very light editing has occasionally been done to adapt the articles for this volume on virtue ethics. Three criteria ground the selection of articles. First, this volume attempts to cover enough of the important aspects of virtue ethics that the reader will gain a fairly complete understanding of the topic. Second, as always in this series, we have attempted to give a fair and objective picture of what is happening in Catholic moral theology by including a range of pertinent perspectives, including those of conservatives and liberals, senior and younger scholars, women and men. Third, the volume attempts to include the most significant contributors to the discussion on virtue, as exemplified in the monographs or important articles they have written, or at least summary essays describing the work of those major contributors. Such a criterion has a twofold purpose: to recognize and thereby give credit to those who have made the most significant contributions, and to make the reader aware of the major figures in the field.

Virtue is a most important subject in moral theology, but until a few decades ago it lived mostly in the shadows of the discipline. In recent decades, writing on virtue has reemerged spectacularly in both philosophical and theological ethics. In the realm of Roman Catholic theological ethics, the primary emphasis of this volume, this return to the language of virtue finds its roots in the mid-twentieth-century turn to the subject.

What is virtue ethics? Most traditional ethical reflection begins with questions about the rightness or wrongness of particular actions.

Virtue ethics starts instead with the insight that our actions, by and large, are not isolated decisions that we make, but arise from our character, the deeper complement of typical patterns of behavior that we exhibit, and the values that we hold. These character traits are not static, but are shaped and reshaped continually by the actions we choose and our reflection on those actions and their meaning in our lives. In an ethics of virtue, questions about actions find their moral valence in light of their effect on character.

The authors in this volume work from (or contribute to the reformation of) the Thomistic/Aristotelian tradition of virtue ethics. In this school of thought, virtues are good habits of character that describe the content of human flourishing, individually and communally. Out of those good habits we tend, by and large, to do morally right actions and thereby become better, more virtuous people overall. Moral theology needs to give attention to principles and particular cases, but virtue alone contributes to the very making of the moral person.

This book is geared for the use of graduate students and upper-level undergraduate students in moral theology. The primary problem facing the editors was the need to make the difficult choices necessary to keep the size and price of the volume reasonable. Readers who find this small buffet of readings in virtue ethics of interest are therefore encouraged to read more deeply in the field and to discover for themselves the many worthy contributions we were unable to represent here.

This volume on virtue unfolds in three parts. The first part considers virtue ethics in general, the second part focuses on virtue ethics in particular spheres, and the third part discusses significant individual virtues in the Christian life.

Part 1, on virtue ethics in general, begins with a summary of Thomas Aquinas's approach to virtue ethics. Thomas Aquinas has been the most significant historical figure in Catholic theology in general and in virtue theory in particular. Stephen J. Pope, the author of this chapter, is professor of theology at Boston College and the editor of the widely acclaimed volume T*he Ethics of Aquinas*. On the U.S. philosophical scene no one has contributed more to the discussion of virtue than Alasdair MacIntyre, whose 1981 book *After Virtue: A Study in Moral Theory* has become a landmark volume. The second chapter in this volume is Brad J. Kallenberg's discussion of MacIntyre's approach.

Kallenberg, with interests in both Christian ethics and philosophical theology, teaches at the University of Dayton. The third chapter comes from Charles E. Curran, a coeditor of this volume and a prominent Catholic revisionist theologian now teaching at Southern Methodist University. Here, Curran develops the Catholic tradition on virtue found in Aquinas and presents a contemporary synthesis. The final chapter in part 1 recognizes the importance of historicity, narrative, and feminism in understanding virtue today. The author, Anne Patrick, emerita professor from Carleton College, has emphasized these aspects in many of her important writings.

Part 2 considers the relationship of virtue to particular spheres of human life—professional life, sexuality, feminism and ecology, and life in the world generally. In chapter 5, William F. May, professor emeritus at Southern Methodist University, develops the role of virtue in the life of professionals such as physicians, lawyers, pastors, and others. This was a seminal article that was fully developed in May's elegant 2001 volume, *Beleaguered Rulers: The Public Obligation of the Professional.* In the following chapter, James F. Keenan recognizes that sexuality involves the virtue of chastity but also needs what he calls "the other cardinal virtues today"—justice, fidelity, self-care, and prudence. Keenan, of Boston College, has been a major contributor to virtue ethics in the Catholic theological tradition. Chapter 7 covers virtue and the very important issue of ecological ethics, which many see from a feminist perspective. Louke van Wensveen, now an independent ethics scholar and consultant in the Netherlands, formerly taught at Loyola Marymount University in Los Angeles and has written extensively on religion and ecology. In chapter 8, Paul J. Wadell reimagines the world in light of the Christian virtue of justice. Wadell, professor at St. Norbert College, has written extensively on the virtues in general and friendship in particular.

Part 3 considers some specific virtues. Jean Porter's chapter deals with the Thomistic virtue of charity and its relationship to the fundamental option and sin. This is the longest chapter in this volume but it recognizes the very important role that Notre Dame's Jean Porter has played in developing Thomistic virtue ethics in the United States. Chapter 10 develops prudence, which in many ways is the most important virtue in the Christian moral life, but has often not been recognized as such. Romanus Cessario, the author of this chapter, teaches systematic theology at St. John's Seminary in the Archdiocese of Boston and has written well-received monographs in both moral and systematic theology. Chapter 11 discusses the significant virtue of courage from the somewhat unique perspective of Stanley Hauerwas of Duke University. Hauerwas is the most productive Protestant ethicist in the United States and has contributed more than any other Protestant scholar to the understanding of virtue. His coauthor, Charles Pinches of the University of Scranton, was an early doctoral student of Hauerwas at Notre Dame and has made his own contribution to moral theology in his several published volumes. The final chapter deals with humility, a very important but often neglected or misunderstood virtue in Christian moral life. The author, coeditor Lisa A. Fullam of the Jesuit School of Theology of Santa Clara University, is author of a recent book on humility.

The editors want to express their appreciation to those who helped in producing this volume. We especially thank the authors whose work we have used and the publications in which their work first appeared. Lawrence Boadt, CSP, the late president of Paulist Press, encouraged us to continue this long-running series. Paul McMahon, the former managing editor of Paulist Press, was most helpful in guiding us and most prompt in responding to all our queries. The editors are very grateful for the assiduous and careful work by our students in preparing this volume, in particular Josh Mauldin and Christopher Dowdy, doctoral students in the graduate program in religious studies at Southern Methodist University, and Katherine Hennessey, doctoral student in ethics and social theory at the Graduate Theological Union in Berkeley, CA. One of the joys of theological scholarship is to join in the process by which students become colleagues. We hope this experience has been helpful for them.

Charles E. Curran and Lisa A. Fullam

Part One

VIRTUE ETHICS
IN GENERAL

1. Virtue Ethics in Thomas Aquinas

Stephen J. Pope

This chapter first appeared in Stephen J. Pope, ed., *The Ethics of Aquinas* (Washington, DC: Georgetown University Press, 2002).

The *Secunda secundae* of Aquinas turns from general ethical considerations to the practical challenge of living a Christian moral life. In it, James A. Weisheipl explains, Aquinas "completely revised Lombard's discussion of moral questions, synthesizing man's return to God through the virtues (*secunda pars*) in much the same order as Aristotle treats man's search for happiness in the *Nicomachean Ethics*."[1] Everything in the *Summa* to this point builds to the culminating discussion of this journey to God. The *Secunda secundae* can thus be read as essentially a long disquisition on the virtues or, just as aptly, though with a somewhat more explicitly religious emphasis, as an extended discussion of what is now called "spirituality."

STRUCTURE OF THE *SECUNDA SECUNDAE*

The *Secunda secundae* first examines specific virtues relevant to all human beings (IIa IIae, qq. 1–170) and then those virtues pertaining to particular callings (qq. 171–89). Most of this section of the *Summa* is concerned with the former, which consists of the three theological virtues of faith (qq. 1–16), hope (qq. 17–22), and charity (qq. 23–46) and the four cardinal virtues of prudence (qq. 47–56), justice (qq. 57–122), fortitude (qq. 123–40), and temperance (qq. 141–70). The treatment of acts pertaining only to certain individuals examines first the diversity of gratuitous graces of prophecy, rapture, tongues, preaching, and miracles (qq. 171–78), then the diversity of active and contemplative lives (qq. 179–82), and finally the diversity of states of life, especially the acts of those seeking to live a life of charity through serving the church (qq. 184–89). While Aquinas referred to the latter as "the state of perfection," this language should not be confused with moral perfection (q. 184, a. 4). "States of perfection" include the episcopal state (q. 185) and the "religious state" of those who have been professed in religious orders (qq. 186–89), which Aquinas described as "a school for attaining to the perfection of charity" (q. 186, a. 3).[2]

From beginning to end, the *Secunda secundae* conceives of the Christian life as essentially one of growth in faith, hope, and charity. The cardinal virtues of prudence, justice, temperance, and fortitude are discussed after the theological virtues because they are understood to be retained and perfected within the Christian life. Because nature is perfected by grace (Ia, q. 1, a. 8), the will is perfected by charity, reason by faith, and the cardinal virtues by the theological virtues. One moves toward the ultimate end most *commonly* through growth in the virtues but in the most *excellent* way through the gifts (Ia IIae, q. 69, a. 1)—dispositions through which one is made more readily amenable to the movement of the Holy Spirit (q. 68, a. 1). Although the sequence of treatment varies from virtue to virtue, each virtue is examined in terms of the same standard conceptual categories. These include the virtue itself, its distinctive acts, its subject and its object, its causes, and its effects. After examining its basic identity, Aquinas expounded the virtues associated with it, the vices opposed to it, and the precepts to which it gives rise. The late treatment of the precepts in this order of presentation indicates that they exist to serve growth in virtue and not vice versa. Each virtue is complemented with a corresponding gift, or gifts, of the Holy Spirit.

Aquinas coordinated the seven central virtues of the Christian life with the seven gifts of the Holy Spirit, long associated by St. Gregory with the Book of Job and by St. Augustine with the seven virtues of the Holy Spirit mentioned in the Gospel of Matthew (ibid.). Faith is complemented by the gift of *understanding* that perfects the apprehension of truth in speculative reasoning and the gift of *knowledge* that perfects good judgment in speculative reasoning; hope by the gift of the fear of the Lord; charity by the gift of wisdom; prudence by the gift of counsel; justice by the gift of piety; courage by the gift of fortitude; temperance by the gift of fear (the last is discussed in Ia IIae, q. 68, a. 4, but not actually in the treatment of the virtue of temperance).

THE THEOLOGICAL VIRTUES OF FAITH, HOPE, AND CHARITY

Aquinas examined faith in light of his standard categories: faith itself (IIa IIae, q. 1), the act of faith (qq. 2– 3), the virtue (q. 4), those who have faith (q. 5), its cause and effects (qq. 6– 7), and the gifts of understanding and knowledge (qq. 8–9). He next turned to what is opposed to the virtue of faith: unbelief in general (q. 10), heresy (q. 11), apostasy (q. 12), blasphemy (qq. 13–14), and the vices opposed to the gifts of knowledge and understanding (q. 15). He concluded with an examination of the precepts relating to faith, knowledge, and understanding (q. 16).

Faith is a gift of grace that allows for an assent of the mind, commanded by the will, to propositions on the basis of divine authority (q. 1; q. 2, a. 2). Such faith generates a firm conviction of the truth of what is believed. This "inner act of faith" is complemented with an "outer act of faith," the public confession of what one believes as a matter of Christian faith (q. 3, aa. 1– 2).

Hope, which receives the briefest treatment among the theological virtues, is examined first as the virtue itself (q. 17) and its subject (q. 18), the gift of fear (q. 19), the opposing vices of despair (q. 20) and presumption (q. 21), and finally the precepts related to hope and fear. Through the theological virtue of hope, the Christian believes that he or she will be granted the good of eternal happiness that lies in the vision of God (q. 17, a. 2). Hope strives for the enjoyment of God himself and ought not be confused with the "mercenary love" (*amor mercenarius*) that uses God as a means to other goods (q. 19, a. 4, ad 3). Hope gives the believer a confident movement toward the future that enables him or her to overcome everything that restricts this movement to God. Hope moves the believer from the desire to avoid punishment that characterizes "servile fear" (*timor servilis*) to the love of God that marks "filial fear" (*timor filialis*; q. 19, a. 5). Grace-inspired confidence leads the Christian away from the twin evils of presumption and despair (q. 21).

Faith precedes hope and hope precedes charity (q. 17, aa. 7–8)— hence the order of Aquinas's presentation. Yet the *Secunda secundae* gives more attention to the theological virtue of charity (qq. 23–46) than to the other theological virtues (qq. 1–22); indeed, it devotes roughly the same number of questions to charity as to the other two virtues combined. The significance of the length of treatment should not be overemphasized, of course. Thomas devotes only nine questions to prudence (qq. 47–56), which he considers foremost among the cardinal virtues. Yet the virtue of charity clearly plays a central role in the schema of the *Secunda secundae*. In charity, people attend the end for which they exist; in this virtue, the human desire for happiness is satisfied completely; it alone, among the theological virtues, is retained in eternal life. Thus, whereas the *Prima secundae* examines the essential components that play a dynamic role in the human quest for happiness (the will, emotions, habits, law, grace), the *Secunda secundae* explains how grace brings these elements into a dynamic and transformative unity in the infused virtue of charity, the "form of all the virtues" (q. 23, a. 8).

The *Summa* examines, first, charity in itself (q. 23), its subject (q. 24), its object (q. 25) and its acts, including love (q. 27), and its effects (qq. 28–33). It treats first its interior effects in joy (q. 28), peace (q. 29), and mercy (q. 30), and then its exterior effects in acts of beneficence (q. 31), almsgiving (q. 32), and fraternal correction (q. 33). This discussion is followed by an inquiry into the four kinds of vice opposed to charity: first, hatred, the vice opposed to charity itself (q. 34); second, the vices opposed to joy: sloth (q. 35) and envy (q. 36); third, the vices opposed to peace: discord (q. 37), contention (q. 38), schism (q. 39), war (q. 40), strife (q. 41), and sedition (q. 42); and last, the vice opposed to beneficence: scandal (q. 43). After the virtue and its opposite vices, this treatise examines the precepts of charity (q. 44) and then completes this analysis with a discussion of the gift of wisdom (q. 45) and the vice opposed to it, folly (q. 46).

Charity is fundamentally the grace-inspired friendship of the human person for God (q. 23, a. 1). It is not to be confused with what modern philosophers came to call "altruism," and even less with philanthropic "charity." The love of friendship includes three marks: benevolence, mutuality, and communication in a shared good (q. 23, a. 1). Aquinas adopted these traits from Book VIII of the *Nicomachean Ethics*, but its unmistakably Christian character is seen in the affirmation that God wills fellowship with humans, and that, through grace, people can become friends with God.

Charity is something created in the soul, and is thus not simply the direct action of the Holy Spirit in the person (q. 23, a. 2); it generates a special kind of love that has as its object divine good (q. 23, a. 4). Charity is the greatest of all the virtues because it enables us to rest in God, the ultimate and principal good (q. 23, a. 7). God is the primary object of charity, and through it one loves all that God loves. It therefore embraces the neighbor (q. 25, a. 1), the soul (q. 25, a. 4), and, indirectly, the body (q. 25, a. 5). Charity respects the natural order, inclining us to love friends and family, parents and children (q. 26, aa. 6–11), while also inspiring love for wrongdoers (q. 26, a. 6) and enemies (q. 26, a. 8).[3] The primary act of charity is the voluntary act of love, which gives rise to the internal blessings of joy (q. 28), peace (q. 29), and the virtue of mercy (q. 30)—the greatest of the virtues that unites a person with a neighbor (q. 30, a. 4)—and to external acts of charity exemplified in corporal works of mercy (such as feeding the hungry and clothing the naked [see Matt 25:31–45]) and in spiritual works of mercy (like comforting those who sorrow [q. 32, a. 2]).

The vices against charity constitute assaults either on charity itself, as in hatred (q. 34), or on the divine good, in the case of sloth vis-à-vis the spiritual life (q. 35); on the neighbor's good, in the case of envy (q. 36); or on the peace that binds neighbors together, by intentionally sowing discord (q. 37), stirring up trouble by speech (q. 38), breaking the unity of the church by schism (q. 39), instigating an unjust war (q. 40), harming others out of personal animosity or strife (q. 41), or plotting sedition against authorities responsible for the common good (q. 42).

Given these and other forms of opposition to charity, it is abundantly clear why charity would be commanded, a matter of precept (q. 44), and not left up to spontaneous inspiration. Yet the climactic expression of charity is found not simply in firm obedience to moral law but in the gift of wisdom (q. 45). The Holy Spirit inspires acute and penetrating judgment by creating in a person an internal and nondiscursive "connaturality" with what is demanded in concrete situations (q. 45, a. 2). The inner promptings of the Spirit enable a person to act in a manner that goes beyond, but not against, the kind of moral excellence found in acquired virtue.

The gift of wisdom does not pertain to all domains of practical knowledge, from baking bread to automobile mechanics, but rather to specific activities of spiritual discernment: "it contemplates divine things in themselves, and it consults them, in so far as it judges of human acts by divine things, and directs human acts according to divine rules" (q. 45, a. 3).[4] The gift of wisdom corresponds to the seventh Beatitude, that of the peacemaker, who sets things in due order and in so doing becomes a child of God (q. 45, a. 6). The disordered life of the fool, in contrast, is marked by the dulling of the spiritual sense. Here inordinate attachment to temporal goods corrupts one's own best judgment, even to the point of creating a distaste for God, and rendering one unaware of one's own foolishness (q. 46, a. 3).

PRUDENCE AND JUSTICE

Immediately after discussing the gift of wisdom, Aquinas turns to its more familiar counterpart, the virtue of *prudence*. Prudence in the Thomistic sense refers to the virtue of practical wisdom, which should not be confused with the "prudential" pursuit of enlightened self-interest found in the modern usage of this term.

Thomas's introduction of this topic begins an extensive discussion of the cardinal virtues that comprises the bulk of what remains of the *Secunda pars*. Were Aquinas building from the natural or acquired to the supernatural, he would have examined first the cardinal and then the theological virtues. The reverse order employed in the *Summa* underscores the fact that the Christian moral life is based first and foremost on grace and the theological virtues; indeed, faith is the first of the virtues to be generated and the last to be lost (IIa IIae, q. 162, a. 7, ad 3; also Ia IIae, q. 62, a. 4). Yet the gift of wisdom does not render the virtue of prudence unnecessary. A person blessed with faith, hope, and charity still needs the virtue of prudence to address the usual array of practical moral difficulties that are part of the human condition.

Following the standard procedure, the *Summa* examines first the virtue of prudence in itself (IIa IIae, q. 47) and then its "parts," those traits that must exist for the complete act of the virtue. These consist of three categories: first, "integral" parts of prudence, for example, memory and docility, which are necessary for its exercise in the full sense (q. 49); second, its various species or "subjective" parts, such as political prudence and domestic prudence (q. 50); and third, the dispositions connected with it—its "potential" parts—like the ability to identify exceptions in cases of law (q. 31). This "treatise" then discusses the corresponding gift of counsel (q. 52); the vices contrary to prudence: imprudence (q. 53), negligence (q. 54), and the vices resembling it (q. 55), such as craftiness (a. 3) and duplicity (a. 4); and finally the precepts as enumerated in the Old Law (q. 56).

The virtue of prudence is unique among the cardinal virtues precisely as a perfection of the intellect rather than of the will or sense appetite (q. 47, a. 2). Defined as the ability to apply right reason to action (q. 47, a. 4), prudence enables one to know how to act in the midst of the contingencies of particular situations (q. 47, a. 5). Aquinas believed that all normally functioning human beings have a natural habit (Ia, q. 79, a. 12) of *synderesis* (q. 47, a. 6, ad 1), an immediate, noninferential grasp of principles, the foremost of which is that one ought to do good and avoid evil (q. 79, a. 12; Ia IIae, q. 94, a. 2). This natural moral knowledge directs one formally to the ends of the moral virtues: that is, it tells a person to be just, temperate, courageous, and so forth, and indicts actions that violate these standards. When someone engages in practical moral reasoning, one reflects on how these given ends might pertain to the concrete situation faced here and now. The person exercising the virtue of prudence, for example, does not ask *whether* to be just, but *what it means* to act justly in this specific situation. Prudence, of course, cannot stand alone: it needs the other moral virtues to exercise its most distinctive act, which is not only to deliberate effectively but even more to command the proper act in light of the preceding process of deliberation (q. 47, a. 8).

Prudence is not defined as simply finding the best means to any end whatsoever, as the false prudence of the "good crook" or the "worldly wise." As a moral virtue, it takes its bearings from the good. It reflects not only on the end of this or that act (as, for example, how to treat justly a needy but dishonest employee) but also about how all of one's acts considered as a whole fit into the end of human life. Because of their disordered ends, sinners can never have the virtue of prudence (q. 47, a. 13).

Conversely, those who have grace always have prudence (q. 47, a. 14), in the sense that infused prudence enables them to make wise decisions with regard to matters necessary for their salvation. Perfect prudence commands the proper means to a particular good end and does so with regard to the good end of the person's whole life (q. 47, a. 13). The relation between the infused virtues and particular acts develops over time. Thus, the infused virtue of young children comes slowly into act and increases gradually as they mature and come into the full use of their reasoning ability (q. 47, a. 14, ad 3).

Justice is examined in sixty-five questions (qq. 57–122), the most extensive coverage of any virtue in the *Summa*. This kind of attention is to be expected, since Thomas wrote for Dominican students of theology, who, in the course of their pastoral work, would be confronted by practical problems of people buying and selling in the marketplace, going to court, and struggling to support their families under difficult economic circumstances. This lengthy discussion is organized into the following categories: first, justice in itself (qq. 57–60); second, the parts of justice (qq. 61–120); third, the gift of piety (q. 121); and last, the precepts of justice (q. 122).

Justice regards rectitude in external relations between people. This rectitude is called *right* (*ius*; q. 57, a. 1), language that should not be confused with modern individual "rights."[5] Positive *right* results from agreement between parties (q. 57, a. 2), as in the case of private contracts. *Natural right* is rooted in the very nature of things as created by God. Creatures have inherent needs and desires whose fulfillment constitutes their flourishing, the reason for their existence in the divine plan. Right exists when one creature's relations to other creatures allow for the satisfaction of their natural needs. This is why, in human communities, taking what belongs to another under extreme stress of need does not constitute theft (IIa IIae, q. 66, a. 7) and also why the rich sin when they fail to give to the poor (q. 66, a. 3, ad 2)—the former fulfills, and the latter violates, what is right.

The strong sense of natural right is seen in the raising of children by their natural parents, (q. 57, a. 3), whereas the weaker sense of natural right is illustrated in legitimacy of the institution of private property, whose social usefulness and common status in the "law of nations" (*ius gentium*) indicate its appropriateness to human nature (q. 57, a. 3, ad 2).

What is right constitutes the deepest intelligibility of human laws, and it is the task of human law to render specific formulations of what is right in particular contexts.

Human laws ought to serve the common good (Ia IIae, q. 90, a. 2; q. 96, a. 1), and that is why violations of right always attack the common good, either directly or indirectly. Aquinas had, as Jean Porter explains, "a great awareness of the communal contexts of the moral life, and more specifically, of the ways in which one can injure another through damaging her standing within the community."[6] Yet for all the significance of the common good, the individual cannot be treated unjustly for the benefit of the wider community (IIa IIae, q. 68, a. 3; although we would of course object to some practices that Aquinas considered to be just, for example, slavery, as in Ia IIae, q. 94, a. 5, ad 4). Inherently wrong legal arrangements cannot be made just simply by the arbitrary declaration of those in power (IIa IIae, q. 57, a. 2, ad 2); hence, the famous axiom that an unjust law is no law at all (Ia IIae, q. 96, a. 4).

There is a sense in which every virtuous act can be said to be just, but Aquinas distinguished, in more precise terms, general justice (*iustitia generalis*), which orders the agent to the common good (also called legal justice [*iustitia legalis*]; IIa IIae, q. 58, a. 6), from particular justice (*iustitia particularis*), which directs the person to particular goods (q. 58, a. 7). Particular justice, which orders a part to the good of a whole, is composed of two species (subjective parts): commutative justice, concerning part to part, and distributive justice, concerning the relation of whole to part (q. 61, aa. 1–2). Just as the heightened respect given to a wise political leader is proportionately equal to his or her contribution to the common good, so the payment of just wages for honest labor respects the equality between what has been given and received by both employers and employees.

Favoritism (q. 63) is the vice opposed to distributive justice. The *Summa* treats in extensive detail the vices opposed to commutative justice (qq. 64–78) through deeds, including murder (q. 64), theft, and robbery (q. 66); words, both inside the court (qq. 67–71) and outside the court (qq. 72–76); and unjust economic transactions (qq. 77–78), including fraud (q. 77) and usury, the charging of interest on money lent (q. 78).

This analysis of the virtue of justice is completed with a lengthy discussion of the virtues "annexed" to justice (its potential parts): religion (qq. 81–100), piety (q. 101), respectfulness for those in authority (qq. 102–5), gratitude (qq. 106–7), vindication (q. 108), truthfulness (qq. 109–13), friendliness (qq. 114–16), liberality (qq. 117–19), and equity (q. 120).

Thomas condemned as unjust a wide range of acts that range from thinking ill of another person without sufficient reason (q. 60, a. 4) to the taking of innocent life (q. 64). Injustice is found in wrongful imprisonment (q. 65), theft (q. 66), backbiting (and even consenting to backbiting as a listener [q. 73, a. 4]), and perjury (q. 98). As indications of his own cultural context, Aquinas regarded as just the practices of maiming criminals (q. 65, a. 1), whipping children and slaves (q. 65, a. 2), and executing heretics (q. 11, a. 3; but not the forced conversion of unbelievers [q. 10, a. 12]).

Readers may expect to find religion treated under the discussion of charity or faith, but the *Summa* instead treats it as a requirement of justice. Justice renders to another person what is his or her due, so in religion believers give to God what is God's due. Yet though justice requires a kind of equality of return (q. 58, a. 11), there is no equality between the creature and God and we can never return anything equal to the benefits we have received from God (q. 81, a. 5, ad 3). Nor can God ever be a debtor to us (Ia, q. 21, a. 1, ad 3). This radical asymmetry accounts for why religion is not one of the integral parts of justice. Religion, however, shares with justice a willingness to repay a debt, specifically the debt of honor to, or reverence for, the first principle of creation and government of all things (IIa IIae, q. 81, a. 3). Devotion (q. 82), prayer (q. 83), sacrifice (q. 85), religious vows (q. 88), and other acts of service and worship that endeavor to give God what is God's due are also morally virtuous (q. 81, a. 5). Yet because of the utter inequality between the worshipper and God, who "infinitely surpasses all things and exceeds them in every way," religion has nothing like the quid pro quo reciprocity that characterizes strict justice and is therefore simply an approximation to it, that is, as a virtue "annexed" to justice (q. 81, a. 4).

In order to understand properly the importance Aquinas attached to religion, it might be helpful to recall his view of the human condition. The state of "original justice" was one of harmony, concordance, balanced proportion, and right relation between humanity and God (Ia IIa, q. 82, a. 3), within the soul and body of each person (Ia, q. 94, a. 1; q. 95,

a. 1; q. 97, a. 1) and between the members of the wider human community (Ia IIae, q. 85, a. 3). The prideful attempt of humanity to grasp more than its due (q. 84, a. 2) destroyed "original justice" and "wounded" human nature (q. 85, a. 3). Our original natural inclination to the good of virtue was diminished but not destroyed by the Fall.

Grace not only works to repair injustice and to restore justice in human society but, even more, to reestablish the justice (or right relation) between human beings and God. The proper justification of the sinner takes place only through the gift of grace accepted freely in faith and with the love of charity. How this is accomplished through the work of Christ is the topic of the *Tertia pars*. The *Secunda secundae*, however, is concerned with religion as the way in which conduct is directed to God. By showing proper honor to God, religious acts are properly proportioned to God (q. 81, a. 2).

The requirements of religion are given precedence to other laws in the scriptures because they are of the greatest importance, even more so than those of other moral virtues (q. 81, a. 6, *sed contra*; on the first three precepts of the Decalogue, see q. 122, aa. 1–3). The rationale for this priority resides in the nature of virtue itself. Whatever is directed to an end takes its goodness from its relation to that end. The virtues are ordered to God as their end, and "religion approaches nearer to God than the other moral virtues, in so far as its actions are directly and immediately ordered to the honor of God" (q. 122, a. 6). For this reason, religion is described as the greatest of the moral virtues (ibid.).

While internal acts of worship are more important than the external acts, one ought not to minimize the importance of the latter as "mere" ritual (q. 81, a. 7). Worship orders humanity to God through external acts, which engage bodies in movement and sense in images in order to draw the entire person into religious reverence (ibid.). Just as his account of our bodily nature led him to acknowledge our need for ritual, so Aquinas's recognition of our social nature encouraged his appreciation for common worship within an ecclesial community. These acts of reverence do not reflect the presumption that they do something for God, who after all is "full of glory to which no creature can add anything," but rather for our own sakes, because, "by the very fact that we revere and honor God, our mind is subjected to Him, and in this consists its perfection" (ibid.). The desire for happiness, then, can only be adequately pursued on the basis of true worship, and especially in its highest form, the Eucharist (IIIa, qq. 73–83).

The gift of the Holy Spirit associated with the virtue of justice is piety (q. 121). Whereas the virtue of piety annexed to justice renders due honor to parents and country, and symbolically to one's human father (q. 101), the gift of piety is that whereby "we provide worship and duty to God as our Father through the inspiration of the Holy Spirit" (q. 121, a. 1). The virtue of religion pays worship to God as Creator, but the excellence of the gift of piety resides in the fact that it inspires us to revere and worship God as Father, and, by extension, and on account of their relation to the Father, to honor all human beings, especially the saints in heaven, and the truth of scripture (q. 121, a. 1, ad 3). Given this context, it makes perfect sense that the bulk of the final question here, dedicated to the precepts of justice in the Decalogue, concentrates not on interpersonal justice but on the duties of religion (the first three precepts; q. 121, aa. 2–4) and the obligations of piety (the fourth commandment, treated in q. 121, a. 5). The remaining article (q. 121, a. 6) accords brief summary treatment to the remaining six precepts concerning justice between people.

FORTITUDE AND TEMPERANCE

The other two cardinal virtues pertain to the internal ordering of the agent, specifically with regard to ways in which the will might be hindered from following right reason. The virtue of temperance enables one to respond reasonably to what presents itself as attractive and the virtue of courage enables one to respond reasonably to what evokes fear.

The *Summa*'s discussion of courage begins with the virtue itself (q. 123), its principal act, martyrdom (q. 124), and its opposing vices, which include disordered fear (q. 125), fearlessness (q. 126), and irrational daring (q. 127). It then examines its parts in general (q. 128) and its parts in particular (qq. 129–38), including confidence or magnanimity (q. 129), magnificence (q. 134), patience (q. 136), and perseverance (q. 137). It concludes with a discussion of the gift of fortitude (q. 139) and its effects (q. 140).

As a general virtue, courage gives the emotional stability required for the exercise of each and every virtue. As a special virtue, it enables the agent to endure or resist challenges to steadfastness of mind, especially in situations involving mortal danger (q. 123, a. 2). The last qualification indicates the special character of courage, its reasonable refusal inappropriately to withdraw from or to be controlled by what generates fear (q. 123, a. 3). Courage is not to be confused with foolish indifference to danger; Aquinas would concur with Mark Twain: courage is "resistance to fear, mastery of fear—not absence of fear."[7] Far from being the same as courage, fearlessness is one of the vices opposed to courage because it lacks proper love of temporal goods (q. 126, a. 1). The courageous person loves life and other temporal goods in due measure and recognizes threats to personal well-being, yet he or she faces danger for the sake of higher goods. The soldier in battle, for example, risks losing his own life for the sake of defending the common good of his country (q. 123, a. 5).

Courage, however, is displayed not only in martial contexts, but wherever people remain steadfast in the danger of death on account of virtue. Abelard, Cicero, and Macrobius divided courage in two: courage as attacking evils and courage as enduring the onslaught of evils (q. 128, a. 1). Thomas clearly believed the latter to be its more important expression.[8] Aquinas maintained that, as it is more difficult to control fear than it is to act aggressively, courage is more characteristically disclosed in endurance than in attack (q. 123, a. 6). Martyrdom, in which one endures the greatest of physical evils, constitutes the supreme act of courage, an act of the highest perfection, which among all the acts of the virtues exhibits most completely the perfection of charity (q. 124, a. 3).

How could the endurance of evils be a cardinal virtue, since virtues move one toward the good? The phrase "cardinal virtue" applies to habits exhibiting characteristics necessary for the exercise of any virtue whatsoever, and Aquinas maintained that the steadfastness of courage is required for the exercise of *any* of the virtues when they are threatened. The final end of the virtue of courage is thus not evil per se, but the good of reason for the sake of which it resists or endures physical evils (q. 123, a. 11, ad 2). And because the fear of death provides the most powerful motive for withdrawing from good, the virtue that properly subordinates this fear to reason is the greatest of the cardinal virtues concerned directly with the emotions (q. 123, a. 12).

Courage faces chiefly the danger of death, but responds in proper measure to other dangers as well. It inspires a balanced, ordered love for temporal goods that overcomes disordered fear concerning their loss (q. 125, a. 1), just as, conversely, it corrects insufficient love of temporal goods and generates a proper appreciation for their place in life (q. 126, a. 2). The activity of other virtues exercised in the face of less extreme kinds of hardships is its "potential" parts. Lesser dangers must still be met with confidence in planning to act and then in being resolute in action, but in neither an ambitious (q. 131) nor a vainglorious (q. 132) way. In its more passive mode courage endures these dangers with patience (q. 136) and perseverance.

The gift of courage so inspires the mind with confidence that it refuses to submit irrationally to fear (q. 139, a. 2). Indeed, it generates confidence of escape from every danger (q. 139, a. 2, ad 1), thus bestowing a special kind of freedom from evil (q. 139, a. 2, ad 2). This gift thus has an affinity with the fourth Beatitude—"Blessed are they who hunger and thirst after righteousness"—in which "hunger" and "thirst" represent the employment of strenuous effort exerted to overcome obstacles to attaining the good (q. 139, a. 2).

Not everyone is blessed with the gift of courage, but every Christian is made aware of the precepts of courage revealed in divine law. Whereas the Old Law instructed the Israelites how to fight for the sake of temporal goods, the New Law teaches spiritual combat for the sake of obtaining eternal life (q. 140, a. 1, ad 1). Such precepts such as Jesus' "Do not fear those who kill the body" (Matt 10:28) thus command endurance of temporal evils for the sake of the ultimate end.

The treatise on the virtue of temperance begins with a discussion of the virtue in itself (qq. 141–42), then its parts (qq. 143–70), both in general (q. 143) and in particular (qq. 144–69), and its precepts (q. 170). It attends to the parts in particular, which encompass three major categories: first, the "integral" parts of temperance, shame (q. 144) and honesty (q. 145); second, the "subjective" parts of temperance, those concerning the pleasures of food (qq. 146–50) and sex (qq. 151–54); and third, the "potential" parts of temperance: continence (qq. 155–56), clemency and meekness (qq. 157–59), and modesty (qq. 160–69).

Temperance is both a general virtue and a special virtue. As general, of course, it is found in all actions exhibiting moderation. As special, the virtue of temperance characteristically orders the sense appetites, especially in matters pertaining to pleasures of touch, such as food, drink, and sex, desires that are especially difficult to control (q. 141, a. 7). Whereas the appetites of animals are regulated by their intrinsic natural ordering, human appetites attracted to the same kinds of goods must be deliberately regulated by reason. Sensible goods offer the greatest pleasures to the sense of touch and often threaten to disturb the reasonable ordering of human action. The virtue of temperance, then, empowers the agent reasonably to use pleasurable objects as needed in this life (q. 141, a. 6)—"need" including not only the bare necessities of life but also the things that make possible a decent life according to one's place in the social order (q. 141, a. 6, ad 2). The meaning of temperance, of course, cannot be set in stone since "the practice of temperance varies according to different times…and according to different human laws and customs" (q. 170, a. 1, ad 3).

Rather than the particularly abstemious mindset of the emotionally constricted, as that name sometimes suggests, the virtue of temperance leads to the moderate fulfillment of natural desires. The *Summa* notes the need to be alert not only to the vicious nature of unchecked sexual desires, but also of insensibility—the rejection of pleasures attending natural operations that are necessary for self-preservation (q. 142, a. 1).

The integral parts of temperance, those necessary for any case of its proper exercise, include shamefacedness, repulsion from the disgrace of acting contrary to temperance (q. 144), and "honesty," the spiritual beauty manifested in the clarity and due proportion of the well-ordered life (q. 145). Thus, the virtue of temperance, more than any other virtue, manifests a certain beauty, just as the vice of intemperance exceeds others in disgrace (q. 143, a. 1).

The subjective parts, or "species," of temperance are differentiated according to the kinds of objects to which they are directed. The virtue of abstinence concerns the proper use of food (q. 146). This includes consumption that observes the mean (q. 146, a. 1, esp. ad 3), as well as acts of fasting for the sake of moral discipline, spiritual growth, and making satisfaction for sins (q. 147, a. 1). Abstinence is contrasted with the vice of gluttony (q. 148). Pleasures of drink are moderated and restrained by the virtue of sobriety just as they are used sinfully in drunkenness (q. 150).

The pleasures of sexual activity are ordered by the virtues of chastity and purity. These virtues properly fall under the cardinal virtue of temperance; however, they also pertain to the virtue of justice when the conduct in question has impact on others, as, for example, in cases of rape and adultery.

Chastity, which "chastises" concupiscence, is a special virtue concerned with disordered sexual desires (q. 151, a. 2). The virtue of chastity concerns sexual acts themselves, whereas the virtue of purity regards the external signs of sexual interest. Virginity as a moral rather than simply physiological condition is a virtue only when embraced for the right reason, that is, for the good of the soul and its spiritual growth, and so that one may have the leisure to be devoted to divine things (q. 152, aa. 3–5). The virtue of chastity is not to be confused with avoiding all sexual pleasures through what would now be described as neurotic psychological aversion. Nor does Aquinas praise a person who avoids sex simply because he or she is, as he puts it, "insensible as a country bumpkin" (*insensibilis, sicut agricola*; q. 152, a. 2; also q. 153, a. 3, ad 3).

Lust, of course, is the vice opposed to chastity. Given the importance of reason, the somewhat suspect status of sexual desire is signaled in the observation that "venereal pleasures above all debauch a person's mind" (q. 153, a. 1). Indeed, the *Summa* argues that even within the morally legitimate context of marriage, sexual intercourse still has some degree of shame because the "movement of the organs of generation is not subject to the command of reason, as are the movements of the other external members" (q. 151, a. 4). Yet, it is important to distinguish lust, which by definition violates the order of reason, from sexual desire per se, which is a created good. Sexual acts in themselves are not sinful, as long as they are directed in the right manner to their proper end, procreation, rather than to the experience of sexual pleasure for its own sake (q. 151, a. 2). The disordered satisfaction of sexual appetite follows not from anything evil in the body but from a refusal of the *will* to be ordered by right reason.

Finally, the "potential" parts of the virtue of temperance are secondary virtues moderating and restraining desires for less powerful pleasures. One set of these virtues controls the inward movements of the will. In this category, the virtue of continence enables the will to stand firm in the face of vehement desires or immoderate concupiscences (q. 143, a. 1). Whereas the intemperate person feels no qualms over the choice of wrongdoing, the incontinent person feels guilt over the wrongdoing he or she has done out of disordered passion (q. 156, a. 3). Strictly speaking, continence is not a perfect virtue because it only exists in the presence of an underlying internal struggle, thus signifying the presence of vehement disordered desires. Continence does have "something of the nature of a virtue, in so far as reason stands firm in opposing the passions" (q. 155, a. 1). The root cause of incontinence is not sexual desire but the *will* refusing either to think about its acts (the sin of impetuosity) or to abide by its own best judgment (the sin of weakness; q. 156, a. 1).

The other potential parts of temperance include the virtues of clemency and meekness. Clemency mitigates external punishment, whereas meekness moderates the passion for revenge (q. 157, a. 1). Note that anger, defined as the desire to punish or to have revenge (*appetitus vindictae*), is not necessarily evil (q. 158, a. 1). Anger is legitimate when emotionally moderate and in accord with right reason ("zealous anger"), that is, when it promotes justice and the true correction of the offender. Like other emotions, it can be evil by either excess or deficiency (q. 158, a. 2).

A set of secondary virtues, those concerned with less difficult matters, belong to the virtue of modesty, which governs the external actions of the body. Humility is essentially the reverence through which people are properly subject to God (q. 161, a. 1, ad 5; q. 161, a. 2, ad 3). In humility, every person, "in respect of that which is his own, ought to subject himself to every neighbor, in respect of that which the latter has of God" (q. 161, a. 3). Humility should not be confused with humiliating self-abnegation before others. The vice directly opposed to humility is of course pride, the disordered desire for exaltation (q. 162, a. 1, ad 2). Pride consists essentially in the willing refusal to be subject to God and the divine rule (q. 162, a. 6). As aversion that amounts to contempt for God, pride is the most grievous of all sins as well as the queen and mother of all the vices (q. 162, a. 8).

Other parts of modesty include studiousness in the pursuit of knowledge (q. 166), opposed by the vice of curiosity by which one pursues knowledge sinfully (q. 167), and the extension of modesty in our conduct toward other people (q. 168) and in our outward apparel (q. 169).

This treatise concludes with a brief discussion of its precepts as indicated in the Decalogue. Among all the vices opposed to temperance,

Aquinas held, adultery would seem most opposed to the love of our neighbor, and for this reason the divine law rightly condemns not only adultery itself but even the intention to commit adultery (to covet; q. 170, a. 1). Similarly, not only is the sin of murder condemned, but also the vice of daring that sometimes leads to murder. More positive common requirements of temperance, Aquinas noted, could not have been given, since the practice of temperance varies according to different times, laws, and customs (q. 170, a. 1, ad 3).

Notes

1. James A. Weisheipl, OP, *Friar Thomas D'Aquino: His Life, Thought and Works*, rev. ed. (1974; Washington, DC: Catholic University of America Press, 1983), 220.

2. "disciplina per quam pervenitur ad perfectionem caritatis."

3. On the order of charity, see Stephen J. Pope, *The Evolution of Altruism and the Ordering of Love* (Washington, DC: Georgetown University Press, 1994) and idem, "The Order of Love and Recent Catholic Ethics: A Constructive Proposal," *Theological Studies* 52 (1991): 255–88.

4. "conspiciendis quidem, secundum quod divina in seipsis contemplatur; consulendis autem, secundum quod per divina iudicat de humanis, per divinas regulas dirigens actus humanos."

5. This distinction is the source of considerable debate within the history of philosophy, with some philosophers regarding Thomas as a precursor to modern rights theories and others regarding his notion of *ius* as contrasting with subjective rights.

6. Jean Porter, *The Recovery of Virtue: The Relevance of Aquinas for Christian Ethics* (Louisville, KY: Westminster/John Knox, 1990), 134.

7. Mark Twain, *Pudd'nhead Wilson,* in *Mississippi Writings* (New York: The Library of America, 1982), 985.

8. See P. G. Walsh, "St. Thomas and his Authorities," in *St. Thomas Aquinas, Summa Theologiae*, vol. 42, *Courage* (IIa IIae. 123–40), ed. Anthony Ross, OP, and P. G. Walsh (London: Blackfriars, Eyre and Spottiswoode, 1963), 241–43.

2. The Master Argument of MacIntyre's *After Virtue*

Brad J. Kallenberg

This chapter first appeared in Nancey Murphy, Brad J. Kallenberg, and Mark Thiessen Nation, eds., *Virtues and Practices in the Christian Tradition: Christian Ethics after MacIntyre* (Notre Dame, IN: University of Notre Dame Press, 1997).

In September of 1995 the Associated Press released a wirephoto showing Russian lawmakers of both genders in a punching brawl during a session of the Duma, Russia's lower house of parliament.[1] Is this behavior an ethnic idiosyncrasy? Do only government officials duke it out over matters of great importance? Or have fisticuffs suddenly become politically correct? No, on all counts.

Pick a topic, any topic—abortion, euthanasia, welfare reform, military intervention in the Balkans—and initiate discussion with a group of reasonable, well-educated people and observe the outcome. Chaos ensues. Of course the volume of the debate may vary according to how "close to home" the issue hits the participants. But any moral discussion, given a group of sufficient diversity, has the potential of escalating into a shouting match...or worse.

An even more striking feature of moral debates is their tendency *never* to reach resolution. Lines are drawn early, and participants rush to take sides. But in taking sides they appear to render themselves incapable of hearing the other. Everyone feels the heat, but no one sees the light.

Many thinkers are inclined to see *shrillness* and *interminability* as part and parcel of the nature of moral debate. But Alasdair MacIntyre begs to differ. In *After Virtue* he offers the "disquieting suggestion" that the tenor of modern moral debate is the direct outcome of a catastrophe in our past, a catastrophe so great that moral inquiry was very nearly obliterated from our culture and its vocabulary exorcised from our language. What we possess today, he argues, are nothing more than fragments of an older tradition. As a result, our moral discourse, which uses terms like *good*, and *justice*, and *duty*, has been robbed of the context that makes it intelligible. To complicate matters, although university courses in ethics have been around for a long time, no ethics curriculum predates this catastrophe. Therefore, for anyone who has taken ethics courses, and especially for those who have studied ethics diligently, the disarray of modern moral discourse is not only invisible, it is considered normal. This conclusion has been lent apparent credibility by a theory called *emotivism*.

Emotivism, explains MacIntyre, "is the doctrine that all evaluative judgments and more specifically all moral judgments are *nothing but* expressions of preference, expressions of attitude or feeling.…"[2] On this account, the person who remarks, "Kindness is good," is not making a truth claim but simply expressing a positive feeling, "Hurrah for kindness!" Similarly, the person who exclaims, "Murder is wrong," can be understood to be actually saying, "I disapprove of murder," or "Murder, yuck!"

If emotivism is a true picture of the way moral discourse works, then we easily see that moral disputes can never be *rationally* settled because, as the emotivist contends, all value judgments are nonrational. Reason can never compel a solution; we simply have to hunker down and decide. Moral discussion is at best rhetorical persuasion.

There are sound reasons for questioning the emotivist picture. In the first place, emotivism is self-defeating insofar as it makes a truth claim about the non-truth-claim status of all purported truth claims! To put it differently, if all truth claims in the sphere of ethics are simply expressions of preference, as emotivism maintains, then the theory of emotivism itself lacks truth value, and thus we are not constrained to believe it if we prefer not to. In addition, emotivism muddies some ordinarily clear waters. Any proficient language speaker will attest to the fact that the sense of "I prefer…" is vastly different from the sense of

"You ought...." The distinct uses to which we put these phrases are enabled precisely because the sense of "You ought" cannot be reduced without remainder to "I prefer."

But MacIntyre is not content to offer first-order arguments against emotivism. Stopping there would have made his book simply another ethical theory—just the sort of thing that emotivism so convincingly dismisses. Instead, what MacIntyre is up to has been called *metaethics*—an exploration into the conditions (or conditioners) of human ethical thought. As a human enterprise, ethics must be shaped in the same way that language, culture, and history shape the rest of our thinking. By investigating the historical conditionedness of our moral life and discourse, MacIntyre undermines emotivism, making a strong case for its own historical conditionedness. Emotivism as a moral philosophy appears to explain why contemporary moral debates are irresolvable. But it cannot account for the oddity that rival positions within these debates all employ incommensurable concepts. Why cannot the Kantian argument ("The taking of human life is always and everywhere just plain wrong") concede even a modicum of legitimacy to the Lockean ("Abortion is the natural right of women") if both views boil down to "I don't/do approve of abortion"? Nor can emotivism explain the oddity that interminable moral debates are conducted with the expectation that such debates *can be* resolved and, in keeping with this optimism, are conducted in such a way that rival positions appeal to principles presumed to be ultimate. In other words, if all value judgments are expressive, how did this belief in ultimate principles arise? MacIntyre suggests that it makes more sense to look for a source of this optimism, and its belief in ultimates, in a tradition that predates emotivism.

In fact, if one looks closely at the modern moral self, it has the appearance of being dislocated, as if it were missing something. The moral self as conceived by the emotivist is "totally detached from all social particularity" and is, rather, "entirely set over against the social world" (32). This autonomous self has no given continuities, possesses no ultimate governing principles, and is guided by no *telos*. Instead it is aimless, having "a certain abstract and ghostly character" (33). If MacIntyre is correct in asserting that "the emotivist self, in acquiring sovereignty in its own realm lost its traditional boundaries provided by a social identity and a view of human life as ordered to a given end," then it comes as no surprise that such a self flounders helplessly and endlessly in a moral quagmire (34). But how did this catastrophe come to pass, and what exactly are the social identity and *telos* that were lost?

THE FAILURE OF THE ENLIGHTENMENT PROJECT

The catastrophe that left the modern moral world in such disarray was a series of failed attempts to provide *rational* justification of morality for a culture that had philosophy as its central social activity. This eighteenth-century culture was called the Enlightenment, and its misguided agenda MacIntyre dubs the Enlightenment Project.

Among the first attempts to justify morality were those of Denis Diderot (1713–84) and David Hume (1711–76). Diderot tried to make human desire the criterion of an action's rightness or wrongness but failed to answer how a conflict of desires, and hence a conflict between an action's rightness and wrongness, could be resolved. Like Diderot, Hume conceived human passion as the stuff of morality because it is passion, not reason, that ultimately moves the moral agent to act. Hume goes further than Diderot by specifying a ruling passion (he calls it "sympathy"), but he can provide sufficient explanation neither for why this passion ought to predominate nor for why his account of the moral life looks suspiciously like that of the English bourgeoisie he emulated.[3]

Provoked by the failures of Hume and Diderot to ground morality in human passion, Immanuel Kant (1724–1804) strove to ground morality in reason alone. He argued that if morality was rational, its form would be identical for all rational beings. Therefore, the moral thing to do is to follow those principles that can be universalized, that is, to follow those principles that one could consistently wish for everyone to follow. This sounds suspiciously like the Golden Rule. What makes it different, however, is Kant's conviction that the principle of universalizability (also called the *categorical imperative*) gets its punch from the requirement that it be willed without falling into *rational* contradiction.[4] Unfortunately, Kant's system has several large flaws, not the least of which is its ability to "justify" immoral maxims such as "Persecute all those who hold false religious beliefs" as well as trivial ones such as "Always eat mussels on Mondays in March" (46).

Søren Kierkegaard (1813–55) heartily agreed with the content of the morality that Kant defended (middle-class German Lutheran piety), but he also perceived that Kant's *rational* vindication of morality had failed as miserably as its predecessors. According to Kierkegaard, all persons are free to choose the plane of their existence. But this leaves open the problem of how to decide which plane to inhabit, since the criteria for making the decision are internal to the plane under consideration. Shall I inhabit the plane of the pleasure-seeking aesthete or that of the ethical rule-follower? To choose according to passion is to be relegated to the plane of the aesthetic. To choose according to reason is to have already chosen the ethical plane. Hence, neither passion nor reason can be the criterion for making the choice. The choice is a criterionless leap. MacIntyre concludes:

> Just as Hume seeks to found morality on the passions because his arguments have excluded the possibility of founding it on reason, so Kant founds it on reason because *his* arguments have excluded the possibility of founding it on the passions, and Kierkegaard on criterionless fundamental choice because of what he takes to be the compelling nature of the considerations which exclude both reason and the passions. (49)

So by Hume's standards Kant is unjustified in his conclusions; by Kant's standards Hume is both unjustified and unintelligible. By Kierkegaard's, both Hume and Kant are intelligible, but neither is compelling. The proof of the Enlightenment Project's failure is the stubborn existence of rival conceptions of moral justification.

WHY THE ENLIGHTENMENT PROJECT HAD TO FAIL

The important thing to realize is that the Enlightenment Project didn't simply happen to fail, it *had* to fail. What doomed the Enlightenment Project from its inception was its loss of the concept of *telos*. The word *telos* is borrowed from classical Greek and means "end" or "purpose." When applied to human morality the term signifies the answer to the question, "What is human life for?" In Aristotle's day (fourth century BC), moral reasoning was an argument consisting of three terms. The first term was the notion of the untutored human nature that so desperately needed moral guidance. The second term was human nature conceived in terms of having fulfilled its purpose or achieved its *telos*. The third term, moral imperatives, was that set of instructions for moving from the untutored self toward the actualized *telos*. In this way moral precepts weren't snatched out of thin air but got their "punch" or their "oughtness" from the concrete notion of what human life was for.[5]

The wristwatch is a good example of how this works. If we ask, "What is the wristwatch for?" the usual answer is that watches are for timekeeping.[6] To put it more technically, we could say that the purpose or *telos* of the watch is timekeeping. Or, to put it in still other terms, we can say that the watch is *functionally defined* as a mechanism for keeping time. Knowledge of this *telos* enables us to render judgment against a grossly inaccurate watch as a "bad" watch. Furthermore, our functional definition also allows us to identify the functional imperative for watches: "Watches *ought* to keep time well."

Because the Enlightenment rejected the traditionally shared concept of what human life is for and started, as it were, from scratch by inventing the idea of humans as "autonomous individuals," the concept of *telos*, so very central to morality, was lost. Having rejected the received account of *telos*, the only remaining option upon which moral principles might be grounded was the *un*tutored human nature—the very thing in need of guidance and, by nature, at odds with those guiding principles!

The results of the failure of the Enlightenment Project were far-reaching. First, without the notion of *telos* serving as a means for moral triangulation, moral value judgments lost their factual character. And, of course, if values are "factless," then no appeal to facts can ever settle disagreements over values. It is in this state of affairs that emotivism, with its claim that moral values were nothing but matters of preference, flourishes as a theory. Second, impostors stepped in to fill the vacuum created by the absence of *telos* in moral reasoning. For example, utilitarianism can be seen to offer a ghostly substitute when it asserts that morality operates according to the principle of *greatest good for greatest number*. But this principle is vacuous because the utilitarians who assert it cannot adequately define what "good" means.[7] Similarly, Kant tried to rescue the (newly) autonomous moral agent from the loss of authority in his or her moral statements by attempting to provide "rational" justification for statements deprived of their former teleological status. Not only did Kant fail but later analytic philosophy cannot advance Kantian arguments without smuggling in undefined terms such as *rights* and *justice*. MacIntyre's point is that tradition alone provides the sense of terms like *good* and *justice* and *telos*. The presence of this moral vocabulary in debates today only goes to show that "modern moral utterance and practice can only be understood as a series of fragmented survivals from an older past and that the insoluble problems which they have generated for modern moral theories will remain insoluble until this is well understood" (110–11). In the absence of traditions, moral debate is out of joint and becomes a theater of illusions in which simple indignation and mere protest occupy center stage:

> But protest is now almost entirely that negative phenomenon which characteristically occurs as a reaction to the alleged invasion of someone's *rights* in the name of someone else's *utility*. The self-assertive shrillness of protest arises because the facts of incommensurability ensure that protesters can never win an argument; the indignant self-righteousness of protest arises because the facts of incommensurability ensure equally that the protesters can never lose an argument either. (71; cf. 77)

NIETZSCHE OR ARISTOTLE?

MacIntyre concludes that we are faced with a momentous choice. The present emotivist world cannot be sustained much longer. Nietzsche saw this clearly. He argued convincingly that every time a person made an appeal to "objectivity," it was none other than a thinly disguised expression of the person's subjective will. When we look at post-Enlightenment ethics through Nietzsche's eyes, we can see that insofar as the Enlightenment Project offers putative moral principles (that is, ones that are devoid of the background context that gives them their clout), it creates a moral vacuum that will inevitably be filled by head-strong people asserting their individual will-to-power; and to the victor go the spoils. To put it differently, the emotivist world is neither stable nor self-sustaining. Rather, it is a battleground of competing wills awaiting the emergence of a conqueror. Once the Aristotelian model of morality was rejected and the Enlightenment Project had failed, the danger of an imminent *Übermensch* (who resembles Hitler more than Superman) must be conceded. The only stopper to this danger is the possibility of recognizing that the Aristotelian model ought not to have been rejected in the first place. We are faced, then, with a momentous choice between Nietzsche and Aristotle. "There is no third alternative" (118).

In Praise of Aristotle

In order for MacIntyre to make a case that the Aristotelian morality ought never to have been discarded, he must first demonstrate the strength of this moral tradition from its origin in Homeric literature to its full-blown Aristotelian Thomistic form of the late Middle Ages.

Heroic Society

Storytelling was the primary tool for moral education in classical Greece. It was for this reason that Homer's epic poems reflect the moral structure of their times. Not only does art reflect life, but literature in particular is the repository for moral stories, stories that have the peculiar ability of becoming embodied in the life of the community that cherishes them. This fact, that human life has the same shape as that of a story, will come up again in our discussion.

The moral structure of heroic society has two other outstanding features. First, morality has a social dimension. The social mobility that typifies our age was entirely absent in Homer's time. Then, one was born into a social structure that was fixed: "Every individual has a given role and status within the well-defined and highly determinate system of roles and statuses" (122). One's social place determined both the responsibility to render certain services to others (for example, it was incumbent on the head of the clan to defend and protect the clan) and the privileges one could expect from others in return. What one lacked in "upward mobility" was compensated by greater security. To know one's role and status in this small social system was to have settled forever the question, "Who am I?" In fact, no one ever thought of asking such existential questions in heroic society because who one *was* was indistinguishable from what one *did*. Within this social framework the word *virtue* (*arête*) describes any quality that is required for discharging one's role. As the clan's warrior-defender, the head of the clan needed courage as well as physical strength and battle savvy. Courage is also intimately linked to another virtue, fidelity. Fidelity and courage become obligatory because the community can survive only if kinsmen can be relied upon to fight valiantly on each other's behalf should the need arise.

This highlights a third feature of the moral structure of heroic societies. Since morality is bound up with the social structure of the clan, questions about moral value are *questions of fact*. Just as what qualifies as a "right" move in the game of chess is predetermined by the agreed-upon object of the game, so, too, the morally acceptable "move" was easily identified for those who participated in the "game." However, there was no way for a person in heroic society to step outside the moral "game" to evaluate it, as is possible with chess. "All questions of choice arise within the framework; the framework itself therefore cannot be chosen" precisely because the person who does try to step outside his or her given social position "would be engaged in the enterprise of trying to make himself [or herself] disappear" (126).

Athenian Society

Life in Athens illustrates an important moment in the life of a moral tradition: growth comes through crisis. In large measure, morality was a subject that received a great deal of attention from the Athenians because of a perceived discrepancy between their moral "scriptures" (the Homeric literature) and life as they knew it. No Athenian could conceive of living like an Achilles or an Agamemnon. This does not illustrate that the heroic society had been mistaken about morality's *social* dimension, but rather, that the social structure since the days of Homer had undergone such a drastic change (with the emergence of the city-state, or *polis*) that morality had necessarily changed shape too. The changes in the social world had the effect of broadening the range of application of the concept of virtue. The term no longer denoted excellence in the performance of one's well-defined social roles (where excellence could be understood only from within such a role), but rather *virtues* signified qualities that were applicable to *human life in general* (or, at least, human life in Athens, which in their minds *was* human life par excellence!). While the Athenians inherited the vocabulary of the virtues from heroic society, the content of these terms was up for grabs.

For example, the Sophists were inclined to see *virtue* as the generic name for those qualities that ensure successful living, and what counts for success was relative to each different city-state. When in Sparta, do as the Spartans do—treasure physical prowess and war craft—but when in Athens do as the Athenians do and hanker after beauty and truth. In response to their appalling relativism, Plato charged the Sophists with failing to discern the difference between mundane virtues and "true" virtue. Plato is willing to grant that the virtues are the means to a happy life, but getting clear about the nature of "true" happiness (and "true" virtue) requires shifting one's focus from the earthly *polis* to contemplate instead the "ideal" world. Plato was convinced that this exercise in contemplation would show that true happiness is the satisfaction of having lived in accordance with one's true nature. Human nature, according to Plato, was composed of three parts. The highest part—that which participates most fully in the realm of the Ideal—is the intellect and is assisted in its function by the virtue of wisdom. The lowest part—that which is shared with the beasts—is the desiring part and is to be constrained by the virtue of prudence. Between lay a motivational wellspring, or high-spirited part, that is assisted by the virtue of courage. A fourth virtue, justice, refers to the state of affairs when all three are in proper order with respect to each other. This set of four virtues is called *cardinal* (from the Latin *cardo,* which means "door hinge") because they are the qualities upon which the truly happy life hangs.[8]

It is important to remember that these two contemporaneous but varying conceptions of the virtues were attempts to align the concept of virtue with the purpose of life as understood in the newly broadened context—that of the *polis*. This broadening was the first movement toward the belief in a universal order, which finds clearer expression in Aristotle.

But Plato did not have the last word even in his own day. His package of virtues, together with the moral order it depicted, was all too neat. The tragic dramatists, such as Sophocles, explored the kinds of real conflicts that might arise *between* virtues or *between* goods. To put it differently, the moral order sometimes makes rival and incompatible claims on a person that can force him or her into a tragic situation of having to make a choice between two or more socially incumbent duties, each of which entails dire consequences. In grappling with this conflict, the Sophoclean protagonist is forced to transcend his or her society while remaining inescapably accountable to the higher moral order.

Here, then, is not simply an argument over which of two lists of virtues is better (Achilles' courage or Oedipus's wisdom) but rather an argument over which narrative form (Homer's epic poetry or a Sophoclean tragedy) best depicts the form of human living. MacIntyre suggests a general lesson to be learned: "to adopt a stance on the virtues will be to adopt a stance on the narrative character of human life" precisely because narrative and virtues are mutually supporting and "internally connected" concepts (144).

Aristotle's Model

To defend Aristotle as the apex of virtue theory, MacIntyre must make a characteristically un-Aristotelian move. He must show that Aristotle lies along the historical trajectory that begins with Homeric literature and is, therefore, indebted to and dependent upon his predecessors.[9] Furthermore, MacIntyre must show that Aristotle's formulation of moral philosophy has advanced beyond that of his predecessors while retaining characteristic features of the overall tradition. To do this MacIntyre focuses on four features in Aristotle's thought.

First, the concept of a moral order, which began to emerge in Plato's thinking, becomes more explicit in Aristotle. However, unlike Plato's conception of moral order, which ruled as it were from above, Aristotle sees this moral order as internal to what it means to be human. Humans are *teleological* beings, which is to say, human living aims at an end, or *telos*. Some ends are intermediate rather than terminal. The ship at which shipbuilding aims may in turn be a means for the practice of war craft, which itself may be a means to a yet more distant end. Aristotle reasons that human action consists of means-end chains, which converge on one ultimate end called the Good. The extent to which humans achieve their *telos* is the extent to which they participate in the Good. In Aristotle's mind, the *telos* can be conceived only in terms of a thing's natural function. Similarly, virtues are function-specific, or more precisely, excellency of function.[10] To illustrate, if the function of a horse is to run, then the *telos* of a horse is racing, and its virtue is its speed. Virtues, therefore, are qualities that assist achievement of the *telos*, and the *telos* of a thing is bound up in the nature of the thing.

The nature of human beings, upon which the notion of the human *telos* depends, is bound up in the metaphysical structure of the soul. According to Aristotle, while we may share the vegetative (growth) and locomotive (movement) soul-stuff with the animals, humans are distinguished in the chain of being by their rational souls. The end of human life, therefore, is rationality, and the virtues are (1) *virtues of character*, which assist living according *to* reason, and (2) *virtues of thought*, which enable proper exercise *of* reason itself.

The notion of a function-specific *telos* represents an advance over earlier formulations of the tradition by providing a clearer account of moral imperatives. As noted earlier in the wristwatch illustration, it is the concept of *telos* that provides human beings with moral imperatives. If the function of a watch is timekeeping, then it *ought* to keep time well. If the function of human beings is rationality, then humans *ought* to live in accordance with, and in right exercise of, reason.

The second feature of Aristotle's moral philosophy is *eudaimonia*. A difficult word to translate—blessedness, happiness, prosperity—it seems to connote "the state of being well and doing well in being well, of man's being well-favored himself and in relation to the divine" (148). *Eudaimonia* names that *telos* toward which humans move. Virtues, then, assist the movement toward *eudaimonia*, but *eudaimonia* cannot be defined apart from these same virtues:

> But the exercise of the virtues is not in this sense a means to
> the end of the good for man. For what constitutes the good

for man is a complete human life lived at its best, and the exercise of the virtues a necessary and central part of such a life, not a mere preparatory exercise to secure such a life. We thus cannot characterize the good for man without already having made reference to the virtues. (149)

The apparent circularity of the relation between *telos, eudaimonia,* and *virtue* is not a mark against Aristotle's system but, rather, an advance over Plato's. For Plato, "reality" not only denoted the world of rocks and doorknobs, it also included the world of intangibles such as "love" and "17"—things whose existence in the realm of Form is every bit as real as the middle-sized dry goods that clutter our sensible world. As Plato saw it, "true virtue" belonged to the realm of Form, and particular human qualities were deemed "virtuous" to the extent that they resembled the "true virtue" of which they were copies. Thus, there could be no inherent conflict or disunity between particular virtuous qualities; any tragic conflict was simply a function of imperfection in copying universal virtue into particular living. In this way, morality was thought to be objective and moral reasoning an exercise of the intellect according to which the mind grasped the Form of "true virtue." Ironically, Plato's doctrine failed even to overcome the relativist claims of the Sophists and tragic dramatists of his own day. Although MacIntyre does not think that Aristotle himself explicitly conquered the problem of what to do when virtues conflict, his model, which defines *telos, eudaimonia,* and *virtue* in terms of each other, does point the way toward conceiving moral reasoning as a *skill* rather than as an exercise of intellect (as Plato and the later Enlightenment thinkers imagined). Such skill could be attained and cultivated only *from within* the form of life in which these concepts were at home.

The third feature of Aristotle's system is the distinction between theoretical reasoning and practical reasoning. Practical reasoning begins with a want, or goal, or desire and always terminates in action. Suppose you are thirsty after a long day of shopping. The major premise of your reasoning process is your (obvious) belief that anyone who is thirsty is well advised to find a drinking fountain. The minor premise of this line of thought is your knowledge that a drinking fountain exists in the northwest corner of this particular department store. Your practical reasoning terminates in your act of walking to the northwest corner of the store and quenching your thirst.

In Aristotle's way of looking at things, moral reasoning is an instance of practical reasoning. It is assisted by virtues of character (which temper, guide, and shape initial desires) and virtues of thought (such as *phronesis*, which enables the perception of practical reasoning's major premises).[11]

Perhaps the most important use of practical reason is its employment in the balancing of human activities. I cannot spend all my time in theoretical contemplation, the highest faculty of reason and thus the highest human good (158), because I would soon starve to death. In order to maximize the amount of time I can engage in contemplation, I must balance this activity with work, civic duty, and the like. This mental balancing act is the domain of practical reason. This explanation also sheds light on why virtuous persons make the best civic leaders, since skill in practical reasoning is also what it takes to run the *polis*.

The fourth feature of Aristotle's moral philosophy that MacIntyre emphasizes is friendship. Friendship, of course, involves mutual affection, but for Aristotle, "that affection arises within a relationship defined in terms of common allegiance to and a common pursuit of goods" (156). This is to say that Aristotle's notion of friendship presupposes, first, the existence of the *polis*, which renders common good possible, and second, that this good itself is the health of the *polis*: "We are to think then of friendship as being the sharing of all in the common project of creating and sustaining the life of the city, a sharing incorporated in the immediacy of an individual's particular friendships" (156).

The emphasis on friendship in Aristotle illustrates one aspect of continuity in this historic tradition, namely, that the moral structure is intimately linked with social relationships.

OBSTACLES TO BE HURDLED

Aristotle is definitely the hero of MacIntyre's account. And at the time *After Virtue* was written (1981, revised 1984) MacIntyre saw Aristotle as the apex of the virtue tradition.[12] However, if MacIntyre is to succeed in rejuvenating the Aristotelian tradition, he must overcome three difficulties in Aristotle's account that threaten to topple the whole project. First, Aristotle's notion of *telos* rests on his distinctive "metaphysical biology." In Aristotle's view, the form guarantees that all humans share a common essence. The essence of humanness is rationality. Rationality is of two sorts, theoretical and practical. The *telos* of human life, then, is actualization of both forms of reason. The goal of theoretical reason is contemplation; the goal of practical reason is life in the *polis*. Aristotle's problem was to give an account of how pursuit of these two forms of rationality could be reconciled. MacIntyre's problem is to provide a replacement for Aristotle's concept of form that will enlighten us as to the *telos* of human life. Traditions provide answers to this question. Second, the virtue tradition sees morality as inextricably enmeshed in the life of the *polis*. What does this do for the applicability of the Aristotelian model today, in view of the extinction of the *polis*? Third, Aristotle retains Plato's belief in the unity of the virtues, which implies that every putative case of tragedy reduces to an instance that is "simply the result of flaws of character in individuals or of unintelligent political arrangements" (157). As Sophocles dramatized, instances of tragic evil were not inconceivable. Can such real conflicts be interpreted as contributing to the moral life rather than confusing it?

In addition to the three problems internal to Aristotle's account, MacIntyre notes one problem external to it. To identify the trajectory from Homer to Aristotle to Aquinas to the present as a single tradition, something must be done to reconcile the diversity in the lists of virtues taken from every age. Not only have the *lists* changed with each successive formulation of the tradition,[13] but *how* virtue is defined at one point in history is at odds with the definition explicated in another age.[14] Thus, the fourth problem MacIntyre must overcome is the challenge of demonstrating the kind of continuity between these formulations that makes these disparate accounts a single, unified tradition.

We now turn to MacIntyre's own "metanarrative" to see if he is successful in his endeavors.

ETHICS À LA MACINTYRE

The disparity between virtue lists and even between the definitions of the term can be reconciled, says MacIntyre, by bringing to light the particular backdrop that each formulation presupposes. The tricky part of his analysis is that each of the central concepts—*virtue, practice, narrative*, and *tradition*—can be defined only, finally, in terms of the other concepts. This does not make the MacIntyrean version guilty of circularity. It simply means that getting a handle on his explanation is not like building a house (which progresses incrementally, brick by brick) but like watching the sun rise—the light dawns gradually over the whole.[15]

Practices

The cornerstone of this backdrop is the idea of practices. MacIntyre defines a *practice* somewhat tortuously as

> any coherent and complex form of socially established cooperative human activity through which goods internal to that form of activity are realized in the course of trying to achieve those standards of excellence which are appropriate to, and partially definitive of, that form of activity, with the result that human powers to achieve excellence, and human conceptions of the ends and goods involved, are systematically extended. (187)

Attention to the grammar of this sentence reveals four central concepts. First, practices are human activities. However, these are not activities of isolated individuals but socially established and cooperative activities. Such activities cannot be executed alone but require participation by like-minded others. In addition to being social, these activities are also complex enough to be challenging, and coherent enough to aim at some goal in a unified fashion. Building a house is a practice, while taking long showers is not. The game of tennis is a practice, but hitting a backhand is not. Medicine is a practice, while gargling mouthwash is not.[16]

Second, practices have goods that are internal to the activity. Some practices, for example, jurisprudence, have external goods—money, fame, power—that come as by-products of the practice. But true practices are marked by *internal* goods—those rewards that can be recognized and appreciated only by participants.[17] For example, I can bribe my son with pieces of candy to learn the game of chess. But at some point he may begin to enjoy the game of chess for itself. At this point he has become a practitioner and member of the greater community of chess players. He has, furthermore, become hooked on its internal reward—the joy of chess—something to which all players have access.

Third, practices have standards of excellence without which internal goods cannot be fully achieved. The joy of chess is in having played *well*. And what counts for excellence has been determined by the historical community of practitioners. The practitioners have recognized that stalemate is not as desirable an endgame as checkmate. And to execute a queen-rook fork is more satisfying than simple *en passant*.

Fourth, practices are systematically extended. As practitioners have striven for excellence day in and day out over the years, the standards of the practice, along with practitioners' abilities to achieve these standards, have slowly risen. Perhaps no field better illustrates this than medicine. Doctors were no doubt sincere when they once treated fevers with leeches, but contemporary physicians possess skills that far surpass those of their predecessors. Yet the dependence of contemporary practitioners upon their predecessors is unquestionable: it is precisely because previous doctors strove for excellence that the specific advances in medicine that have been made *have* been made. But increase in technical skill does not quite capture what is meant by the notion of systematic extension. It also includes the way technically proficient doctors have come to appreciate how the health of a patient is a function of a larger system. Thus, the practice of medicine is slowly being extended to encompass care for the whole patient in all his or her psychosocial complexity.[18]

Against the backdrop of practices, virtue can be defined as "an acquired human quality the possession and exercise of which tends to enable us to achieve those goods which are internal to practices and the lack of which effectively prevents us from achieving any such goods" (191). The clan leader who *practices* war craft and the church father who *practices* evangelism are assisted by the qualities of courage and humility respectively. Against this backdrop many of the discrepancies between virtue lists can be reconciled as a matter of differences of practice.

In our smorgasbord era it is tempting to think of practices as self-contained exercises. In fact, many practices are so complex that they have become an entire tradition in themselves. Medicine, science, and war craft all have attending epistemologies, authoritative texts, structured communities and institutions, and histories of development. Other practices are parts of clusters that contribute to the identity of a tradition. For example, the Christian tradition defines itself as a socially expanding movement called "the kingdom of God." At its core, therefore, Christianity seems to consist primarily of the practice of community formation. Subpractices that contribute to community formation can be categorized under the rubrics of *witness, worship, works of mercy, discernment*, and *discipleship*.[19] Other schemes can be imagined of course, but my point is that Christianity cannot be explained or understood without reference to a distinctive cluster of practices. In order to participate in the tradition called Christianity one must necessarily participate in these practices. To put it another way, to participate in the community is to participate in practices because communal life is the point at which the practices intersect. Furthermore, knowing the constitutive practices of Christianity tells us a great deal about how Christians ought to live. If virtues are cultivated by striving for excellence in the practice of practices, then we are unable to grow in Christlikeness unless we participate in Christianity's practices.

Narrative

A second crucial concept that serves as a backdrop to our understanding of the virtues is *narrative*. MacIntyre explains narrative this way. Imagine that a woman approaches you at a bus stop and says, "The name of the common wild duck is *histrionicus histrionicus histrionicus*." Now, what would you make of this person? Truth is, you can't make anything of her, or of her action, without more information. Her act is completely unintelligible. But now suppose it becomes known that this woman is a librarian, and she has mistaken you for the person who earlier had asked for the Latin name of the common wild duck. We can now understand her action because it has been put into a context. The contexts that make sense out of human action are *stories* or *narratives*. To explain an action is simply to provide the story that gives the act its context. We can imagine any number of stories that might make sense out of the bus stop incident (for example, perhaps she is a Russian spy whose password is the sentence in question). But we will also say that the explanation of her action is rendered more fully if we can tell the story that takes her longer- and longest-term intentions into account and shows how her shorter-term intentions relate to the longer-term ones. So we might discover that she has rushed out of the library in search of a particular patron because she has been put on a standard of performance under threat of losing her job. Her longer-term intention is to save her job. Her longest-term intention might be uncovered in telling the story of how she is the sole provider for her paraplegic son. MacIntyre reasons that if human actions are intelligible only with respect to stories that contextualize intentions, then that which unifies actions into sequences and sequences into a continuous whole is the story of one's life. My life as a whole makes sense when my story is told.

This has important consequences for the problem of Aristotle's "metaphysical biology." Imagine we had the opportunity to ask Aristotle, "How can I know that I am the same person as the me of ten years ago?" He would likely reply, "Though your body changes through growth and decay, your form, or essence, is immutable." But this answer is not likely to fly very far for a modern audience. In contrast, MacIntyre suggests that *narrative* provides a better explanation for the unity of a human life. The self has continuity because it has played the single and central character in a particular story—the narrative of a person's life. MacIntyre puts it this way: the unity of the self "resides in the unity of a narrative which links birth to life to death as a narrative beginning to middle to end" (205).

Just as practices have a characteristically social dimension, so also do narratives. Humorist Garrison Keillor reminisces about the distinctive characters who populated the Lake Wobegon, Minnesota, of his childhood. But notice how in identifying themselves as "Norwegian bachelor farmers" such folk have immediately linked who they are with others who share these ethnic, gender, and occupational features. I cannot explain who I am without utilizing some social place markers that identify me with certain strata of my community. If pressed to go beyond this first-level answer to "Who am I?" where can one go but to say that I am also someone's neighbor, child, sibling, student, mate, friend, constituent, or employee? In occupying these roles we simultaneously become subplots in the stories of others' lives just as they have become subplots in ours. In this way, the life stories of members of a community are enmeshed and intertwined. This entanglement of our stories is the fabric of communal life: "For the story of my life is always embedded in the story of those communities from which I derive my identity" (221). Our stories are concretely embedded, or our stories intersect, in those practices in which we are coparticipants. For example, the role of ethics professor links the instructor with the rest of the faculty in general and one group of students in particular, within the wider practice of graduate education.

This construction overcomes the fear that the Aristotelian account of the virtues cannot be sustained after the extinction of the *polis*. In MacIntyre's construction, virtues are those qualities that assist one in the extension of his or her story, and, by extrapolation, the extension of the story of his or her community or communities. The question, "What ought I to do?" is not a question of one's political duty as it was in Aristotle's day, but it *is* a question whose answer must be preceded by the logically prior question: "Of which stories am I a part?"

Although none of us will ever have the clear moral parameters that were to be had in the well-defined social framework of Aristotle's *polis*, the concept of narrative embeddedness still explains the presence of natural boundaries and moral momentum. In 1994 a U.S. postal worker lost his job and retaliated by going on a killing spree. Our responses to his actions were telling. People reacted by saying he "flipped out," "snapped," "went berserk," or "had gone insane." Our expectation is that postal workers (even unemployed ones) aren't killers, and once a postal worker type, always a postal worker type.[20] This illustrates our deeper belief that *rational* human behavior is action that stays within the boundaries of "character." To step outside these boundaries is not merely to act irrationally but to lose one's sanity. This is because the narrative shape of human life carries with it a certain degree of moral momentum. For example, my wife can bank on the fact that I won't wake up tomorrow morning and say, "Today I think I'll become an ax murderer." There is a certain momentum in who I am; I will generally stay "in character." The transition from who I was yesterday to who I am today will be a smooth one, marked only by minor changes. A drastic change in character—whether for the better or for the worse—is always taken to be the result of a long-term, preexistent (though perhaps not publicly visible) process.

Tradition

The third term that forms the backdrop to all the various accounts of virtue is the notion of *tradition*. MacIntyre defines tradition as "an historically extended, socially embodied argument, and an argument precisely in part about the goods which constitute the tradition" (222). This definition has three components. First, MacIntyre's understanding of tradition is really the logical extension of his treatment of narrative. To be "historically extended" is to be narratively extended. Just as the self has the unity of playing a single character in a lifelong story, so too the community has its own continuity—despite loss and gain of members—because the community itself is a character of sorts in a narrative that is longer than the span of a single human life. For example, Christians in the Reformed tradition feel kinship with John Calvin because they can tell the story (recount the history) of the Reformed Church from Calvin's Geneva to their present church community.

Second, a tradition is "socially embodied" because traditions are lived in community. A tradition has its inception in the formation of the community that is defined by those who have pledged corporate allegiance to the tradition's authoritative voice or text.[21] In that this prophetic word shapes the practices of communal life, the community is said to "embody" the tradition's persona in that age. For example, early Christians prayed because their scriptures exemplify, illustrate, and command the practice of prayer. Outsiders, who have no access to the authoritative text, can still read the nature of the Christian tradition off the lives and practices of the community's members. Should the community die off or disband, the tradition passes out of existence (at least until another group rallies in the same way around the same text). In this way the tradition has the quality of being "socially embodied." However, because the application of the authoritative text or voice is done afresh in every successive generation, the tradition remains a live option only so long as the discussion about the text's relevance and meaning is sustained. Hence, third, traditions are necessarily long-standing arguments. But let's get clearer on the notion of historical extension because this will help us evaluate the current status of the virtue tradition.

Just as selves and communities are characters in their respective stories, so too traditions are also characters in an even wider narrative.

When we recount Christian, Jewish, or Muslim history, we are telling the story of just such a character. The viability of any one tradition is not merely its historical survival, however, but its *historical extension*. MacIntyre uses this term to describe the growth a tradition undergoes through time as it overcomes obstacles raised against it. In his sequel to *After Virtue* called *Whose Justice? Which Rationality*? he defines a tradition as

> an argument extended through time in which certain funda-
> mental agreements are defined and redefined in terms of two
> kinds of conflict: those with critics and enemies external to
> the tradition...and those internal, interpretive debates through
> which the meaning and rationale of the fundamental agree-
> ments come to be expressed and by whose progress a tradition
> is constituted.[22]

For example, early Christians faced a crisis when they tried to reconcile three seemingly inconsistent beliefs: God is one, Jesus is divine,
and Jesus is not the Father. The well-known "solution" to this quandary
came when the Cappadocian fathers borrowed Platonic resources to
frame the doctrine of the Trinity. This enabled Christians to believe all
three propositions without logical contradiction. The universal adoption
of their formulation as orthodoxy at Constantinople (AD 381) freed the
Christian tradition to move on to tackle the next obstacle in its path.[23] We
don't know how long the trinitarian problem might have been sustained
had the Cappadocian fathers not entered the debate. We *do* know that by
AD 325 the stakes were very high—unacceptable proposals were deemed
heretical, and their authors were banished from the community (or
worse). Were it not for belief in God's sovereignty over history, it would
be tempting to wonder how long Christianity might have lasted had not
the trinitarian problem been overcome.

If virtue theory is itself a tradition in the sense just described then
we can see that its viability depends upon overcoming the obstacles that
threaten the Aristotelian version. We have already seen how *narrative*
overcomes the problem of Aristotle's metaphysical biology and how
practices overcome the problem of discrepancies in the virtue lists. The
extinction of the *polis* is a third crisis that must be overcome. For

Aristotle, the *telos* of life, together with the attending virtues, can be expressed only in terms of life in the *polis*. One reason the virtuous person was identical to the virtuous citizen was that without the prosperity and leisure engendered by the shared life of the city-state, the highest *telos* (for Aristotle, metaphysical contemplation) was an impractical and impossible ideal. But by exercise of practical reason the *polis* flourished in such a way that contemplation could be maximized (at least by the elite). However, a more fundamental reason virtue was tied to the *polis* was that the Good, at which human life aims, was thought to be a *corporate* Good that could not be possessed by isolated individuals but only jointly in community. The *polis* was the by-product of pursuing this corporate Good together. To put it differently, the Good *was* this corporate life. But now the *polis* is no more. Therefore, in order for the virtue tradition to be extended, there must be an alternative way to understand the social dimension of virtue. Of course, this is ground we have already covered. The narrative shape of human existence—that is, that human sociality is identical to the embeddedness of our respective narratives—shows the way to preserve the sociality of virtue theory even in the absence of the *polis*.

Narrative extends the Aristotelian tradition in another way as well. MacIntyre credits the high medieval age with conceptualizing the genre of our narrativity to be akin to the quest for the Holy Grail: "In the high medieval scheme a central genre is the tale of a quest or journey. Man is essentially *in via*. The end which he seeks is something which if gained can redeem all that was wrong with his life up to that point" (174–75). MacIntyre goes on to say that this move was *un*-Aristotelian in at least two ways. First, it placed the *telos* of life beyond life, in contrast to Aristotle, who imagined the *telos* of life to be "a certain kind of life." Second, it allowed for the possibility of positive evil in contrast to the Aristotelian scheme, which understood evil as always the privation of a good. These two features gave the medieval view an advantage over Aristotle in dealing with the problem of tragic evil. In the eyes of the medieval person, the achievement of the human *telos* counterbalanced all evil, even evils of the tragic sort envisioned by Sophocles. Thus, the fourth objection that threatened *Aristotle* (that is, tragic evil) has been overcome by the Aristotelian *tradition*:

> The narrative therefore in which human life is embodied has
> a form in which the subject…is set a task in the completion
> of which lies their peculiar appropriation of the human good;
> the way toward which the completion of that task is barred
> by a variety of inward and outward evils. The virtues are
> those qualities which enable evils to be overcome, the task to
> be accomplished, the journey to be completed. (175)

MacIntyre concludes, therefore, that tragic choices are real but
that the inevitability of such choice does not render morality unintelligible or criterionless (as the emotivist claims, thereby concluding that
moral choices boil down to matters of preference). Rather, such choice
plays a central role in the development of character by providing an
occasion for moral agents to exercise and build virtue when they sustain
the quest for good precisely at the time it is most costly to do so. If "the
good life for man is the life spent in seeking for the good life for man,
and the virtues necessary for the seeking are those which will enable us
to understand what more and what else the good life for man is," then
tragic evil is overcome because evil, even evil of the tragic sort, cannot
diminish this kind of good (219). Instead of detracting from this kind of
goodness, tragic evil can even be thought to *contribute* to the moral fiber
of the life so lived. This solution to the problem of tragic evil employs a
view of life that has come out of a particular historical cross-section of
the tradition. Because the medieval period provides them with the
resources for overcoming this obstacle, adherents to this tradition are
warranted in retaining this feature from their corporate past. So then, not
only are practices and narratives sources for understanding the human
telos, but tradition itself contributes to this understanding.

Identifying the genre of a tradition's narrative also makes sense
out of the fractal symmetry that can be seen when we look at the way in
which the narrative unity of (1) a life, (2) a community, and (3) a tradition are mutually nested. Individual, community, and tradition, while
telling different parts of the master story, nevertheless share equally in
the genre of that story. Thus, if the genre of the tradition is that of a
quest, the genre of a human life is also that of a quest. And if human life
is a quest, then human virtues are those qualities that assist it:

The virtues therefore are to be understood as those dispositions which will not only sustain practices and enable us to
achieve the goods internal to practices, but which will also
sustain us in the relevant kind of quest for the good, by
enabling us to overcome the harms, dangers, temptations
and distractions which we encounter, and which will furnish
us with increasing self-knowledge and increasing knowledge of the good. (219)

RETROSPECT

Looking back, we can see not only that the virtue tradition that
MacIntyre has recounted fits his definition of tradition but that it is one
in which he represents the most recent advance! He has succeeded in
overcoming four important obstacles to the Aristotelian model by eluci-
dating the story about stories, or what has been called the metanarrative
about the narrative quality of human life. In so doing he has clarified
how the notions of *telos, virtue, practice, narrative*, and *tradition* form
a mutually supporting and interlocking web of concepts.

Let us recall now the master argument of *After Virtue*. MacIntyre
challenged us to reconsider the emotivist conclusion (namely, that
morality is by nature nothing more than matters of preference) by arguing that the Enlightenment Project's move to repudiate all things social
(that is, virtues and practices) and all things historical (that is, narrative
and tradition) was a major misstep. He argued further that moral imperatives can be derived from an answer to the question, "What is human
life for?" In the same way the functional definition of a watch ("A watch
is for timekeeping") entails its virtue (accuracy), its functional imperative ("A watch *ought* to keep time well"), and its ground for being evaluated ("This grossly inaccurate watch is a *bad* watch"). To have a grasp
on the human *telos* affords us with moral virtues, moral imperatives, and
sufficient grounds for moral judgment. Furthermore, because narratives
intersect at social practices, and practices constitute traditions, and traditions are historically (that is, narratively) extended, to understand
virtue adequately as those qualities that assist pursuit of *telos* at all three
levels, virtue itself must be given a threefold definition:

The virtues find their point and purpose not only in sustaining those relationships necessary if the variety of goods internal to practices are to be achieved and not only in sustaining the form of an individual life in which that individual may seek out his or her good as the good of his or her whole life, but also in sustaining those traditions which provide the practices and individual lives with their necessary historical context. (223)

Aristotle's notion of virtue as "excellency of function" has thus been expanded. Human virtues are learned qualities that assist us in achieving the human *telos*, which can be understood by considering (1) the functional definition of the human person, which is provided by the master story of the tradition, (2) the internal goods of those practices that constitute the tradition, and (3) those roles that arise at the intersection of our life stories. To put it differently, moral imperatives arise from that understanding of the human *telos* that arises within the context of those practices, narratives, and tradition in which we locate ourselves.

CONCLUSION

In the end there is much unfinished business. MacIntyre himself bemoans the marked absence of moral communities in the modern world. But this is not the only problem that must be addressed in the wake of *After Virtue*. For example, if the answer to "What is human life for?" is supplied to each of us by our respective practices, narratives, and traditions, doesn't this still leave us with an incurable problem of moral pluralism if not one of downright relativism? Are there some criteria for adjudicating multiple traditions? Further, if MacIntyre's project succeeds, are we in the Western world not faced with the dilemma of being inheritors of at least two conflicting traditions (namely, Aristotelianism and political liberalism)? Or can MacIntyre's thesis possibly succeed if, in fact, the Aristotelian tradition *died* with the Enlightenment? With what resources can it be exhumed and resuscitated?

MacIntyre is not unaware of these perplexities. Some of the objections earned responses in the second edition of *After Virtue* while others he has made the central concern of later books. But the mere presence of these objections does not count against his system because they become the fodder for enlivening the debate by which the tradition is extended. The question, "Is MacIntyre's moral philosophy the *final* word?" is wrongheaded. The better question is, "Is it the best one so far?"

Notes

1. Sergei Shargorodsky, "Russian Lawmakers Do Battle," *The Sun* (San Bernardino, CA), 12 September 1995, A5.

2. Alasdair MacIntyre, *After Virtue*, 2nd ed. (Notre Dame, IN: University of Notre Dame Press, 1984), 11–12. Hereafter, page numbers in parentheses in the text refer to this book.

3. Alasdair MacIntyre, *Whose Justice? Which Rationality?* (Notre Dame, IN: University of Notre Dame Press, 1988), 300–325.

4. This can be understood by means of the following illustration. Consider first the case where lying is simply speaking the opposite of the truth, A person faced with the question of whether to lie on a given occasion should easily realize that lying cannot be universalized without rational contradiction. For if everyone lied, then lying would become the normal mode of communication. If everyone always lied, we would simply adjust our expectations and hence could navigate just fine. For example, one day my eight-year-old son declined my offer of a peanut butter sandwich but then reminded me with a grin that Tuesday was "opposite day." Once I knew the plan, we had no trouble communicating because I could bank on the opposite of what he said. ("Do you like it?" "No, it's awful. I hate it!") Similarly, in a world where lying was the universal practice, deception could not exist because lying, in effect, would have become the means of truth telling. Of course, this would fly in the face of what we understand by the term *lying*. So we run headlong into a rational contradiction: *lying* cannot be universalized because when universalized, lying ceases to be lying. Therefore, the opposite of lying must be universalizable; or to put it differently, truth telling is the categorical imperative.

Now imagine the case that lying is not simple opposite-saying but distortion of truth—a mixture of truth and error. It should be clear that the sort of confusion that would be produced by universalizing this brand of lying would be on the scale that disables all communication—*including deception*. In such a world "intent to deceive" has no meaning. So, once again, we run up against a rational contradiction: universalization of lying leads to the state of affairs in which what is universalized, that is, lying, is logically impossible.

5. Admittedly, the Aristotelian model of morality makes moral imperatives appear hypothetical—as means to socially conceded ends—but theistic morality has the same basic shape. The primary difference is that the theistic version contends that the human *telos* is divinely determined, a determination that has the effect of bestowing a categorical status on moral imperatives.

6. Of course, it could also be argued that watches make fashion statements, have sentimental value, and so forth. But for sake of the illustration, let us imagine that watches are useful only for timekeeping.

7. Please note, however, that the situation in the wake of the Enlightenment Project's failure is far worse than merely a state of being unable to settle disagreements. MacIntyre argues that the disagreements themselves are wrongheaded in the first place. Seventeenth-century empiricists thought themselves adequate to the task of dealing with *brute* facts, when the truth of the matter is that facts cannot be perceived apart from a conceptual framework that recognizes, sorts, prioritizes, and evaluates the facts. Value-laden theory is required to support observation as much as vice versa. This insight was overlooked when, in the transition to the world of "modern" science, the medieval notion of final cause (that is, causes that proceed according to *teloi*) was rejected in favor of making efficient causes the whole ball of wax. When this scientistic view becomes adopted by ethicists, what emerges is a mechanistic account of human action framed in terms of "laws of human behavior" with all reference to intentions, purposes, and reasons for action omitted. The "facts" of human behavior are thus construed free from value concepts (such as "good"), and human action is thereafter presumed to be predictable and manipulable like all other physical bodies. This presumption is embodied in the central character of the emotivist era: the bureaucratic manager. Unfortunately for the manager we do not possess lawlike generalizations for human behavior. In fact, human behavior is systematically unpredictable for a number of reasons. Both the expert manager and the attending virtue of "effectiveness" are fictions that expose the poverty of the Enlightenment Project (cf. *After Virtue*, 93–99).

8. Plato goes on to argue that society is, or ought to be, arranged along the same lines. The bronze class of society are those working folk whose citizenship is assisted by the virtue of prudence. The silver class comprises the warriors in whom the high-spirited part of the soul dominates. The quality they need above all is courage. The gold class, of course, is made up of the philosopher-kings, whose role in society is not merely to rule but to contemplate truth with the aid of the virtue of wisdom. Social justice, in Plato's view, signified keeping the classes in the proper order, which amounted to maintaining the status quo. In this way Plato's system is by nature conservative: change (including progress) was bad; stability was good.

9. Frederick Copleston notes that Aristotle, like Hegel, saw himself to be systematizing and improving upon previous philosophy. See *A History of*

Philosophy, 9 vols. (New York: Doubleday, 1985), 1:371–78. Yet while Aristotle appreciated his Platonic heritage, he conceived his own work in terms of "getting it right" in those places Plato "got it wrong." What is un-Aristotelian, therefore, is MacIntyre's historicist claim that Aristotle's work lies along a trajectory that stretches from Plato to the Middle Ages and beyond, a claim that necessarily relativizes Aristotle's contribution to the conceptual framework he shared with his predecessors. Thus the "new ground" Aristotle broke must be seen as nothing more than *intrasystematic* improvements.

10. In *Nicomachean Ethics*, Aristotle writes, "[E]very virtue causes its possessors to be in a good state and to perform their functions well." *Nicomachean Ethics*, trans. Terence Irwin (Indianapolis, IN: Hackett Publishing, 1985), 1106a.

11. Since right action follows in straightforward fashion from the initial desire and major premise, and since differences in initial desires as well as differences in major premises boil down to variations in the exercise of the respective virtues, moral quandaries are nonexistent for Aristotle. When in a bind, he can always defer to the maxim, "The morally right action is that taken by the virtuous person."

12. In later works, MacIntyre becomes convinced that Aquinas had succeeded in surpassing Aristotle on several points. See Alasdair MacIntyre, *Whose Justice? Which Rationality?* and *Three Rival Versions of Moral Enquiry: Encyclopaedia, Genealogy, and Tradition* (Notre Dame, IN: University of Notre Dame Press, 1990).

13. For example, the early church fathers champion humility as a virtue, while Aristotle repudiates it as a vice (182)!

14. For example, Aristotle sees virtues as the means to internal ends, while Benjamin Franklin sees virtues as means to external, even utilitarian, ends (184).

15. This illustration comes from Ludwig Wittgenstein, *On Certainty*, ed. G. E. M. Anscombe and G. H. von Wright, trans. Denis Paul and G. E. M. Anscombe (New York: Harper Torchbooks, 1969, 1972), §141.

16. For an extended discussion of practices see chapter 7 of *After Virtue*.

17. It is often, but not always, the case that internal rewards are shared among all practitioners without diminution.

18. The changing mode of the physician-patient relationships is detailed by William F. May in *The Physician's Covenant* (Philadelphia: Westminster, 1983).

19. For an alternate list of constitutive Christian practices see Craig R. Dykstra, "No Longer Strangers: The Church and Its Educational Ministry," *Princeton Seminary Bulletin* 6, no. 3 (1985): 188–200.

20. We would even say that someone who sincerely harbors paranoia that the mail carrier is a killer is mentally maladjusted.

21. For an extended account of how traditions are born and develop see chapter 18 of MacIntyre's *Whose Justice? Which Rationality?*

22. *Whose Justice? Which Rationality?* 12.

23. The next major debate was the doctrine of Christ: if Christ was God the Son, how are we to understand the relation of his divine and human natures while preserving the unity of his person?

3. Virtue: The Catholic Moral Tradition Today

Charles E. Curran

This chapter first appeared in Charles E. Curran, *The Catholic Moral Tradition Today* (Notre Dame, IN: University of Notre Dame Press, 1999).

Virtue has played an important role in Catholic moral theology as exemplified in the work of Thomas Aquinas. Here virtue is understood as a good habit or stable disposition inclining the person toward the good.[1] However, the manuals of moral theology, which were the textbooks used before Vatican II, with their narrow focus on sinful acts paid basically no attention to virtue.

In the past decades philosophical ethics have paid more attention to virtue. Many have realized there is more to ethics than the quandary ethics that discusses whether or not particular acts are right or wrong. In philosophical ethics the dissatisfaction with the unencumbered self of much contemporary thinking has occasioned the return by some to the tradition of Aristotle and the virtues.[2]

Protestant ethics has tended to be suspicious of a virtue ethics approach because of its understanding of justification and its fear of any ethic based on the principle of human flourishing and striving for perfection. Protestantism has generally insisted on God's gracious gift and has been fearful of the latent Pelagianism (we are saved by our own efforts) in Catholic understandings of salvation and morality. However, in this country Stanley Hauerwas, while recognizing traditional Protestant problems with virtues, has proposed an approach to character and virtue that has sparked a great interest.[3] Recall that Hauerwas's emphasis on a narrative theology and virtue comes within the context of a morality based primarily on what is required for life in the church and does not directly address life for the world at large. Gilbert Meilaender, writing from a Lutheran perspective, has problems with the eudaimonistic aspect of virtue ethics and the emphasis on human flourishing that seem to detract from the role of God's gift of salvation. Meilaender's virtue ethics tries to hold on to the tension between the self-mastery of moral virtue and a self that is perfectly passive before God; the tension between a virtue we claim as our possession and the self perfectly passive before God; the tension between virtue as a possession and as continually reestablished by divine grace; the tension between a self that can see itself only in part and a self whole before God.[4] These examples show that Protestants today are proposing the role and importance of virtue and character in the moral life, even though they may have some significant differences with the Catholic approaches.

VIRTUE IN THE CATHOLIC TRADITION

The Catholic tradition has generally seen virtue as a part of human flourishing and the call of God to strive for perfection in response to God's gift. The Catholic tradition has always insisted on a proper love of the self and the importance of happiness and self-fulfillment not with the individual as the absolute and the ultimate but as a part of God's gracious reign and love. Love of God, love of neighbor, and love of self ultimately fit together. The Christian brings the human to its greatest perfection. The virtues are seen in this context of this theologically grounded vision of human flourishing and happiness.

There is a persistent tension between Aristotle and Christianity (especially as interpreted by Augustine) and between philosophy and theology in the writings and legacy of Thomas Aquinas. This also comes through in recent interpretations of the Thomistic approach to virtue. Jean Porter in her 1990 book *The Recovery of Virtue* deals only with the philosophical aspect of Aquinas and brackets the theological.[5] In his 1991 book on *The Moral Virtues and Theological Ethics*, Romanus Cessario insists on the theological aspects of Aquinas's approach by developing the Thomistic notion that the Christian moral virtues are infused and not acquired.[6] Likewise, Thomas O'Meara has strongly maintained that the Dominican tradition of Thomism (that espoused by members of the Order of Friars Preachers) is theological with regard to the virtues. This means the virtues must be rooted in grace with emphasis on the infused virtues and not the acquired virtues. Just as grace changes the basic being of the individual person, the infused virtues affect and change the powers or faculties of the person.[7]

Contemporary Catholic debates about the virtues have historical precedents beginning in Aquinas's day. Medieval theologians after Aquinas did not always accept his position on the infused virtues. Some medieval theologians accepted only the acquired moral virtues but now under the influence and direction of the theological virtues.[8] Such debates illustrate a tension between the role of God's gift and the human response that will always remain in theological ethics. The danger in the Catholic tradition has most often been toward Pelagianism—overemphasizing the human response. This same tension also affects our understanding of the virtues. Here too, we see the need for both God's gift and the human response, but the Catholic tradition will not be as paradoxical as the Lutheran in its manner of holding on to these two aspects. For the Catholic tradition, grace is a true possession of the believer as a result of God's gracious gift. Lutheran thought tends to see grace as imputed to the believer, but it does not intrinsically transform the person.

The recognition of historical consciousness, social location, diversity, pluralism, and individual vocations also influences our interpretation of the virtues today. Is it still possible to propose the virtues that should characterize Christian life today in the midst of such diversity and pluralism? Here again the particular and the universal come into tension. The unique individual will have a particular character because of the way in which the different virtues are put together in her life. Everyone creates her own personal synthesis. In addition, within the Christian community some individuals are called to bear witness to specific attitudes or virtues to the exclusion of others. Some are called to be pacifists; others are called to embrace celibacy, others voluntary poverty. Yes, much individual diversity exists, but there still remains a minimal understanding of those virtues that must form a part of every Christian life. One can spell out the virtues of the Christian life common to all Christians only in the sense of a loosely arranged minimum common to all.[9]

Other aspects of the Thomistic approach might also not be so appropriate today. Thomas carried on the tradition by speaking about the cardinal virtues—prudence, justice, fortitude, and temperance. Cardinal in this meaning does not necessarily imply the most important or significant. Cardinal refers to a logical primacy. The cardinal virtues are the logical hinges (the Latin word *cardo*) on which all other virtues can build and be grouped together in a logical way. They are logically prior but not existentially more important.[10] Thus, for example, justice is the cardinal virtue and religion fits under justice. Most people would be willing to admit that religion, which attempts to give to God what is God's due, is more important than justice, which deals with neighbors and others. However, justice fits perfectly the logical requirements of giving everyone what is due to them. Religion does not fulfill this criterion perfectly because we can never give God what is due to God. Since religion lacks the logical perfection of justice, it cannot be a cardinal virtue.[11]

Thomas Aquinas, in keeping with his emphasis on hierarchical ordering, maintained that the cardinal virtues could not be in competition with one another. Ultimately justice was the supreme arbiter and no real conflicts could exist.[12] But today we are much more conscious of the tensions we face between different virtues. The tension between forgiveness and justice comes to the fore in many aspects of public life but also at times in private life.[13] Fidelity and truthfulness seem to conflict in some situations. The fact that such conflicts exist does not detract from the role and importance of the virtues but reminds us of the tensions and conflicts based on human finitude and sinfulness that we all experience in human and Christian existence today.

How should we understand and develop the role of the virtues? Thomas Aquinas distinguished between the theological and the moral virtues. The theological virtues, faith, hope, and charity, which are gifts from God and infused, have God as their immediate object. The moral virtues, which are also gifts of God and infused, do not have God as their immediate object but rather human beings, and are explained in terms of the four cardinal virtues. In Aquinas there is a twofold basis for the way in which the moral virtues are developed on the basis of the four cardinal virtues. The first way grounds the virtues in the four different faculties or powers that they modify. Many today reject such a Thomistic faculty psychology. But for Aquinas, the cardinal virtues of prudence, justice, fortitude, and temperance and all the virtues related to them refer to the four faculties of intellect, will, irascible appetite (overcomes obstacles in the way of the good), and concupiscible appetite (desires what is pleasing). A second approach in Aquinas is based on the relation between the person and the goods of value. The first relationship is the practical knowledge of the good to which the cardinal virtue of prudence belongs. Fortitude and temperance govern the relationship with oneself and justice directs the relationship with others through external actions.[14] Here are some traces of a relational model in Aquinas.

This chapter will discuss the virtues in light of the relationality-responsibility model of the moral life. This model sees the moral life in light of the individual's multiple relationships to God, neighbor, world, and self, and the need to act responsibly within these relationships. The chapter will discuss the general virtues that affect our basic orientation and all our relationships and then discuss the virtues that modify our particular relationships with God, neighbor, world, and self.

GENERAL VIRTUES

The traditional theological virtues of faith, hope, and love, although generally described as gifts of God having God as their immediate object, basically modify the fundamental orientation of the person that includes in an implicit way the fundamental relationships described in the model. The theological virtue of charity well illustrates such an understanding. In the Catholic tradition the theological virtue, due to God's prevenient love for us, refers to the love that we give in response to God's gracious gift. The biblical approaches to love have recognized in many ways that the love of God is intimately connected with love of neighbor, world, and self although individual biblical authors often emphasize different aspects of love.

Thomas Aquinas's approach to charity also includes the four fundamental relationships described in the model. Charity is primarily friendship with God—the love of God for God's own sake brought about by the Holy Spirit working in us. The first and formal object of charity is God, but love also reaches to others including enemies because they are loved for God's sake. Aquinas in the same way recognizes that a person can love oneself in charity. However, Aquinas distinguishes between other rational creatures and irrational creatures. Since love of God is friendship, we cannot love or have friendship with irrational creatures. However, irrational creatures (his term) can be loved with charity insofar as through charity we wish them to be conserved for the honor of God and the usefulness of human beings.[15] Today I would want to see the material part of creation more directly related to charity, but still Thomas Aquinas recognized that the love of God includes neighbors, self, and, in some way, material creation. However, in keeping with much of the Catholic tradition, he is perhaps too anthropocentric and does not give enough importance to the material world itself. The exact meaning of love in the Christian tradition has been constantly debated. Amidst these debates the Catholic tradition with its emphasis on inclusiveness, as illustrated by Thomas, sees love as affecting all our relationships—God, neighbor, world, and self.

Faith involves our fundamental recognition of God in Jesus and through the Spirit as our Creator, Redeemer, and Sanctifier.[16] Faith primarily involves a personal relationship with God. In the Bible faith is a surrender to and a total commitment to God that, however, affects the person in all other aspects of life. The Thomistic tradition with its faculty psychology tied faith to the intellect, but faith must be seen as affecting the total person. Whereas the Catholic approach at times has overstressed the intellectual aspect of faith and the truths to believe, one can never forget that faith does involve an intellectual aspect and there are truths of faith. But faith is much more than just an intellectual assent to truths for it involves our relationship with God and affects the totality of our being. The prayer for the liturgy of the Twentieth Sunday in Ordinary Time speaks of God being present in all things and beyond all things. Such a perspective is the fruit of faith.

Faith also reminds us that we are not self-sufficient monads. We surrender ourselves to the gracious God but this involves not just a passive response but the commitment to live out our existence as God's people. Faith in God for the Catholic includes membership in the church, the community of faith, and affects our relationships with other believers, nonbelievers, and the whole world that God has made. In the world we journey together by faith, which gives a direction and an intentionality to all we do as believers.

In our contemporary world the virtue of hope has come to the fore, for this virtue deals with the meaningfulness of human existence in this world.[17] Do we really live in a vale of tears? Is there any meaning to this world with all its problems and atrocities? For believers in God the relationship between our faith in God and our life in the world becomes most significant. What is the meaning of our existence as we strive to live in this world? In this vein, John Courtney Murray once raised the question if life in this world is simply like basket weaving, which does not have any real inherent meaning.[18]

Hope as a theological virtue is based on the power and promise of God to bring us to the fullness of life.[19] Hope was central to the life of God's covenant people in the Hebrew Scriptures. Yahweh made a promise to the people, and Yahweh was faithful to that promise to safeguard and protect his people and bring them forth from the bondage of Egypt into the Promised Land.

In the Christian tradition Augustine developed an understanding of hope with the primary emphasis on the hope of the individual for eternal life after death. On the other hand, Joachim of Fiore in the fourteenth century emphasized the effect of hope on human history and pointed out different stages of development in human history. In the modern era scientific progress, Enlightenment thinking, the theory of evolution, and the emphasis on progressive history encouraged a belief in evolution and progress in history. Contemporary liberation theologies concerned with the poor, the racially oppressed, and women all have been rooted in the effect of eschatology on history and the need to bring about development and changes in history more in accord with the reign of God. But for Christian theology hope cannot be reduced to a secular theory of progressive development.

Hope influences the personal and social life of the Christian. In personal life the believer hopes that death is not the end, but God's all enduring love will change death into life. Suffering is a fact of life in our world. Even in the midst of sorrow and suffering the Christian person lives in the hope of the resurrection. In personal suffering the Christian participates in the paschal mystery of Jesus with its dying and rising. In social life our relationship to the world is not just a time of passive endurance but a vocation to make the reign of God more present in our world. The most significant question today concerns the relationship between hope and history, between the eschatological future and the contemporary historical realities. The fivefold stance of creation, sin, incarnation, redemption, and resurrection destiny sheds considerable light on this question. Creation is good and God's redemption is already present and working in our world, but sin remains and the fullness of the reign of God will only come at the end of time. The stance points out the opposite extreme dangers of either putting the reign of God completely into the future with nothing in the present, or putting the fullness of the reign of God into history while having nothing more in the future. Christians are called to strive to bring about greater justice, freedom, and peace in our world while recognizing that the fullness of justice and peace will only come at the end of time and history. In all our relationships, despite the frustrations and negative aspects, we strive to grow and develop.

In personal life and in social life the Christian struggles to make the reign of God more present. However, it always remains a struggle. The Christian approach avoids both naive optimism and a pervasive pessimism. We are called to grow in all our relationships, but this growth will always be difficult, suffer reverses, and never be ultimately successful. In the mid- to late-twentieth century people were too optimistic all over the world but especially in our country. People often naively thought that change and progress could come quickly, easily, and without great problems. Today in the world and in the United States a greater pessimism reigns. The problems are manifold, answers are hard to come by, and people often retreat into their own private lives in the light of the seemingly insoluble problems with which we live. Christian hope supplies the motivation and the energy to work for a better world with the knowledge that change will never be easy and the fullness of the reign of God will only come as God's gracious gift on the other side of time and history. The Christian continues to struggle even when there are no accomplishments but only problems. Hope ultimately does not depend on tangible and visible results but on our trust in the promise of God who can turn sorrow into joy and death into life. The Christian struggling for justice in all aspects of life bears witness to the promise of God that will never be totally verified in human history. Only Christian hope enables believers to carry on the struggle even in the absence of visible signs of success.

With regard to the life of the church, pre-Vatican II Catholicism was rightly accused of triumphalism based on a practical tendency to equate the church with the reign of God.[20] Vatican II insists on a pilgrim church that is not the reign of God but at best the sacrament and witness to the reign of God. This pilgrim church is also a sinful church that is always in need of reform and renovation.[21] Today many progressive Catholics have been greatly frustrated by the problems of the institutional church and its failure to change. One often hears the question: Is there any hope for the church? In a sense such a question betrays a poor notion of hope. Hope does not depend ultimately on human accomplishments or works but on the promise and presence of God. There is always hope, but we have to struggle to bring about change and make the church itself a better witness to the reign of God.

The Aristotelian-Thomistic tradition sees virtue in the middle between the opposite extremes. Thus generosity stands in the middle between the extremes of prodigalness and miserliness. The opposite extremes of hope in terms of excess or defect are presumption and despair, which the manuals of moral theology developed as the two primary sins against hope.[22] The notion of virtue as a middle between two extremes of excess and defect continues to have some meaning for us today in many areas. In the case of hope today we might see the opposites as an easy optimism and a negative pessimism. Hope thus affects the Christian person in all one's relationships and is very often a distinguishing feature of Christian life in this world. The Christian hopes in good times and in bad, in life and in death, in joy and in suffering.

There are other general virtues that affect all our relationships. We are called and challenged to grow in our multiple relationships and, thus, creativity plays a very important role in Christian life. We try to find ways to improve, deepen, widen, and develop our multiple relationships. The *kairos* in the biblical understanding is a special time given by God—the opportune moment.[23] The Christian person takes advantage of these opportunities to grow in relationships. The emphasis on historicity, growth, and development in the moral life underscores the importance of creativity in all our relationships. Note how this compares with the stress on obedience in the legal model. In the context of law, obedience became the primary and seemingly the only virtue. However, creativity becomes much more important in the relationality-responsibility model.

The emphasis on the subject in contemporary thought also stresses the need for the virtue of creativity. There is no one model of character combining the virtues that everyone is to follow. Each individual is unique. Again there are many common elements in the Christian moral life, but each individual puts them together in a unique way. As a result of this, the creativity of the individual assumes an even greater role in developing oneself in terms of these multiple relationships. In keeping with the importance of creativity some contemporary moral theologians have insisted on the important role of imagination.[24]

However, creativity exists in tension with the need for fidelity. We are not free to do anything we please. The existing relationships are to be strengthened and deepened, not abandoned and overturned. Fidelity plays a significant role in the covenantal relationship between God and us, and it must also be present in all our relationships. Without doubt the Catholic tradition, until recently with the advent of historical consciousness, did not give enough importance to creativity. But one cannot absolutize creativity because we are all conscious of both our limitations and, in the relationality-responsibility model, of our involvement with others. Thus, the inclusive Catholic approach today once again insists on a "both-and" approach. Bernard Häring, who contributed the most to the renewal of Catholic moral theology before and after Vatican II, perceptively entitled his second three volumes on moral theology *Free and Faithful in Christ.*[25]

From an ethical perspective the insistence on both creativity and fidelity avoids the dangers of a one-sided consequentialism and of a one-sided deontology. Creativity or freedom is often associated with doing good or achieving good consequences. But we are limited human beings and exist in multiple relationships that direct our creativity. The Catholic tradition has recognized that one cannot directly kill innocent civilians in the course of war no matter how much good one wants to accomplish.[26] On the other hand, fidelity has never been proposed as an absolute. For example, vows, which are promises made to God, can be broken if the matter of the vow or the persons involved have substantially changed. The Catholic Church has always given dispensations from some religious vows or promises.[27] Thus, both creativity and fidelity characterize all our different relationships. Other general virtues affecting all our relationships include truthfulness and honesty. However, the purpose here is not to discuss exhaustively all these virtues but rather to illustrate the most significant virtues and how they shape the Christian person as both subject and agent.

PARTICULAR VIRTUES

In addition to the general virtues that affect the total person and all her relationships, there are also particular virtues affecting the particular relationships. A brief sketch of some of the more significant virtues affecting our particular relationships follows.

Relationship to God

The Christian sees all life and reality as a gift from God. God gives, we receive; God calls, we respond. The fundamental disposition in the Christian with regard to God is openness and readiness to receive the gift. The believer must constantly be open to recognize, receive, and respond to the gift of God's gracious love in all its dimensions. The significant biblical figures are those who were open to hear and respond to the call of God—Abraham and Sarah, Moses, the prophets, and in the New Testament, Mary. Mary is the model of all believers since she was most open to the Word of God and totally responded to it—be it done unto me according to your word (Luke 1:38). Jesus is pictured in the same type of relationship with his heavenly Father (John 17). Discipleship in the community of the disciples of Jesus entails this fundamental openness to God's life-giving words and deeds. The Gospels frequently insist on the need to be open and ready when God comes—be vigilant and watchful (Mark 13:32–35, Matt 25:1–13, Luke 12:35–48).

Openness is a virtue that many Americans today gladly accept. We talk about the importance of being open and the dangers of being closed. However, being open is much more challenging in reality than it seems. Being open to God (and others) stands in opposition to self-centeredness and self-sufficiency. The person who is closed in on oneself can never hear the promptings of the Spirit. This fundamental openness to God goes against the self-sufficiency and absolutization of the individual that is so persuasive today.

This openness to God and the need for vigilance continues throughout our life. God is constantly coming to us. The Spirit is always prompting us. The danger is that we become so preoccupied with self in our daily concerns that we are deaf and blind to the call and sight of God. As mentioned before, Christian theology speaks about the *kairos*—the time or the moment in which God comes to us (Eph 5:16, Col 4:5). The Christian has to be open to hear the call of God and seize the opportunity in the midst of all the daily duties, obligations, and distractions of our lives. True openness thus calls for a contemplative aspect to our being that allows us to truly discern the call of God amidst the din and cacophony of the many voices we hear. God comes to us not only in the depths of our hearts but also in the circumstances and relationships of our daily lives especially in the needs of others. The spiritual tradition often recommends time for contemplation and retreat precisely so that one can truly be more disposed to hearing the call of God in daily life and acting upon it.[28]

The first Beatitude in Matthew 5:3 proclaims, "Blessed are the poor in spirit for theirs is the kingdom of God." The notion of being poor in spirit underscores the emphasis on openness. The poor in spirit recognize that they depend on God for all things and by their posture of open arms signify their watchfulness and need to receive from God. Both the materially poor and the poor in spirit are important biblical concepts, but the danger exists among affluent Christians of overemphasizing the poor in spirit at the expense of the role of the materially poor. Nevertheless, there always remains an important role in the Christian life for the poor in spirit.[29]

Thankfulness or gratitude is another important virtue in our relationship with God that again comes from the initiating gracious act of God's gift. Whatever we have is received as gift from God. Praise and thanks are fundamental Christian attitudes. The liturgical emphasis of Roman Catholicism illustrates the emphasis on praise. The Eucharist is at the heart and center of Catholic life and the very Greek word means thanksgiving. According to the beginning of the Eucharist prayer, we do well always and everywhere to give thanks but especially in this Eucharist.[30]

At times even in the Catholic tradition, the praise aspect of the sacraments has been diminished or forgotten. The older format and name of the sacrament of reconciliation was confession—the confession of sins according to number and species to the priest. The experience of the sacrament involved little or no praise or thanksgiving. But the primary reality of every sacrament is the worship and praise of God for mercy and forgiveness. The Catholic tendency toward Pelagianism has in instances such as this downplayed the aspect of God's gracious initiative to which our first response is gratitude. Ironically, the Latin word for confession actually means to give praise and thanks. The *Confessions* of Augustine are not the memoirs in which he tells all including his early life but rather his praise and thanks to God. Penance celebrates the reconciling mercy and forgiveness of God and praises God for these gifts.[31]

Relationship to Others

Justice in the Catholic tradition has been the most significant virtue involving our relationships with others. Modern papal social teaching, beginning with Pope Leo XIII's encyclical *Rerum novarum* in 1891, used the Thomistic understanding of justice to develop the official teaching.[32] Subsequent hierarchical teaching has followed somewhat the same approach as exemplified in the pastoral letter of the United States bishops on the economy. The recent documents as illustrated by this pastoral letter continue to see this Thomistic approach to be consonant with, and a good way of organizing, the different aspects of justice found in the scripture.[33]

Justice in this tradition involves giving the person what is her due. The ultimate question concerns the meaning and reality of what is due. The basic reality of justice itself is complex precisely because of the undergirding anthropology that emphasizes the social nature of human beings. Justice involves three different types of relationships—one individual to another individual, society (or the state) to the individual, and the individual to society (or the state). Each of these relationships brings into play a different type of justice. Notice how the Catholic recognition of the social and political nature of human beings emphasizes that the individual is not an isolated monad but lives in relationship to others in the general society and in the political order of the state.[34]

Commutative justice governs the relationship of one individual to another, but this individual can also be what has been called a moral person or corporation. Thus commutative justice involves all sorts of contracts, agreements, or relationships involving a one-to-one relationship. Commutative justice has two distinctive characteristics—arithmetic equality and blindness or not being a respecter of persons. This type of justice is concerned only with the reality or thing itself and not with the person. Sears must charge the same price for a refrigerator whether you buy it or the richest person in the world buys it. The same price is for all regardless of who the person is. In this approach justice is blind because it pays no attention to the condition of the person. Commutative justice covers all contracts and relations of individuals and/or corporations to each other. What is due in this case depends on the reality itself and is independent of the nature of the persons involved.[35]

Distributive justice involves the relationship between society or the state and the individual. An important difference exists between society and the state. Society is the broader reality referring to all aspects of social life, whereas the state is the strictly political order where the power of coercive law exists. The state as a lesser part of society embodies the fundamental principle of a limited constitutional government. The government does not control all aspects of life in society and its powers are limited. However, government exists to promote the public good of society and not just to protect and promote individual goods.[36] For our limited purposes we cannot delve into the different ramifications of the role of the state and society with regard to justice.

Society basically has two realities to distribute—goods and burdens. With regard to the distribution of goods one important aspect is the distribution of material goods or wealth. What is a just distribution of such goods? The Catholic tradition continuing the biblical and Aristotelian-Thomistic approaches insists on the fundamental importance of human need but recognizes other criteria of just distribution as well. John A. Ryan, the most significant figure in Catholic social ethics in the United States in the first half of the twentieth century, defended every person's right to the minimum of goods necessary to satisfy basic human needs. Ryan with the tradition recognized other canons of distribution such as equality, effort and sacrifice, productivity and security.[37]

John A. Ryan here underscored what is a significant aspect in Catholic social teaching today—the right of every human being to a minimally decent human existence. The Pastoral Constitution on the

Church in the Modern World states: "[T]he right to have a share of earthly goods sufficient for oneself and one's family belongs to everyone."[38] The pastoral letter of the United States bishops on the economy maintains: "Distributive justice requires that the allocation of income, wealth, and power in society be evaluated in the light of its effects on persons whose basic material needs are unmet."[39] Pope John Paul II, in his 1991 social encyclical *Centesimus annus*, insists: "It is a strict duty of justice and truth not to allow fundamental human needs to remain unsatisfied...."[40]

The right of human beings to a minimally decent human existence and the obligation of society to meet these fundamental needs is grounded in the realization that the goods of creation exist primarily to serve the needs of all. All other rights whatsoever, including those of private property and free commerce, are to be subordinated to this social destination of the goods of creation. The doctrine of creation recognizes that God made the world and material creation to serve the needs of all God's people, not just a few. (However, the goods of creation and ecological realities have some meaning in themselves apart from human needs.) Such an approach does not necessarily deny the right to private property, but this right to private property is always ordered to serve the destination of the goods of creation to serve the needs of all.[41]

Another basis for the fundamental importance of human need in distributing material goods comes from the traditional Christian emphasis of coming to the assistance of those in need. Christianity often sees our relationship to others in terms of God's relationship to us. Our needs, not our merits or accomplishments, are the basis for God's gracious gift to us, and, therefore, we should respond to the needs of others in the same way. Pope Paul VI's *Populorum progressio* quotes St. Ambrose to the effect that, in giving what you possess to the poor, you are really handing over what is theirs.[42] Peter Lombard, who wrote the textbook for theology in the Middle Ages, defined justice as coming to the assistance of the poor.[43] To this day Catholics remain divided over the nature of the obligation of almsgiving. In the light of his Aristotelian categories, many theologians maintain that Thomas Aquinas sees the obligation in terms of charity and not strict justice.[44] Some commentators, however, see a relation to justice in Aquinas's teaching on almsgiving.[45] Others accept

Peter Lombard's position of seeing an obligation in justice to help the poor.[46]

Contemporary liberation theology has developed the notion of a preferential option for the poor. Throughout the Hebrew and Christian Scripture God is portrayed as the protector and defender of the poor. Liberation theology begins with this approach and, as noted earlier, develops an epistemology coherent with such a preferential option as opposed to a neutral, universal, value-free perspective of the human knower. This preferential option for the poor wants to avoid an exclusivity that understands God as loving only the poor. But the preferential option for the poor certainly grounds the need to provide all human beings with the material goods necessary for a minimally decent human existence.[47]

Need is a fundamental canon of just distribution but is not the only canon—effort, sacrifice, productivity, and scarcity are also mentioned by Ryan.[48] This perspective has guided the Catholic approach, which in matters of political and economic ethics develops a position between the extremes of individualistic capitalism and collectivistic communism. The Catholic position calls for a basic and decent human minimum for all but allows for differences in material goods based on the other canons of distribution. Effort, productivity, risk, and scarcity can justify greater material goods for certain people. Thus, the Catholic tradition does not require an absolute equality for all, but it does not allow the free market to completely determine how goods are distributed. Extreme inequality in wealth and income also threatens the solidarity of the human community. Society and the state have the obligation to make sure that all individuals have this basic minimum and that extreme inequalities do not exist.[49] The individual Christian person with the virtue of distributive justice is inclined toward working in this direction.

Society distributes not only goods but also burdens to its members. What is the just distribution of these burdens? Perhaps the most significant burden in political society is taxation. Here the Catholic tradition has insisted on the need for progressive taxation. Those who have more should pay not only arithmetically more but proportionately more taxes.[50]

The virtue of distributive justice is ultimately rooted in an anthropology that recognizes the relational social nature of human beings. We are not isolated monads, but we are members of the human community with responsibilities for one another precisely because we are all children of a gracious and loving God. Distributive justice, precisely because it takes into consideration the social aspect of human beings, by definition differs from commutative justice. Whereas commutative justice is blind, no respecter of persons, and deals with arithmetic equality, distributive justice is not blind, definitely considers the person involved, and insists on proportionate, not arithmetic, equality. Thus, for example, if one were to consider the obligation of paying taxes solely on the basis of some type of contract by which we pay society for what it provides for us, then the criteria of commutative justice would come into play. But taxation involves distributive justice precisely because it is part of our obligation to the total society in which we live and is not merely the tax we pay for the services provided for us.[51]

The 1986 pastoral letter of the United States Catholic bishops on the economy caused quite a stir in this country because of its negative critique of the American economy. The bishops elaborated and developed the requirements of distributive justice for our society. The letter did not call for the abolishment of capitalism but for limits on the free market in order to ensure the requirements of distributive justice for all our citizens. The precise challenge for our country today is to secure economic rights for all just as our country has gradually faced the challenge to secure political rights for all.[52] Distributive justice further reminds us of the danger of a narrow individualism which is so often prevalent in our society. The Catholic approach stresses the solidarity of all in the human family and the need to have a concern for others, especially the poor and the needy.

Legal justice, also known as social or contributive justice, guides the relationship of the individual to society and the state. In the past the primary consideration in this category involved obedience to just laws made for the common good of society. Today the emphasis is more on the need for the individual to participate and contribute to the life of society—hence the name contributive. All others have an obligation to make sure that every individual is able to fully participate in the life of the total society.[53]

In sum, justice in the Catholic tradition is a complex reality that, as a virtue, disposes the individual person to act in accord with the demands of the three types of justice outlined here. Many other virtues also guide and direct our relationships to other human beings, but justice remains a very significant virtue with important ramifications especially for our relationships in society.

Our relationships to others are not just to others as particular individuals but as members of different organisms, institutions, or social communities. In the classical tradition piety is the virtue that disposes children to act properly toward their parents and family, and individuals toward their country.[54] Today it seems more accurate to speak of patriotism as the virtue directing the love of one's own country. Once again this virtue is in the middle. The defect comes from a lack of appreciation and respect for one's country. More often than not problems arise from an exaggerated and absolutized love and reverence for one's country. Every state or country is human, limited, and subject to being wrong. The Christian tradition has always recognized that our obligation to God limits and directs our obligation to Caesar (Matt 22:21). To absolutize one's own country is epitomized in the saying, "My country right or wrong." Patriotism calls for a critical love of one's country. Today we are conscious that individual states and countries also have an obligation to the whole world. Our global existence today relativizes every country, race, tribe, or ethnic group. The primary danger remains in absolutizing or idolizing what is only a part that should be seen in the service of the whole.

Relationship with the World

Our relationship with the world calls for care, concern, reverence, and solidarity with our environment. We might call this virtue ecological stewardship. Stewardship is the name of the virtue that Christians have traditionally used to describe our relationship with the earth and the environment. However, in the past there have been some difficulties in the Christian and Catholic tradition, and we have not recognized the importance of the environment in itself. Some of the ecological neglect in the Christian tradition can be traced to the Genesis command (1:26) to subdue the earth and have dominion over the fish of the sea and the birds of the air and every living thing that moves upon the earth. Such a command has been interpreted to give human beings a right to interfere in the ecological world for their own purposes and needs without any further consideration. Moreover, the spirit/matter distinction that has been strong in certain periods of Christian history has tended to downplay all that is material, including the world of nature. The Catholic tradition has often employed hierarchical perspectives for its understanding of human relationships and, thus, has insisted on the dominion of humans over nature and creation. Christian theology, both Protestant and Catholic, has tended especially in the last centuries to be very anthropocentric in its approach. James M. Gustafson has insisted on a theocentric ethic in place of the anthropocentric ethic that is so characteristic of our times and, in the process, gives much more significance to the patterns and processes of nature.[55] In the United States society the exaggerated emphasis on individualism has given free rein to the individual to do whatever one wants with regard to nature and ecosystems. Modern technology, in the service of that individualism, has accepted no boundaries or limits in its quest to shape the world in accord with what human beings want.

We are, however, beginning to experience the need for ecological stewardship and awareness. We have a responsibility to the ecosystem and cannot see the earth merely as a means to fulfill our human wants. A Catholic perspective here should develop the understanding of the earth's sacramentality. All of God's creation is a sacrament and sign of the presence of God. Thus creation itself has a meaning that even incorporates this aspect of reverence and awe because it makes God present to us.[56] Ecofeminism brings together ecology and feminism on the basis of the common theme of exploitation by the powerful, especially white males.[57] In the United States we are also learning from the tradition of Native Americans, who have had such a great respect for the earth and all that is in it.[58]

A problem for Catholic moral theology concerns identifying the exact relationship between human beings and the earth or the ecosystems of our world. In a sense most people recognize that human beings are superior to animal and plant life. A human being has more importance than a dog, a cat, a tree, or a plant. In one sense human beings can and should in some way use the so-called lesser forms of life on our planet, especially when truly human needs are involved and not merely wants. But all of created reality and the environment and ecosystems in which we live are not simply means to be used by human beings. Creation and the environment have a value and meaning in themselves. They cannot be totally subordinated to human beings. The genetic makeup of human beings is very close to the genetic makeup of animals. As a result ecological stewardship calls for awe and reverence with regard to all of God's creation even though at times the lesser will serve the higher.[59] Ecological concern as a virtue produces an attitude of respect and reverence for all God's creation together with the recognition that at times the lesser can be used for the true good of the greater.

Stewardship has also been considered as the virtue that directs our attitude toward the material goods of this world. The classical ethic of Aristotle recognized that human happiness and well-being require a sufficiency of material goods such as food, clothing, shelter, but external goods are not the highest good and the basis for our happiness.[60] The Catholic tradition has built on this approach in the light of its own biblical origins. Material goods are necessary for human existence but they are not the most important or the most humanly satisfying goods. True human happiness and fulfillment can never consist merely in the accumulation of material goods. In fact the quest for material goods often becomes an obstacle in the way of human fulfillment and Christian discipleship. Recall the biblical story of the rich young man who went away sad in response to the call of Jesus because his possessions were many (Matt 19:16–30). There can be no doubt in our contemporary society that the problems of consumerism and materialism abound. The Christian vision appreciates the need for material goods but recognizes their limits. Consumerism and materialism flourish in an ethos that stresses individual wants. Our wants and desires have to be moderated for truly human and Christian purposes as will be mentioned shortly in discussing the virtue of temperance. The emphasis on individualism and wants paves the way for a gross overexaggeration of the importance of material and consumer goods. The same basic attitudes have contributed to the exploitation of our earth and are the source of many of the ecological problems we face today. Stewardship disposes the person to have a proper relationship to the world and to material goods.

Relationship to Self

Other virtues modify the person as subject and agent in terms of the relationship with oneself. The Catholic tradition in theory, despite some practical contradictions, has insisted on a proper love for self.[61] All are made in the image and likeness of God. God has called each individual by her own name. We can and should love ourselves, but here again proper self-love avoids the two opposite extremes. An excessive or exaggerated love of self goes too far by making self the center of the world and failing to appreciate our dependence on God and our multiple relationships with others. Without doubt individualism and an inordinate love of self constitute very strong temptations in our world today. But these problems do not take away from the importance of and need for a proper love of self. The extreme, by defect involving a lack of love of self, is often described in psychological terms as insecurity or a poor self-image. In religious language the person fears that she is evil or sinful and God does not and perhaps cannot love her. The Christian understanding of a proper love of self overcomes and corrects this Christian, human, and psychological defect of not truly appreciating one's own self. The Christian understands oneself as a unique gift of God, an image of God called to become a child of God. The individual person can never be the center of the world or the most important reality, but proper love of self recognizes this relationship to God and dependence upon God and relationship with many others.

Honesty and a self-critical attitude should also mark the Christian's attitude to oneself. In a sense the virtue of honesty gives some direction to the proper love of self. Honesty and a self-critical attitude are necessary if there is to be any growth in our multiple relationships. From the Christian perspective the call to conversion reminds us of the need to recognize and strive to overcome the sinful elements that are still a part of our lives. There can be no growth without a recognition of the need to change. The Catholic ascetical tradition has long recognized this reality. The sacrament of reconciliation makes us conscious of our continuing sinfulness and the need for forgiveness and reconciliation in all our relationships. Every eucharistic assembly begins with calling to mind our sinfulness, although the danger exists that this ritual can become a rote practice that does not meaningfully involve the members of the assembly. The Catholic tradition has also recommended the need for a daily examination of conscience as a way to be critical and to be able to grow in our multiple relationships. Being self-critical does not mean to deny the gifts we have received and our own personal talents.

Here again one can see the stance at work. As human beings we experience the goodness of creation and the presence of God's redeeming love in us, but we are also conscious of our limitations, our finitude, our sinfulness, and our lack of eschatological fullness.

The danger of making oneself the center of the world and living in accord with an absolutization of oneself remains very strong. In this context the Kantian notion of the importance of universality can be a very significant practical means of exercising this self-critical attitude. The Kantian categorical imperative insists that one can do a particular action only if one is willing to let all other persons in a similar situation do the same thing.[62] I have difficulty with the ultimate metaphysics and ethics of the Kantian approach because it tends to be purely formal and does not have much material content. However, his categorical imperative serves as a very good means to ensure that we continue to be self-critical. The great danger consists in the fact we tend to be willing to make exceptions for ourselves. Applying the Kantian principle of universalizability constitutes an excellent practical means of overcoming this danger.

Integrity constitutes an important virtue for the Christian and for all human beings. Integrity calls for cohesiveness and coherence. All the aspects of our lives should fit together; especially words and deeds have to be consonant. The danger for all of us is to talk a good game but not to live in accord with what we say. Integrity is especially important for those in leadership and teaching roles—for example, parents with regard to their children. Integrity also argues against giving primary importance to appearances and wanting to seem to be better or to have more than others. Especially in our consumer society that overvalues material possessions, people are often tempted to give too much importance to appearances whether it is in terms of the size of one's home or the cost of one's automobile.

The virtue of temperance, which traditionally has been labeled one of the four cardinal virtues, regulates and moderates what the tradition calls the "concupiscible appetites," which deal with physical pleasures such as food, drink, and sex. These appetites are common to human beings and other animals and humans must, therefore, live them out in a truly human way.[63]

Here again virtue finds itself in the middle between the extremes of excess and defect. The stance again indicates the basic goodness of these appetites and their limits with the danger that sinfulness can affect and distort them. The proper function of the virtue of temperance is to moderate and direct these appetites, not to deny, suppress, or annihilate them. Alcoholic beverages, for example, are not evil or bad. Like all other human realities involved with the concupiscible appetites, alcoholic beverages are limited goods that can be abused. I have always been intrigued by the fact that many of the best wines and liqueurs in the world have been named after monks! These monks apparently saw no incompatibility between their religious life and alcoholic beverages. But drink, food, and sex are limited human goods that can be abused. The virtues of sobriety and chastity recognize the good involved in these appetites but also order these appetites in a truly human way because of the dangers of abuse.

Most often the extreme vice opposed to the median of the virtue of temperance comes from the side of excess. Gluttony and drunkenness illustrate such abuses. Likewise, in sexuality the primary abuse comes from failing to see human sexuality in the context of loving human relationships. However, in the Catholic tradition in practice (and in many other religious and Christian traditions), the danger of abuse often comes from defect with regard to the concupiscible appetites, especially sexuality. The fear and denial of sexuality have often appeared and fostered a very repressive attitude toward sex. Many factors have influenced this negative attitude to sexuality in the past. Too often a Greek philosophical background distinguished between the spirit, which is good, and matter, which is evil. Paul the apostle does speak about a struggle between spirit and flesh but too often the tradition has inaccurately understood the flesh in terms of the problems connected with sexuality. In reality, spirit for Paul means the whole person who is under the influence of the life-giving Spirit, whereas flesh refers to the whole person, body and soul, under the control of sin (Rom 8:4–20). Many Christian heresies from early Gnosticism to eighteenth-century Jansenism and down to the present day have denigrated the material aspect of human existence especially with regard to sexuality.[64] Undeniably, sexuality has often been abused, but the abuse does not negate the proper use. Thus, the virtue of chastity moderates but does not deny or repress human sexuality.

Christian asceticism has often been seen in the light of the concupiscible appetites. All recognize that these appetites can readily get out of control and need to be directed. There continues to be an important place for this exercise (asceticism literally means exercise) in our world today, but asceticism is always in the service of true human good and not aimed at repression or denial.

Both the general virtues and the particular virtues modify the person as subject and agent. These dispositions truly constitute the character of the individual person. These virtues thus make the individual a better person and dispose that person to act for the good. The virtues thus play a very significant role in human moral life and in the theoretical reflection on that life. The Catholic tradition has understood vice to be the opposite of virtue. There is no need for a long separate discussion on vice or the habits disposing the person to do evil. Very often the extreme vices have already been mentioned in the discussion of the individual virtues.

Notes

1. Thomas Aquinas, *Summa Theologiae*, Ia Iae, qq. 55–67.

2. Charles Taylor, *Sources of the Self: The Making of the Modern Identity* (Cambridge, MA: Harvard University Press, 1989).

3. Stanley Hauerwas, *Character and the Christian Life: A Study in Theological Ethics* (San Antonio, TX: Trinity University Press, 1975).

4. Gilbert C. Meilaender, *The Theory and Practice of Virtue* (Notre Dame, IN: University of Notre Dame Press, 1984), 122.

5. Jean Porter, *The Recovery of Virtue: The Relevance of Aquinas for Christian Ethics* (Louisville, KY: Westminster/John Knox, 1990).

6. Romanus Cessario, *Moral Virtues and Theological Ethics* (Notre Dame, IN: University of Notre Dame Press, 1991).

7. Thomas F. O'Meara, "Virtues in the Theology of Thomas Aquinas," *Theological Studies* 58 (1997): 254–85.

8. Odon Lottin, *Morale fondamentale* (Tournai, Belgium: Desclée and Cie, 1954), 467–70.

9. James F. Keenan, "Proposing Cardinal Virtues," *Theological Studies* 56 (1995): 711–15. Keenan does, however, propose his own list of cardinal virtues—prudence, justice, fidelity, and self-care.

10. George P. Klubertanz, *Habits and Virtues* (New York: Appleton-Century-Crofts, 1965), 201–3.

11. Ibid., 241.

12. Keenan, *Theological Studies* 56 (1995): 718–19.

13. For example, Donald W. Shriver, *An Ethic for Enemies: Forgiveness in Politics* (New York: Oxford University Press, 1995).

14. Klubertanz, *Habits and Virtues*, 202–3.

15. Thomas Aquinas, *Summa Theologiae*, IIa IIae, qq. 23–25. For an overview of faith in Catholic systematic theology, see Avery Dulles, "Faith and Revelation," in *Systematic Theology: Roman Catholic Perspectives*, ed. Francis Schussler Fiorenza and John P. Galvin, 2 vols. (Minneapolis, MN: Augsburg Fortress, 2000) 1, 92–128.

16. For the theological virtue of faith, see Romanus Cessario, *Christian Faith and the Theological Life* (Washington, DC: Catholic University of America Press, 1996).

17. For a contemporary Catholic understanding of hope, see Dermot A. Lane, *Keeping Hope Alive: Stirrings in Christian Thinking* (New York: Paulist Press, 1996).

18. John Courtney Murray, *We Hold These Truths: Catholic Reflections on the American Proposition* (Kansas City, MO: Sheed and Ward, 1960), 175–96.

19. For an overview of the historical development in the theology of hope, see Michael Scanlon, "Hope," in *New Dictionary of Theology*, ed. Joseph A. Komonchak, Mary Collins, and Dermot A. Lane (Wilmington, DE: Michael Glazier Books, 2004), 492–98.

20. For the famous intervention of Bishop de Smedt of Bruges on triumphalism at the first session of Vatican II, see Gérard Philips, "History of the Constitution," in *Commentary on the Documents of Vatican II*, ed. Herbert Vorgrimler, 5 vols. (New York: Herder and Herder, 1967), 1, 109.

21. Dogmatic Constitution on the Church, nn. 48–51, in *Vatican Council II*, ed. Flannery, 407–13.

22. Marcellinus Zalba, *Theologiae moralis summa*, 3 vols. (Madrid: Biblioteca de Autores Cristianos, 1957) 1, 731–33, 812–17.

23. Paul Nevenzeit, "Time," in *Sacramentum Verbi: An Encyclopedia of Biblical Theology*, 3 vols., ed. Johannes B. Bauer (New York: Herder and Herder, 1970), 3, 911–15.

24. Daniel C. Maguire, *The Moral Choice* (Garden City, NY: Doubleday, 1978), 189–217; Philip S. Keane, *Christian Ethics and Imagination: A Philosophical Inquiry* (New York: Paulist, 1984).

25. Bernard Häring, *Free and Faithful in Christ* (New York: Seabury Press, 1978).

26. Zalba, *Theologiae moralis summa*, 2, 302–13.

27. Ibid., 127–35.

28. Thomas Merton, *Contemplation in a World of Action* (Garden City, NY: Doubleday Image, 1973).

29. Albert Gelin, *The Poor of Yahweh* (Collegeville, MN: Liturgical, 1964).

30. Leo C. Hay, *Eucharist: A Thanksgiving Celebration* (Wilmington, DE: Michael Glazier Books, 1989).

31. For worship as a central aspect in the sacrament of reconciliation, see James Dallen, *The Reconciling Community: The Rite of Penance* (New York: Pueblo, 1986).

32. Paul Misner, *Social Catholicism in Europe: From the Onset of Industrialization to the First World War* (New York: Crossroad, 1991), 213–20.

33. National Conference of Catholic Bishops, *Economic Justice for All* (Washington, DC: USCCB Publishing, 1997), nn. 28-125, 15–63.

34. For an overview of the Thomistic approach to justice, see Josef Pieper, *Justice* (New York: Pantheon, 1955); Daniel C. Maguire, "The Primacy of Justice in Moral Theology," *Horizons* 10 (1983): 72–85. Maguire has frequently emphasized the importance of justice in social ethics; see Daniel C. Maguire, *A New American Justice: Ending the White Male Monopoly* (Garden City, NY: Doubleday, 1980), and his most recent work *The Moral Core of Judaism and Christianity: Reclaiming the Revolution* (Minneapolis, MN: Fortress, 1993). For my development and analysis of the Thomistic understanding of justice, see Charles E. Curran, *Tensions in Moral Theology* (Notre Dame, IN: University of Notre Dame Press, 1988), 110–37. For a different reading of the Thomistic tradition, which sees legal justice as a general virtue, see Jeremiah Newman, *Foundations of Justice* (Cork, Ireland: Cork University Press, 1954).

35. Catholic Bishops, *Economic Justice for All*, n. 69, 35–36.

36. John Courtney Murray emphasized a distinction between society and the state in his theory of religious freedom; see John Courtney Murray, *The Problem of Religious Freedom* (Westminster, MD: Newman, 1965), 28–31.

37. John A. Ryan, *Distributive Justice: The Right and Wrong of our Present Distribution of Wealth* (New York: Macmillan, 1916), 243–53.

38. Pastoral Constitution on the Church in the Modern World, n. 69, in *Catholic Social Thought*, ed. David J. O'Brien and A. Shannon (Maryknoll, NY: Orbis Books, 2000), 213.

39. Catholic Bishops, *Economic Justice for All*, n. 70, 36.

40. *Centesimus annus*, n. 34, in *Catholic Social Thought*, ed. O'Brien and Shannon, 464.

41. *Populorum progressio*, n. 22, in *Catholic Social Thought*, ed. O'Brien and Thomas, 245.

42. Ibid., n. 23, 245.

43. Petrus Lombardus, *Sententiarum Libri IV* (Lyons: J. Sacon, 1515), lib. 3, dist. 33, cap. 1.

44. Aquinas, *Summa Theologiae*, IIa IIae, q. 32, a. 1; see Odon Lottin "La nature du devoir de l'aumône chez les prédécesseurs de Saint Thomas

d'Aquin," in *Psychologie et morale au XIIe XIIIe siècle* (Louvain, Belgium: Abbaye du Mont César, 1949), III–1, 299–313.

45. L. Bouvier, *Le précepte de l'aumône chez Saint Thomas d'Aquin* (Montreal: Immaculata Conceptio, 1935).

46. Hermenegildus Lio, *Estne obligatio justitiae subvenire miseris?* (Rome: Desclée, 1957).

47. Donal Dorr, *Option for the Poor: A Hundred Years of Catholic Social Teaching*, rev. ed. (Maryknoll, NY: Orbis Books, 1992).

48. Ryan, *Distributive Justice*, 243–53.

49. Catholic Bishops, *Economic Justice for All*, nn. 61–95, 32–49.

50. Ibid., n. 76, 38–39.

51. For my in-depth defense of progressive taxation, see Charles E. Curran, *Toward an American Catholic Moral Theology* (Notre Dame, IN: University of Notre Dame Press, 1987), 93–118.

52. Catholic Bishops, *Economic Justice for All*, 49.

53. Ibid., n. 71, 36–37.

54. Aquinas, *Summa Theologiae*, IIa IIae, 101.

55. James M. Gustafson, *Intersections: Science, Theology, and Ethics* (Cleveland, OH: Pilgrim, 1996).

56. Kevin W. Irwin, "The Sacramentality of Creation and the Role of Creation in Liturgy and Sacraments," in *Preserving the Creation: Environmental Theology and Ethics*, ed. Kevin W. Irwin and Edmund D. Pellegrino (Washington, DC: Georgetown University Press, 1994), 67–111.

57. Elizabeth A. Johnson, *Women, Earth, and Creator Spirit* (New York: Paulist, 1993).

58. Jana Stone, *Every Part of This Earth Is Sacred: Native American Voices in Praise of Nature* (San Francisco, CA: Harper, 1993).

59. For a similar position taken by the bishops in the United States, see United States Catholic Conference, "Renewing the Earth: An Invitation to Reflection and Action on the Environment in the Light of Catholic Social Teaching," *Origins* 21 (1991): 425–32; also Daniel M. Cowdin, "Toward an Environmental Ethic," in *Preserving the Creation*, ed. Kevin W. Irwin and Edmund D. Pellegrino (Washington, DC: Georgetown University Press, 1994), 112–47; Charles M. Murphy, *At Home on Earth: Foundations for a Catholic Ethic of the Environment* (New York: Crossroad, 1989); Drew Christiansen and Walter Grazen, eds., *And God Saw That It Was Good: Catholic Theology and Ecology* (Washington, DC: United States Catholic Conference, 1996). For a more radical approach, see Thomas Berry, *The Dream of the Earth* (San Francisco, CA: Sierra Club, 1988). For developments away from anthropocentrism in the teaching of John Paul II, see Daniel M. Cowdin, "John Paul II and

Environmental Concern: Problems and Possibilities," *Living Light* 28 (1991): 44–52.

60. Aristotle, *Nicomachean Ethics*, nn. 1097–98, 13–20.

61. Aquinas, *Summa Theologiae*, IIa IIae q. 26, aa. 3–5.

62. Roger J. Sullivan, *An Introduction to Kant's Ethics* (Cambridge: Cambridge University Press, 1994), 28–45.

63. Josef Pieper, *The Four Cardinal Virtues: Prudence, Justice, Fortitude, and Temperance* (Notre Dame, IN: University of Notre Dame Press, 1966), 145–206.

64. For my evaluation of the Catholic sexual tradition, see Charles E. Curran, *A Living Tradition of Catholic Moral Theology* (Notre Dame, IN: University of Notre Dame Press, 1992), 27–57; see also Christine Gudorf, *Body, Sex, and Pleasure: Reconstructing Christian Sexual Ethics* (Cleveland, OH: Pilgrim, 1994); Gareth Moore, *The Body in Context: Sex and Catholicism* (London: SCM, 1992).

4. Narrative and the Social Dynamics of Virtue

Anne Patrick

This chapter first appeared in *Changing Values and Virtues*, ed. Dietmar Mieth and Jacques Pohier (Edinburgh: T.&T. Clark, 1987).

In the past, questions of personal virtue were discussed in isolation from topics of social ethics. Studies of culture, however, suggest that virtue is a thoroughly social phenomenon, for groups of all types are distinguished by the sorts of traits and dispositions they foster in their members. Besides recognizing the historicity of virtue, then, an adequate theory will appreciate its sociality as well. This involves acknowledging that an agent's social context determines to some degree the ideals for character he or she will develop. Societies promote ideals through such means as laws, rewards and punishments, rituals and prayers, and, above all, narratives. Myths, legends, histories, biographies, fables, dramas, and other works of fiction convey clear messages about what sorts of characters are valued and despised. Whether or not individuals personally embody the traits prized by the group, they generally internalize the values contained in important cultural myths and judge their own worth in light of these common norms. Narrative thus plays a key educational role by communicating and reinforcing the values and virtues esteemed by a culture. Moreover, narrative also serves to criticize views of value and virtue once their favored status in a society is seen as ambiguous. The critical role of narrative, in fact, is an important part of the dynamics of change where value and virtue are concerned.

In describing the formative role of narrative I am not suggesting that every agent in a society will adopt a uniform set of ideals, for especially in modern pluralistic cultures value options are constantly competing for adoption by individuals, with agents choosing among this plurality and designing their own value paradigms. As a result, ideals for character vary among members of any society. But the element of choice is far from completely autonomous, for social realities strongly influence an individual's sense of value and virtue, establishing the limits within which personal freedom operates.

In thus emphasizing the social dimensions of virtue, I am applying the insights of psychologist G. H. Mead and theologian H. Richard Niebuhr to the realm of virtue, a move supported by other work in sociology, cultural anthropology, and, indeed, moral theology. As Mead, Niebuhr, and others have shown, the human person is constitutively social.[1] One would not develop as a human being in the absence of social relationships; one's very self is structured by the values bound up in the linguistics and mythic patterns of the culture or cultures in which one is raised. Certain narratives contribute markedly to this structuring of the personality because they express the worldview and ethos of the group in a way that at once engages emotions, intellect, and imagination, effectively conveying the message of what is valued and how values should be prioritized.

Among contemporary Christian ethicists, Stanley Hauerwas is known for emphasizing the historical and social dimensions of virtue, and for attending to the role of narrative in shaping both communities and individuals. His works go well beyond older tendencies to isolate considerations of personal virtue from discussions of social ethics. His position is summarized in the claim: "Our capacity to be virtuous depends on the existence of communities which have been formed by narratives faithful to the character of reality."[2] Hauerwas stresses the primary function of narrative in relation to values and virtues, namely, its role in forming communities and selves. But the norm of adequacy to reality in his theory suggests the importance of the secondary function of narrative, that of correcting the limitations of operative myths by critiquing inadequate ideals for character. Recently John Barbour has combined insights from Hauerwas, classics scholar James Redfield, and his own literary investigations to argue the role played by tragedy, and in modern times tragic novels, in critiquing dominant ideals of virtue. Such works portray the human costs of attempting to live out certain characterological ideals to their fullest, thus inviting reconsideration of societal norms.[3]

My analysis will add to the work of these thinkers in the following way. First, I describe certain tensions now felt within Catholicism as involving a conflict between two paradigms of value and virtue, "patriarchal" and "egalitarian." My assumption is that the latter is gaining ascendency in Catholic consciousness, and this accounts for the increasingly defensive articulations of the patriarchal paradigm by those in power who espouse it. Then, to illustrate the two functions of narrative with respect to paradigms of virtue and also to contribute substantively to the case for the egalitarian configuration, I next discuss two stories. The first is a report of a recent beatification ceremony, which illustrates one way in which traditional values and virtues have been communicated to Catholics. My discussion combines personal narrative with feminist critical analysis of the ideals bound up in the story. The second narrative is a longer work of fiction, *The Good Conscience* by Carlos Fuentes. My analysis indicates how Fuentes employs a genre linked with issues of character formation, the *Bildungsroman*, to critique the constellation of attitudes concerning Christian virtue that I term the patriarchal paradigm. From all of this I conclude that what is especially needed by Catholics today are narratives that illustrate the power and validity of the egalitarian paradigm for virtue.

CURRENT CONFLICT OF CATHOLIC PARADIGMS FOR VIRTUE

The debate concerning "authority and dissent" in the Catholic Church, evident recently in the United States in Vatican disciplinary action against Professor Charles Curran of Catholic University and Archbishop Raymond Hunthausen of Seattle, has yet to be analyzed in relation to Catholic ideals for character. What I would claim, however, is that these cases, as well as certain others involving hierarchical censure of loyal dissenters since Vatican II, are symptoms of a conflict well under way between competing paradigms for Christian virtue. The cases have ecclesiological, political, and economic dimensions as well, but to understand them fully it is necessary to recognize that part of what is at issue is precisely what it means to be a "good Catholic." In other words, ethical issues of character and virtue are central to these debates. Whether or not they have expressed this explicitly, each side espouses a different normative constellation of values and virtues. Positions vary in details from case to case, but they tend to line up with either the patriarchal paradigm or the egalitarian one. This analysis assumes, of course, the artificiality of any typology; thus the description that follows is partial and suggestive rather than elaborate and definitive.

A patriarchal paradigm for virtue has long enjoyed ascendency in the Roman Catholic community. Its shape has been affected by the otherworldly spirituality, the theological and social patterns of domination and subordination, the misogynism, and the body-rejecting dualism characteristic of Western culture. This paradigm understands virtue to involve the control of passion by reason and the subordination of earthly values to "supernatural" ones. It articulates many ideals for character, but tends to assume that these are appropriately assigned greater emphasis according to one's gender and social status. All Christians should be kind, chaste, just, and humble, but women are expected to excel in charity and chastity, men are trained to think in terms of justice and rights, and subordinates of both sexes are exhorted to docility and meekness. For various reasons this paradigm has come to function in a way that sees chastity as the pinnacle of perfection, absolutizing this virtue as defined by physicalist interpretations of "natural law" and stressing its necessity for salvation. Avowedly higher values of charity and justice are understood to be important, but only relatively so. This point would be denied by hierarchical defenders of the patriarchal paradigm, but such a denial is unconvincing in view of continued insistence that there is no parvity of matter where sexual sin is concerned, whereas violations of charity and justice admit of varying degrees of gravity.

Biblical grounding for the patriarchal paradigm derives in part from interpreting the Beatitude, "Blessed are the clean of heart, for they shall see God" (Matt 5:8), in a way that internalizes sexual taboos and establishes sexual purity as a focal sign of religious devotion. For this paradigm, "purity of heart" is interpreted in a narrow, sexual sense, rather than in the broader sense of singleness of purpose. This paradigm is based on a metaphor of domination, which emphasizes the control of the lower by the higher; the unruly body must be disciplined and tamed by dispassionate reason. Further scriptural warrant is found in the Pauline declaration, "I chastise my body and bring it into subjection" (1 Cor 9:27). The emphasis on discipline through control from above extends beyond sexual matters to include social ones as well; hence the high value placed on obedience to legitimate authority in this paradigm. In fact, the idea of hierarchical control of the "mystical body" closely parallels the premium placed on domination of the flesh by the will in traditional understandings of chastity. It would seem also that the tendency to apply military "solutions" to political problems is a secular manifestation of the same paradigm.

In contrast to the anthropological dualism of the patriarchal paradigm, the egalitarian paradigm understands reason itself to be embodied, and women and men to be fully equal partners in the human community. Instead of control, the notion of respect for all created reality is fundamental to this paradigm, which values the body and the humanity of women and promotes gender-integrated ideals for character. Rather than understanding power as control over, this paradigm operates with a sense of power as the energy of proper relatedness. Ideals of love and justice are not segregated into separate spheres of personal and social ethics, with responsibility for realizing them assigned according to gender; instead, love and justice are seen to be mutually reinforcing norms that should govern both sexes equally.

Perhaps because of the exaggerated attention given by advocates of the patriarchal paradigm to sexual purity, advocates of the other paradigm tend not to be concerned with the virtue of chastity per se, though a reinterpretation of this virtue may be inferred from what they have written on love and justice, and also on particular sexual questions. This paradigm sees sexuality as a concern of social justice as well as of personal virtue, and attends particularly to the Beatitude, "Blessed are they who hunger and thirst for justice, for they shall be satisfied" (Matt 5:6).[4] It recognizes that the focal sign of religious devotion cannot be the directing of one's energy to controlling bodily impulses and other people, but rather must involve a stance of ongoing commitment to the well-being (which is at once spiritual and material) of oneself and others. This entails concern for building social relations of respect, equality, and mutuality.

Both paradigms recognize that suffering is part of the Christian life, but they understand the last Beatitude quite differently. The patriarchal paradigm tends to foster an apocalyptic mentality, in which the "righteous" see themselves enduring persecution from godless enemies in this world, but ultimately vindicated in the next. The egalitarian paradigm acknowledges that forces of evil long structured into unjust power relationships will seek to destroy those who dedicate themselves to the campaign for just social and economic relationships. But, with Jesus' own paschal experience in mind, advocates of this model recognize that the campaign has in principle been won, even here and now on earth, thanks to the graciousness of the Ground and Source of life and the continued involvement of God in human history.

Presently the egalitarian paradigm is capturing the imaginations of the devout through a process involving many factors. Among these are new narratives and new critiques of old narratives. To illustrate this aspect of the dynamics of change, I turn now to an example of a narrative designed to foster the patriarchal paradigm, and show why such stories are losing their power over contemporary believers.

A NARRATIVE WITH FADING POWER

Throughout its history the Catholic Church has communicated ideals of character to the faithful by designating certain persons as saints or "blessed ones." To appreciate the role played by hagiographical narrative in relation to the patriarchal paradigm of virtue, it is useful to study a brief news story from the *New York Times* for 16 August 1985.

> KINSHASO, Zaire, Aug. 15—Pope John Paul II today beatified a Roman Catholic nun who chose to be killed rather than surrender her virginity. The nun, Marie Clementine Anwarite, demonstrated the "primordial value accorded to virginity" and an "audacity worthy of martyrs," the pope said. He said he forgave the man, a Col. Piero Colombe, who killed the nun in an incident in Zaire's civil war in 1964. (page A–4)

How do contemporary believers respond to such a story? My own reaction testifies to major changes in one Catholic's perception of values and virtues, for I responded very differently to this story than I did to a similar one some decades ago. St. Maria Goretti was canonized in 1950, when I was in elementary school, and I recall being greatly influenced during childhood and adolescence by the story of her repulsion of the sexual advances of the youth who stabbed her to death in 1902. Here was an exemplar for teenage girls, a model of virtue whose concern was not for her physical well-being but rather for the spiritual values at stake. A biographer quotes her as declaring during the encounter with her assailant, "No, God does not wish it. It is a sin. You would go to hell for it."[5] These words reveal much about the values Maria espoused and the religious world she inhabited. This was a world where sexual pleasure outside of sacramental marriage, if deliberately indulged, was always grounds for damnation, a world where death was preferable to yielding to rape. The Vatican's selection of this young woman for canonization in 1950 was clearly an effort to articulate the value of premarital chastity in a society that was questioning the absoluteness of this norm. Moreover, the saint's preeminent concern for the spiritual welfare of her assailant ("It is a sin. You would go to hell for it.") functioned to reinforce the emphasis on a young woman's responsibility for the sexual behavior of a dating couple typical for Catholic education of the day. None of this troubled me consciously during the years when the examples of Maria Goretti and the male "patrons of youth" (John Berchmans, Aloysius Gonzaga, and Stanislaus Kostka) were held up as the ideal for holiness. Gradually, however, one outlives these teenage saints, and imperceptibly one's notion of heroic virtue may change. The extent of the transformation in my own case was evident when I reflected on the Anwarite beatification some months ago.

Several items about this report disturbed me. Paramount was the flagrant injustice of the basic situation of attempted rape and actual murder. This situation is faced frequently by women around the globe, with all too many suffering one or both dimensions of the threatened evil: forced sexual contact and/or death. Moreover, I am now aware that unjust patterns of relationships between the sexes contribute to the frequency with which women experience such predicaments, and that schooling in traditional "feminine" virtues of docility and submissiveness to male authority increases the likelihood that a woman will suffer violence.

Also intensely disturbing is the explicit value statement, "the primordial value accorded to virginity," with its clear implication that the woman's life is of lesser value than a physical condition that in fact is not typical for the majority of mature women of all cultures. Marie Clementine's virginity was, to be sure, "consecrated virginity," and the religious significance of this detail should not be minimized. Nonetheless, the aspect of formal religious dedication should not obscure the basic fact of the case, namely, that a woman was lifted up as a model for the emulation of the faithful because "she chose to be killed rather than surrender her virginity."

Any person's right to physical integrity, privacy, and sexual autonomy is of course a high value. But is this value greater than the value of the person's physical life? To be sure, the threat of death is not necessarily removed by a woman's submission to rape, but if we assume that some virginal victims are presented with two real alternatives, the Anwarite beatification explicitly raises the question of whether rape is a greater evil than death.

But is this to put the question wrongly? One might object that the chief value at stake in these instances was not virginity per se but rather God's will. There is a point to this objection insofar as the question of subjective culpability or merit is concerned, for the formal value of God's will is indeed a preeminent one for believers. The obligation to follow a certain conscience is exceptionless. But to point to this formal value does not suffice to answer the substantive question concerning what God "wills" a woman to do when threatened with death if she does not submit to rape. Answers to this question can hardly be universal or absolutely certain, for as with other ethical decisions, the right choice must be discerned in view of the relevant circumstances, values, and principles involved in each case. This fact leads to further questions: Is such overriding emphasis on sexual "purity" a good thing? Is it right to emphasize one sort of response to the threat of violent attack by a rapist ("take my life, but not my virginity") by idealizing it to the extent that virginity assumes a "primordial value" for females, one greater than their own lives, with the result that other responses, which might be equally moral, are ruled out of consideration by devout women?[6] The answers to these questions bring one to the point where concerns about virtue and action intersect most conflictedly in contemporary Catholicism because they hinge on the issue of knowledge of God's will, and more particularly on the question of what constitutes the basis for claims of the hierarchy to have certain knowledge on matters of sexual ethics.

Further, these stories invite questions about what they imply concerning the nature of rape. Do they recognize that rape is primarily an act of hostility and aggression, or do they contribute to the prevalent and inaccurate myth that somehow a victim derives pleasure from being seized and "taken," thereby reinforcing a problematic tendency to blame the victim of this crime?[7] And what does the lack of attention to the social causes of male sexual aggression imply? One might have hoped that by 1985, if not 1950, church leaders would recognize the past teachings about the "unnaturalness" of masturbation and homosexuality and the "naturalness" of rape feed into the insecurities of young males and contribute directly to patterns of seduction and rape. Finally, why would any woman prefer death to the violation of her virginity? To answer this question is to solve the problem of who is the subject of virtue, for such a choice on a woman's part is largely a function of her socialization. Her choice makes sense in light of the ideals for character dominant in her culture, values she has appropriated to govern her decisions.

This story brings clearly to mind the cultural influences on character. Early in the history of Christianity, the biblical emphasis on sexual purity among the Hebrews, the doctrine of Mary's perpetual virginity, assumptions that Jesus eschewed sexual activity, and emphasis on eschatological virginity combined with a body-rejecting dualism present in Greco-Roman culture to yield an ethos that encouraged the development of persons who saw their own bodies as the locus of a contest between the powers of good and evil, with goodness demanding a vigilant campaign against one's sexual inclinations. Over the centuries new stories entered the culture—stories of virgin martyrs, ascetic monks and nuns, repentant profligates, and the like—all of which joined with legal practice and other social determinants and an otherworldly eschatology to create a world where a decision to die rather than lose one's virginity made very good sense.

A person growing up in such a world understands that an ideal character requires sexual abstinence, or "perfect continence" (at least before marriage, when sexual activity becomes permissible), and judges the self according to this cultural norm, whether or not he or she achieves it in practice. Such a view of chastity may have been on balance beneficial to Christians in the past. What is evident today, however, is that an ideal of character with this notion of chastity as its linchpin is no longer accepted uncritically by Christians, although a clearly delineated alternative understanding of chastity has yet to be articulated. Catholic society today is reassessing its ideals of character with respect to sexuality, even though the transformation has not been the locus of much attention in discussions of virtue among theorists of the moral life. Instead, Catholic moral theologians have concentrated on gingerly trying to question formerly absolute prohibitions of certain sexual acts without unleashing a plague of ecclesiastical penalties on their lives. We are at a moment in history when one understanding of chastity is increasingly recognized as inadequate and when a more adequate one has not come fully into focus.

At this juncture, however, we can recognize that the task of moral theology in bringing a new interpretation of chastity into an egalitarian paradigm of virtue has been made easier because of ethical reflection already done by two groups working mainly outside the circle of traditional moral theology. These are the feminist scholars of religion, whose contribution to a rethinking of chastity is inferable from more general explorations of gender and ethical ideals, as well as from explicit attention to sexual questions, and the literary artists, particularly the novelists, who have been testing various ideals for character and virtue ever since moral philosophy began to concentrate its energies so markedly on decisions and actions in the eighteenth century.[8]

A now classic feminist critique of ideals for virtue is Valerie Saiving [Goldstein]'s article "The Human Situation: A Feminine View."[9] Saiving argues that traditional Christian understandings of sin and virtue reflect experiences typical for males who enjoy some status and power in society. For such men, pride has been recognized as the most harmful inclination, with temptation to sensual indulgence at others' expense also a recurrent danger. Thus exhortations to cultivate humility and self-sacrifice are appropriate. But to universalize this analysis, and especially to apply it to women, whose social location is quite different, is to exacerbate the moral problems most women face. For given the disparate social experiences of the two sexes, the temptations of women are different from those of men. Instead of pride being the greatest danger, for women the chief temptation is to fail to have a centered self, to yield up responsibility for one's identity and actions to other persons and environmental factors. Whereas men are tempted to abuse their power, women tend to abdicate their possibilities for using power properly by surrendering it for the sake of approval and security. What women in patriarchal society need are not exhortations to humility and self-sacrifice, or stories of saints who preferred death to rape. Women need instead new models for virtue and new stories that communicate them. I look forward to the day when such narratives are characteristic of popular Catholicism.

In the meanwhile, a second resource for the constructive work still to be done by storytellers and theologians is the large body of serious fiction that critiques the inadequacies of the patriarchal paradigm of virtue. A particularly interesting example is an early work by the Mexican novelist Carlos Fuentes, *The Good Conscience*.

CHASTITY AND PSYCHOLOGY OF SOCIAL INJUSTICE

Originally published in 1959, *The Good Conscience* provides an incisive analysis of the ambiguity of Catholic teaching and practice with respect to values and virtues. A prominent theme in this novel is that of the co-option of Christian moral energy in the service of an unjust social structure. By reducing Christian morality to sexual purity, the wealthy Mexican class into which Jaimé Ceballos is born succeeds in distracting itself from the poverty and injustice surrounding it, and to which its own defensive greed contributes. The novel depicts Jaimé's transformation from a sensitive, idealistic child, who befriends a fugitive labor organizer and a Marxist Indian youth, into a hardening egoist who will follow in the footsteps of the hypocritical uncle whose values he has always despised. At the book's end we find Jaimé dealing with the guilt he feels over having failed to show love and respect for his parents, by visiting a brothel after his father's funeral. There he commits a sin that can be more easily named and absolved in the confessional than the pride and insensitivity to others that have become part of his character. Thus by reducing the moral life to a routine of sexual sin and confession he comes to have "good conscience," as the work's ironic title puts it.

Earlier scenes establish the connection between affirming one's own embodiment and rejoicing in the mysteries of creation and God's love. They also show how such feelings are linked with a disposition to care for others, whereas alienation from the body is associated with alienation from other people. Indeed, through several examples from the lives of Jaimé and his family, Fuentes shows how moral theology and pastoral practice emphasizing sexual sins contribute to neurotic patterns of individual behavior as well as to social injustice. To be more precise, the novel demonstrates just how the patriarchal paradigm of virtue is implicated in some of the most besetting problems of Catholicism today: injustice to women and the blindness of the middle and upper classes to matters of social and economic justice. We see in this novel what rigid patriarchal authority has done to one family system, and we can infer what it has done and is doing to the church. Jaimé's was a home in which the truth could not be spoken, and where sexuality above all was a taboo subject. What Fuentes's narrator says of this home brings to mind how pastors and moral theologians alike have been silenced on matters of sexuality: "The first rule in this family was that life's real and important dramas should be concealed."[10]

CONCLUSION

This essay has focused on the social context of virtue and on the dynamics of transformation of ideals for character, emphasizing how the interplay of cultural factors, especially models and stories, affects the ranking of values and virtues. My argument implies that the virtue of chastity needs to be brought in from the wings of ascetical theology, where candidates for vowed celibacy ponder its intricacies in light of physicalist interpretations of natural law, and placed on center stage for scrutiny by moral theology, at least for whatever time is required to develop a rational and coherent set of ideals for character with respect to sexuality. Such a reinterpretation must certainly take into account the insights of thinkers who have shown how inadequate understandings of chastity reinforce the complicity of the churches in perpetuating social injustices of various types. What is needed even more, however, are new narratives that go beyond criticism and theory to provide models that demonstrate—with a power scholarly prose can never attain—the goodness and beauty of lives governed by the egalitarian paradigm for virtue.

Notes

1. This claim is developed in George Herbert Mead, *Mind, Self, and Society: From the Standpoint of a Social Behaviorist*, ed. C. Morris (Chicago: University of Chicago Press, 1934), and applied to the question of moral agency in H. Richard Niebuhr, *The Responsible Self* (New York: Westminster John Knox Press, 1963). Other works that strongly influence my view of the social and historical dynamics of virtue include Thomas Luckmann, *The Invisible Religion* (New York: Macmillan Publishers, 1967), and Clifford Geertz, *The Interpretation of Cultures* (New York: Basic Books, 1973).

2. Stanley Hauerwas, *A Community of Character* (Notre Dame, IN: University of Notre Dame Press, 1981), 116.

3. John D. Barbour, *Tragedy as a Critique of Virtue: The Novel and Ethical Reflection* (Chico, CA: Scholars Press, 1984).

4. Works that reflect the values of the egalitarian paradigm include Margaret Farley, "New Patterns of Relationship," *Theological Studies* 36 (1975): 627–46, and Margaret Farley, *Personal Commitments: Beginning, Keeping, Changing* (San Francisco: HarperCollins, 1986); Beverly Wildung Harrison, *Making the Connections*, ed. C. Robb (Boston: Beacon Press, 1985); and Joan Timmerman, *The Mardi Gras Syndrome: Rethinking Christian Sexuality* (New York: Crossroad Publishing Company, 1984).

5. Maria Cecilia Buehrle, "St. Maria Goretti," in *New Catholic Encyclopedia*, ed. Catholic University of America (New York: McGraw-Hill, 1967), 1: 632.

6. One wonders what Augustine would have thought of the language used to praise Marie Clementine, for his insight in *City of God*, 18, is entirely absent from the report of the ceremony: "[B]odily chastity is not lost, even when the body has been ravished, while the mind's chastity endures" (trans. H. Bettenson; Baltimore 1972) at p. 28. Despite the body-rejecting dualism implied in his analysis, Augustine is correct to recognize that chastity involves a disposition of the subject that perdures despite bodily violation. His analysis betrays his male bias, however, especially in the assertion that an act of rape "perhaps could not have taken place without some physical pleasure" on the part of the victim (I, 16: p. 26). It can only be lamented that in the late twentieth century

Catholic women were being exhorted to an even more regressive understanding of chastity than that of the fifth-century Augustine.

7. For an informed ethical and pastoral analysis, see Marie M. Fortune, *Sexual Violence: The Unmentionable Sin* (New York: Pilgrim Press, 1983).

8. For an account of this relationship between fiction and moral philosophy see James T. Laney, "Characterization and Moral Judgments," *The Journal of Religion* 55 (1975).

9. Valerie Saiving, "The Human Situation: A Feminine View." Originally published in *The Journal of Religion* (1960), the article also appears in *Womanspirit Rising*, ed. C. Christ and J. Plaskow (San Francisco: Harper & Row, 1979), 25–42.

10. Carlos Fuentes, *The Good Conscience* (New York: Farrar, Straus, and Giroux, 1974), 26.

Part Two

VIRTUE ETHICS IN PARTICULAR SPHERES

5. Virtues in Professional Life

William F. May

This chapter first appeared in *Annual of the Society of Christian Ethics* (1984).

The Benthamites, observed Melville, would never have urged Lord Nelson to risk his life on the bridge of his ship. The loss of so brilliant a tactician would have looked bad on a cost/benefit analysis sheet; his heroism would not have produced the greatest balance of good over evil. Melville's comment slyly suggests that the field of ethics does not reduce to the utilitarian concern for producing good. Ethics must deal with virtues as well as principles of action, with being good as well as producing good. This essay will explore some of the virtues central to professionals and to those upon whom they practice.

Let it be conceded at the outset that virtue theory does not cover the whole of ethics. The terrain of professional ethics covers at least four major areas:

1. Quandary or case-oriented ethics that searches for rules and principles helpful to the decision maker in making choices between conflicting goods and evils, rights and wrongs. Some have called this approach dilemmatic or problematic ethics, or, alternatively, ethics for the decision maker. One hopes to arrive at principles that will establish priorities. This dilemmatic approach has dominated the field of professional ethics partly because of its intrinsic prestige in philosophical and theological circles and partly because of its cultural notoriety. The mass media already focus attention on headliner quandaries (whether or not to pull the plug on the comatose patient); and medical, business, and legal

education largely organizes itself around case study. What more natural way to recommend professional ethics as a subject than to adopt the case method and highlight moral quandaries that a purely technical professional education does not help one resolve!

2. The moral criticism of systems, institutions, and structures. Quandary ethics alone emphasizes too much the perplexities that the individual practitioner faces. It does not examine critically the social institutions that generate professional services, the reward systems that shape professional practice, the complexities of interprofessional and interinstitutional relations, and the delivery systems that allow some problems to surface as cases and others not. On the whole, structural questions attract liberals and radicals more than conservatives; and social scientists and political theorists are better equipped to explore these questions than conventionally trained ethicists.

3. Professional regulation and self-discipline. The problem of defective or unethical performance preoccupies the layperson more than professionals, either professional practitioners or ethicists. Practitioners accept only reluctantly responsibility for a colleague's behavior. Moralists do not find the issue of professional self-discipline intellectually interesting at the level of a quandary. The bad apple is self-evidently a bad apple. This neglect of the subject of professional self-regulation is morally and intellectually regrettable. Professionals wield enormous power; they must accept some responsibility as their colleague's keeper. Meanwhile, their reluctance to discipline the bad performer raises interesting moral issues for the ethicist about the relations between institutions, their members, and the communities they serve.

4. The subject of virtue. While virtue theory may not deserve preeminence of place, it constitutes an important part of the total terrain. Unfortunately, contemporary moralists, with some recent exceptions, have not been too interested in the clarification and cultivation of those virtues upon which the health of personal and social life depends. Reflection in this area appears rather subjective, elusive, or spongy ("I wish my physician were more personal"), as compared with the critical study of decisions and structures.

Especially today, however, attention must be paid to the question of professional virtue. The growth of large-scale organizations has increased that need. While the modern bureaucracy has expanded the opportunities for monitoring performance (and therefore would appear to lessen the need for virtue), the specialization it fosters makes the society increasingly hostage to the virtue of experts working for it. Huge organizations can easily diffuse responsibility and cover the mistakes of their employees. The opportunity for increased specialization that they provide means that few people—whether lay or professional—know what any given expert is up to.

Professionals had better be virtuous. Few people may be in a position to discredit them. The knowledge explosion has also produced an ignorance explosion; even the expert knowledgeable in one domain is ignorant and therefore dependent in many others. Knowledge admittedly creates power, but ignorance yields powerlessness. Although institutions can devise mechanisms that limit the opportunities for the abuse of specialized knowledge, ultimately one needs to cultivate virtues in those who wield that relatively esoteric and inaccessible power. One important test of character and virtue: what does a person do when no one else is watching? A society that rests on expertise needs more people who can pass that test.

I will begin more abstractly with some definitions of virtue and then explore a range of virtues, particularly those pertinent to the so-called helping professions.

GENERAL CONSIDERATIONS OF VIRTUE

A Principle-Oriented Definition of Virtue

It should be noted that a principle-oriented moral theory does not altogether ignore the question of virtue; rather, it tends to subordinate the virtues to principles. Beauchamp and Childress, in the first edition of their *Principles of Biomedical Ethics*, gave the following definition: "virtues are settled habits and dispositions *to do what we ought to do* (where ought judgments encompass both ordinary duties and ideals)."[1] This definition subordinates virtues to principles, agents to acts; that is, the question of one's *being* to one's *doing*. This subordination systematically correlates *specific virtues* with specific rules and ideals. Thus the virtue of benevolence correlates with the principle of beneficence, non-malevolence with nonmaleficence, respect with autonomy, and fairness with justice.

This scheme, while helpful, fails to acknowledge the importance of the virtues not simply as correlates of principles and rules, but as human strengths important precisely at those times when men and women dispute over principles and ideals. In professional settings, where the arguments sometimes grow fierce, we need, to be sure, modes of reasoning and social mechanisms for resolving disagreements. But philosophical sophistication about the debates between Mill vs. Kant and Nozick vs. Rawls does not necessarily resolve the disputes among us. Sometimes, the philosophers merely transpose the dispute to a more elegant level of discourse. The debate rages on. In nineteenth-century England, a fierce quarrel once broke out between two women shouting at one another from second-story windows on opposite sides of the street. An Anglican bishop, passing by with friends, predicted, "These women can't possibly agree; they are arguing from opposite premises."

Just as important as principles may be those virtues that we bring to a dispute: a measure of charity and good faith in dealing with an opponent, a good dose of caution in heeding a friend who approves only too quickly what we think and say, humility before the powers we wield for good or for ill, the discipline to seek wisdom rather than to show off by scoring points, sufficient integrity not to pretend to more certainty than we have, and enough bravery to act even in the midst of uncertainty. Even with the best of theories and procedures, the moral life only too often pushes us out into open terrain, where we must shoulder uncertainties and muster the courage to act.

Further, a theory of the virtues that merely correlates them with principles fails sufficiently to deal with a range of moral life that does not conveniently organize itself into deeds that we can perform, issues about which we can make decisions, or problems that we can solve.

At the close of a lecture that T. S. Eliot once gave on a serious moral issue before an American academic audience, an undergraduate rose to ask him urgently, "Mr. Eliot, what are we going to do about the problem you have discussed?" Mr. Eliot replied, in effect, in his no-nonsense way, "You must understand that we face two different types of problems in life. In dealing with the first kind of problem, we may appropriately ask the question, 'what are we going to do about it?' But for another range of human problems, the only fitting question is not 'what are we going to do about it?' but 'how does one behave toward it?'" The first kind of question presses for relatively technical and pragmatic responses to problems that admit of solution; the second recognizes a deeper range of challenges—hardy perennials—that no particular policy, strategy, or behavior will dissolve. Gabriel Marcel likened these problems to mysteries rather than puzzles. They call for moral responses that resemble ritual more than technique. They require behavior that is deeply fitting, decorous, appropriate. Most of the persistent problems in life fall into this category: the conflict between the generations, the intricacy of overtures between the sexes, the mystery of birth, the ordeal of fading powers and death. "I could do nothing about the death of my husband," a college president's spouse once said to me. "The only question put to me was whether I could rise to the occasion." The humanities, at their best, largely deal with such questions and less so through the deliverances of technical philosophy than through historical narrative, poetry, drama, art, and fiction. In the medical profession, the dividing line between Eliot's two types of questions falls roughly between the more glamorous systems of cure and the humbler action of care.

Both kinds of moral challenge call for virtue. But in the second instance, the virtues supply us not merely with settled habits and dispositions to *do* what we ought to *do* but also to *be* what we ought to *be*. Virtues come into focus that do not tidily correlate with principles of action: courage, lucidity, prudence, discretion, and temperance. Faced with these challenges, we function not simply as agents producing deeds but partly as authors and coauthors of our very being.

None of this self-definition comes easy. Thus inevitably virtues must contend with adversity—not simply the objective adversity of conflict between principles and ideals to which I have already referred but also the subjective adversity of the temptations, distractions, and aversions we must face. Virtues thus do not simply indicate those habits whereby we transform our world through deeds but also those specific strengths that partly grow out of adversities and sustain us in the midst of them.

A Virtue-Oriented Theory of Virtue

Alasdair MacIntyre offers a useful start on this second way of interpreting the virtues: "A virtue is an acquired human quality the possession and exercise of which tends to enable us to achieve those goods which are internal to practices and the lack of which effectively prevents us from achieving any such goods."[2]

This definition emphasizes two important points. (1) Virtue is an acquired human quality (rather than an inherited temperament). The two should not be confused. Our annoyance with some people results from their inherited psychic makeup but we confuse their grating temperament with objectionable character. (2) We should prize the virtues primarily because they make possible the goods internal to practice rather than those goods that flow externally and secondarily from practices. The virtues make possible the intrinsic goods of studying rather than the rewards or results that flow externally from studying such as grades, job, and so on.

The role of public virtue in the thought of the American Revolutionaries illustrates this distinction between external and internal good. Next to liberty, the Revolutionary thinkers invoked the term *public virtue* most often in their rhetoric. They defined public virtue as a readiness to sacrifice personal want and interest to the public good. Such virtue, of course, had a kind of utilitarian significance at the level of external outcome. A general readiness of citizens to make personal sacrifices helped win the Revolutionary War. But if public virtue had only an instrumental value, then the Revolutionaries should have been content to see the virtue vanish once the war was won. The justification of the practice lay in the results alone. The Revolutionaries, however, prized public virtue as an internal good characteristic of a republican nation. Public virtue belongs to the very soul of a republic apart from which it could not be itself. Public virtue supplies the glue that holds a republic together. The Revolutionary thinkers quite self-consciously followed Montesquieu on this matter.[3] A despotic government rules by fear; a monarchy governs by the aristocratic aspiration to excellence; but a republic, which cannot rely on fear or on an aristocratic code of honor, must depend upon public virtue to create a public realm, to be a *res publica*.

Further, if the good that it produces, and not the good that it is, alone justifies a virtue, then one might be content with counterfeits or illusions of virtue if these *simulacra* could get the job done. In the best of all possible strategies, a Benthamite might be tempted to use a Nelson look-alike on the bridge both to reap the benefit of an inspiring example and to ensure the continuing services of a brilliant tactician.

Utilitarians orient so exclusively to results that they see no good in the noble deed per se—independent of the good it produces. Thus Mill wrote, "The utilitarian morality does recognize in human beings the power of sacrificing their own greatest good for the good of others. It only refuses to admit that the sacrifice is itself a good."[4] Once dismissing goods internal to practice, utilitarians less noble than Mill find it easy not just to instrumentalize but to corrupt practice for the sake of outcome.

Not that a virtue-oriented theory of virtue entirely escapes its own set of difficulties when it neglects the question of principles. The question—what should I do?—should not completely collapse into the question—who shall I be?—and this for at least four reasons: First, many virtues do correlate with principles and ideals. Without clarification of a principle of gratitude it would be difficult to distinguish gratefulness from mere obsequiousness (not an insignificant issue for court life in the eighteenth century and office life in the twenty-first century). Second, without some common commitment to principles of justice, candor, and so on, it would be difficult to construct a society in which specific configurations of the virtues might flourish.

Third, an exclusive preoccupation with the question, *who* am I? and an indifference to the question, what *ought* I to do? produces an excessively narcissistic, perhaps even adolescent, character. The external world quickly fades into theatrical background for one's own expressive acts that command center stage. Scripture sharply reminds us, "by their fruits you shall know them." One's being does not free-float behind one's deeds; it should manifest itself in doing. Max Weber distinguished between value-expressive and goal-oriented actions. Value-expressive acts become more self-expressive than valuable if they do not reckon seriously with the question of what shall I do, and if they fail to contend with that question in the harsh glare of principles under which we commonly stand. Thus, I prefer to say that the moral life poses the question of being good, as well as (and not rather than) doing good.

Finally, MacIntyre is gloomy about the possibility of practicing the virtues at all in the large-scale organization. The bureaucracy, perforce, orients to results, to external outcomes, while the virtues evince goods wholly internal to a practice. I do not deny the existence of tension between the two sorts of goods, especially in a large institutional setting. The pressure for results can tempt us to corrupt those goods internal to practice; efficiency in producing outcomes can distort all else. Yet some large-scale organizations do exist that have not abjectly surrendered everything to the bottom line and that have signaled their commitment to the goods internal to the practices that they support and organize.

Some commentators would distinguish between moral rules and moral ideals and establish a sharp line between the two. They deem rules mandatory and ideals optional; rules oblige and ideals merely encourage. Character and virtues have to do chiefly with the latter. This move runs the danger of reducing character and virtue essentially to the order of the aesthetic. It becomes a matter of purely optional preference and taste as to which goods one pursues, and which roles one plays.

This reduction of character to an aesthetic option overlooks the imperativeness of ideals. Just because an ideal hovers beyond our reach in the sense that we can seldom directly realize it does not remove it to the merely optional. One may live under a double responsibility—both to respect the ideal but also to recognize the unavoidable difficulties in the way of its even partial realization in an imperfect world. But this double responsibility does not reduce the ideal to the status of the merely elective. One lives under the imperative to approximate the ideal; and this task of approximation is not merely optional. For example, one may only rarely be able to realize Jesus' command to love one's enemies, but one may still live under the obligation to approximate this law of perfect love in a very imperfect and violent world. So Niebuhr saw the issue in his debate with the pacifists in World War II.

Further, the reduction of an ideal to the merely optional neglects an important feature of moral ordeals. Helen Featherstone—mother of a disabled child and author of a book about the care of such children—reports that the birth of her child made her feel a little like a person facing the decision as to whether to risk his life to save a drowning person.[5] So to expend your life may be heroic, but the challenge itself hardly seems optional—whether one plunges in or walks away, one comes out of the event an altered person. The challenge wells up at the core of one's being and not at some outermost reach of life where much seems merely optional. Most ideals impinge upon us as more than mere electives even when we can only approximate them. Here I stand, I can do no other.

The virtues reflect not only commitments to principles and ideals but also to narratives, the exemplary lives of others, human and divine. Much of the moral life mediates itself from person to person and from communities to persons. As the saying goes, virtues are caught as much as they are taught. The influential narratives, moreover, may be records of divine action, not simply accounts of exemplary human conduct.

Philosophers and theologians generally differ in their assessments of the place of religious narratives (mythic and ritual) in the moral life. Philosophers sympathetic to religious traditions often hold that religious narratives, at their best, illustrate moral principles. Jesus' sacrificial life, for example, illustrates the principle of beneficence. Kant typified this approach when he held that the really thoughtful person could ultimately dispense with the inspiring example and respond directly to the principle. Thus religion, at the most and at its best, supplies us with morality for the people: it offers principles heightened and warmed up by inspiring examples.

Religious thinkers, on the other hand, tend to hold that sacred narratives about God's actions and deeds do not merely illustrate moral principles derived from elsewhere. Rather, these decisive sacred events open up a disclosive horizon from which the believer derives the commands, rules, virtues, and principles that govern his or her life.

The rabbis, for example, emphasize that the Bible includes two kinds of material, narrative and imperative (*agada* and *halacha*), which both illuminate and reinforce one another. Christian theologians have argued further that the narrative materials provide the disclosive foundation for the imperatives. For example, the Scriptures of Israel urge the farmer, in harvesting, not to pick his crops too clean but to leave some for the sojourner, for "you were once sojourners in Egypt." Thus God's own actions, his care for Israel while a stranger in Egypt, measure Israel's treatment of the stranger in her midst. Similarly, the New Testament reads, "Herein is love: not that we loved God but that God first loved us. So we ought to love one another." The imperative derives from the disclosive religious event.

The question occurs, of course, as to whether these particular scriptural passages simply illustrate and reinforce a more general principle of beneficence, in which case biblical religion, at least in this instance, folds under moral philosophy. Does the imperative to love distinctively derive from the narrative or does the narrative merely illustrate a general principle?

A close look at the passage makes it clear that the narrative pushes the believer toward a notion of love different from the philosopher's virtue of benevolence. The general principle of beneficence presupposes the structural relationship of benefactor to beneficiary, of giver to receiver. How shall I act so as to construct a better future for others? The question slots one in the position of a relatively self-sufficient philanthropist beholden to no one. But these scriptural passages put human giving in the context of a primordial receiving. Love others as God loved you while you were yet a stranger in need. Thus the virtue in question differs from self-derived benevolence. It bespeaks a responsive love that impels the receiver reflexively beyond the ordinary circle of family and friendship toward the stranger. The scriptural notion of service differs in source and substance from modern philosophical notions of benevolent or philanthropic love.

SPECIFIC VIRTUES IN PROFESSIONAL PRACTICE

The second part of this essay turns from general considerations to specific virtues germane to professional practice. Let it be noted at the outset that I do not claim that professionals display a distinctive set of virtues beyond the reach of others. Along that road lies a claim to uniqueness—a gnostic pretension to superiority in knowledge and virtue that swiftly corrupts into professional highhandedness, condescension, and even lawlessness. This essay settles for much less—simply a discussion of the virtues, the moral strengths particularly required in a professional setting. A theory of professional virtue must fall under a more inclusive doctrine of vocation or calling.

Virtues Connected with Truth-Telling

It may be useful to begin with the virtues that figure in the debate over the quandary of truth-telling in medicine. That point of departure lets us begin with the role of the virtues in a principle-oriented theory of ethics but then move beyond it.

Often the debate over truth-telling in medicine turns on contending views of the truth's impact on the patient's welfare. Shall I tell the patient the truth and run the risk of frightening him so badly as to interfere with a successful operation? Or shall I avoid telling him the facts in order to protect him? In the latter case, he also suffers. I and others encircle the patient with silence. I subject him to a kind of premature burial. When the debate over truth-telling unfolds in this way, both parties presuppose the same disposition of character or virtue: *benevolence*. They differ merely on how one makes good on this attitude through truly beneficent action directed to the patient's good or welfare.

The argument, however, can take a second form. The first party again urges the therapeutic lie for the sake of the patient's good. But this time, the advocates for categorical or, at least, prima facie truth-telling cite the patient's rights, rather than his welfare. The caretaker owes the patient the truth as a rational creature. The professional abuses the patient if she manages him with something other than candor. The blunt truth may, to be sure, harm the patient, but a lie, in the nature of the case, wrongs him; it subverts his dignity. It subjects the seriously ill patient to a fatal condescension. Thus, two different principles contend in the debate: the patient's welfare vs. the patient's rights; and, correspondingly, two different virtues come to the fore: benevolence vs. honesty and respect.

(Debate over the issue of truth-telling, of course, can be joined at a very different level, especially when professionals kibitz *en famille*. In this variant, pro–truth-tellers argue that honesty is the best policy because the physician becomes vulnerable to lawsuits—if she does not inform patients fully of the risks that surgery entails or if she does not allow a dying man or woman to make appropriate financial arrangements. Opponents of truth-telling counter that it is easier to manage a dying patient by illusive hope. Both sides decide the issue straightforwardly on the basis of the interests of the staff rather than the patient. Suddenly the virtues of benevolence and honesty vanish and the self-protection of the professional becomes decisive. On the surface, the objective choices would appear to be the same—to tell or not to tell the truth—and yet the virtue or lack of it with which the professional delivers the truth to the patient can alter for the latter its impact and meaning. A very different human environment surrounds a patient when the virtues of benevolence or honesty operate in truth-telling rather than the grubby motives of self-protection alone.)

So far in this analysis, the virtues simply function as subjective correlates to objective moral principles/obligations. Benevolence coordinates with beneficence; candor correlates with the principle of autonomy. But, further, the virtues with which the professional dispenses the truth may condition the very reality he or she offers the patient. This complication displays itself most fully in the link between the truth and yet another virtue, that is, fidelity.

The philosopher J. L. Austin drew the distinction, now famous, between two different kinds of utterances: descriptive and performative. Ordinary declarative or descriptive sentences report a given item in the world. (It is raining. The tumor is malignant. The crisis is past.) Performative sentences do not merely describe the world, but *alter* the world of the person to whom one delivers the declaration. Promises are such performative utterances. (I, John, take thee, Mary.) The promise introduces an ingredient into the world of the hearer that would not be there apart from the vow. As performative occasion, the marriage ceremony appropriately wastes no time on romantic declarations of love with Wagnerian trombones in the background. The ceremony functions to change the world for two people; it concentrates sparingly on an exchange of vows.

The professional relationship, though less comprehensive and intimate than marriage, similarly depends upon the promissory and the fiduciary. Taking a client implies a promise to help a distressed person within the limits of one's professional resources. To that degree, the promise alters the world of the patient/client. Correspondingly, to go back on a professional promise is world-altering. For this reason, the conditions under which a professional can withdraw from a case must be carefully limited.

We need not enter into the details of Austin's original and subsequently refined distinction between descriptive and performative speech. Suffice it to say that the question of the truth in professional life must include the fact of performative utterances. The talented lawyer, in an important way, alters the world of her troubled client when she promises to take his case. The moral question for the professional becomes not simply a question of telling truths, but of being true to one's promises. Conversely, the total situation for the patient includes not only his disease but also whether others ditch him or stand by him in extremity.

In the background of this expanded sense of the truth lies the scriptural sense of the statement: God is truth. First and foremost, the assertion means that God can be trusted. He keeps his promises, his covenants, if you will. God's truth is a being-true. The philosophers Josiah Royce and Gabriel Marcel have emphasized the way in which human fidelity can participate in and signify the "being-true" of God. To this degree, human fidelity—albeit derivatively—helps create the real.

The professional's fidelity per se will not eliminate the disease or the crime, but it can affect mightily the context in which the trouble runs its course. Thus the virtue of fidelity begins to affect the resolution of the dilemma itself. Perhaps more patients and clients would accept the descriptive truth if they experienced the performative truth. The anxieties of patients in terminal illness compound because they fear that professionals will abandon them. Perhaps also patients would be more inclined to believe in the doctor's performative utterances if they were not handed false diagnoses and prognoses. That is why a cautiously wise medieval physician once advised his colleagues, "Promise only fidelity."

Truth-telling also involves the virtue of prudence and its social specification as discretion. Moralists oriented to quandaries tend to concentrate on the question as to whether one ought to tell the truth. However, the practitioner knows, or learns painfully, that she must face the equally important question as to how she speaks the truth—directly or indirectly, personally or with a sparing impersonality. The theologian Karl Barth once observed that Job's friends were metaphysically correct in what they had to say about suffering, but existentially false in their timing. They chose a miserable moment to sing their theological arias on the subject of suffering.

Theorists oriented to principles tend to downgrade prudence because they rely on general rules rather than the concrete insight of the practitioner. Correspondingly, they trivialize prudence into a merely adroit selection of means in the pursuit of ends, into a crafty packaging of policies. The virtue of prudence, to be sure, deals with fitting means to ends. But, as a virtue, it consists of much more than the "tactical cunning" to which Machiavelli and the modern world diminishes the virtue.

The medievalists gave a primary place to the cardinal virtue of prudence on the grounds that Being precedes Goodness. An openness to being underlies both being good and producing the good. The marks of prudence include (a) *memoria*—being true to the past (rather than retouching, coloring, or falsifying the past); (b) *docilitas*—openness to the present, the ability to be still, to be silent, to listen; (c) and *solertia*—readiness for the unexpected. This essential openness to the past, present, and future fairly summarizes what the distressed subject needs from the interventionist in the helping professions and long precedes Freudian wisdom on the subject of the therapeutic relationship.

Prudence demands much more than a facile packaging of what one has to say. Discretion presupposes metaphysical perception, a sense for what the Stoics called the fitting, a sensibility that goes deeper than tact, a feel for behavior that is congruent with reality. Without *discretio* the professional does not reckon with the whole truth. He may tell the truth, but he does not wholly serve the truth when he tells it. He may be using the truth to serve his own vanity; or to satisfy his craving for power over his client; or to indulge himself in the role of nag, policeman, pedant, or judge.

Perseverance and Integrity

Two virtues deserve attention in any account of professional education and the formation of persisting professional identity. Perseverance is a lowly virtue but indispensable to the acquisition of technical competence under the trying conditions of lengthy professional training today. A young physician once conceded to me that medical school required more stamina than brains. I liked him for saying it. He instantly became my primary care physician because I thought he would have the sense to turn over my case if any complications required a referral. Most holders of PhDs would have to confess the same about their own graduate school education—it took more stamina than brains—though it takes the virtue of modesty to concede that fact.

Perseverance is one of the rather inconspicuous marks of courage. Thomas Aquinas once defined courage as the habit of keeping one's aversions and fears under control. Courage isn't fearlessness, a life free of aversions; it is a matter of keeping one's dislikes, one's laziness, one's fears under bridle for the sake of the good. Courage is firmness of soul in the face of adversity. Without such courage, the practitioner fails of that detachment, that disengagement of feelings, indispensable to the delivery of effective service. Most discussions of detachment emphasize the need to disengage one's likes, one's wants, and one's interests for the sake of a steadfast delivery of services. That goes without saying. But vastly more important, the social worker, the minister, the nurse, and the physician must learn to keep their aversions and frustrations with the client under control. Norman Mailer once defined the professional writer as someone who can keep at it even on a bad day.

Some thinkers rightly associate integrity with character itself. Since character is a moral structure rather than a mere temperamental state, one needs a virtue that summarizes this inclusive structure, when it is at one with itself.

Integrity draws on the images of uprightness and wholeness. Integrity gets tested at the outset in the forward scramble for admission to professional schools and in the competition for grades and position. Integrity has to do with moral posture: the upright professional refuses to put his nose to the ground, sniffing out opportunities at the expense of clients and colleagues; he equally refuses to bow before the powerful client or patient, the influential colleague, and outside pressures. Integrity also signifies a wholeness or completeness of character; it does not permit a split between the inner and the outer, between word and deed. As such, it makes possible the fiduciary bond between the professional and the client.

But nothing so demonstrates the indissoluble link between the virtues and objective principles and ideals as the virtue of integrity. The completeness or roundedness of integrity differs from mere self-sufficiency. While referring to the self in its wholeness, integrity also points beyond the self toward the person, the ideal, the transcendent that gives shape to the person's life. The virtue refers to the inclusive self, to be sure, but the self turns out to be ecstatic—pitched out beyond itself toward that in which it finds its meaning. Thus, we say that a man has lost his integrity when his core identity with those ultimate aims and purposes that ground his life breaks asunder.

Public-Spiritedness

This virtue orients the professional to the common good. The term *profession* and the more ancient, though less often invoked words, *vocation* and *calling*, have a public ring to them that the terms *job* and *career* do not. Career reminds us of the word *car*, the automobile, a self-driven vehicle. A career is a kind of self-driven vehicle through life; it enters the public thoroughfares, but for the driver's own private reasons and toward his own private destination. It ill behooves a professional to sever his calling from all question of the common good and to instrumentalize it to private goals alone. Professionals are often licensed by the state; the society invests in their education; they generate their own public standards of excellence; and they are expected to conform to these standards and to accept responsibility for their enforcement in the guild. Apart from public-spiritedness, the professional degenerates into a careerist and his education becomes a private stock of knowledge to be sold to the highest bidder.

The notion of the just and public-spirited professional suggests more than a minimalist commitment to commutative justice, that is, to the fulfillment of duties to others based on contracts. Public-spiritedness suggests a more spacious obligation to distributive justice (above and beyond exchanges through the mechanism of the marketplace). Professionals have a duty to distribute goods and services targeted on basic needs without limiting those services simply to those who have the capacity to pay for them. Some would deny this obligation altogether. Others would argue that the services of the helping professions should be distributed to meet basic human needs, but the obligation so to distribute rests upon the society at large and not on the profession itself. Thus, some lawyers have argued, the society, not the legal profession, has the duty to provide services to the poor. This approach would eliminate *pro bono publico* work as a professional obligation in favor of a third-party payment system.

Still others, myself included, would perceive the obligation to distribute professional services to be both a public and a professional responsibility. Professionals exercise power through public authority. The power they wield and the goods they control are of a public magnitude and scale. Although the state has a primary responsibility for ministering justice (an old term for distributive justice), professional groups as well have a ministry, if you will, to perform. When the state alone accepts responsibility for distributive justice, a general sense of obligation diminishes, and the social virtue upon which distribution depends loses the grounds for its renewal. Professionals particularly need to accept some responsibility for ministering justice to sustain that sensibility in the society at large. Physicians in the nineteenth century, for example, doing *pro bono publico* work, helped to dramatize the need for sanitation laws in our cities.

It should also be noted that such *pro bono publico* work does not merely serve the private happiness of those individuals who receive services, it eventually redounds to the common good and fosters public happiness. Those who receive help are not merely individuals but parts of a whole. Thus the whole, in so serving its parts, serves its own public flourishing; it rescues its citizens, mired in their private distress, for a more public life. In the absence of *pro bono publico* work, we signal, in effect, that only those clients who can pay their way into the marketplace have a public identity. To this degree, our public life shrinks; it reduces to those with the money to enter it. Public-spirited professionals not only relieve private distress, they help preserve our common life, in a monetary culture, from a constant source of its perishing.

Benevolence

The professional transaction also depends upon a pair of virtues associated with giving and receiving. Fidelity, benevolence, compassion, and public-spiritedness emphasize the pole of giving in professional life (the professional transaction also depends upon a virtue associated with the pole of receiving—humility). The virtue of benevolent service is the sine qua non of the professional relationship. The professional gives; the client receives. The client depends upon the specialized service that the professional has to offer to meet his needs. The professional, of course, is paid for her work and, like any seller, should be legally accountable for the delivery of goods promised. Compliance with contractual standards is essential; but the legal minimum should hardly be the norm. The professional transaction includes giving and receiving, not just buying and selling. Contractualism based on self-interest alone suppresses the donative element in the professional relationship. It encourages a minimalism, a grudging tit for tat—just so much service for so much money and no more. This minimalism fails to suffice—particularly in those professions that deliver help to persons with contingent, unpredictable, future needs that cannot be wholly foreseen in a contract and can only be covered by the habits of service. The word *benevolence* only palely reflects the donative element in the professional relationship; the earlier Western tradition used the stronger words, *covenant*, *love*, and *compassion*. They bespeak an exposure to the needs of others, beyond calculation, an efficacious suffering with. But our earlier discussion provides ample warning that the virtues of giving should not be celebrated alone. Unqualified and unchecked, they verge on the messianic. They require their check and counterpart in the virtues of hope and humility.

Fidelity, as we have seen, calls for a deep-going, core identity, a covenantal tie between the professional and the patient or client in his plight. Fidelity promises a service and self-expenditure that do not defect, despite the client's misery. However, drawing this close to misery and deprivation threatens to suck the professional into a whirlpool. The interventionist risks getting mired down in the mess and confusion of another's life. Inevitably, therefore, the demand to keep faith with others raises the question of the place of the virtue of hope in the helping professions. What is the metaphysical horizon in which professional interventions take place?

Sociologists are fond of describing modern professional authority as knowledge-based power. But what leads us to prize this power? Chiefly, the hope and expectation that the professional will fight against or shelter us from some evil that besets us. Mired down in disease, suffering, ignorance, uncertainty, aging, traumas, perilous transition, or crime, we grant the professional some provisional power; we hope, in exchange, to get some help in overcoming or containing the negativity that threatens to engulf us.

In effect, the modern professional's authority resembles in origin the Hobbesian and Lockean accounts of the state's derivation of authority—not from a *Summum Bonum* but a *Summum Malum*. The king in the Hobbesian state and the modern professional acquires his authority reflexively in the fight against negative and destructive power. Meanwhile, the metaphysical plight of their clients tempts professionals to respond in two ways: one, to play the role of savior, the anointed defender and guardian of the woe-beset, or, alternatively, to find some way to shield oneself from the stricken, radioactive client. These two responses in turn subdivide, but all share in common a metaphysical gloom. Savior-activists, on the one hand, see themselves as either military or parental figures, either conducting a war against disease, death, ignorance, injustice, and crime, or making parental decisions on behalf of those too weak to cope. Thus, the modern hospital has converted itself into a battleground where professionals fight an unconditional battle against death, often imposing more suffering than they relieve; while the total institution has grown apace across the last 160 years handling the negativities of madness, crime, retardation, dependency, and decrepitude, on the assumption that the negative absolutely has to be eliminated (through the ministrations of the professional), and, when it cannot be eliminated, it has to be sequestered.

The self-protectors, meanwhile, recoil from the messianic in the opposite direction, relying on various devices to protect themselves from the contaminating client. Some self-protective professionals retreat behind the shield of a purely technical competence. Others adopt the pose of benefactors who give only out of their margins and surplus. The ideal of philanthropy offers a doctrine of love without ties. Still others rely on a minimalist ethic of commercial contract—so much work for so much pay.

It may be a good deal healthier to begin with the assumption that the negative is not absolute and therefore that its elimination is not the precondition of a truly human existence. Once the negativities of sickness, suffering, ignorance, crime, and death are not treated as absolutes, then professionals may be less tempted to hike their pretensions to a messianic level or to hunker down into purely self-interested defense.

Where, however, does one find theological warrant for a more hopeful vision of the setting in which professional intervention takes place? In my own effort to puzzle over this problem as a Christian theologian, I have found myself drawn to the "suffering servant" passages in Isaiah. Remarkably enough, the texts locate the servant in the very arena of human deprivation and need. "He was despised and rejected by men; a man of sorrows and acquainted with grief, and as one from whom men hide their faces, he was despised and we esteemed him not." Further, this passage does not suggest that he is engulfed by this entry into the site of deprivation and death. Quite the contrary; in and through his outpouring of service, the will of the Lord actually prospers in his hand. This asserted link between prosperity and his own dying contrasts starkly with our ordinary scenario for social action. Ordinarily, we assume some kind of dualistic battle in which either we gradually prevail over death (in which case death diminishes) or we find our resources gradually thinned out by death (in which case we diminish). But this passage suggests that he makes his own dying, his own self-expenditure, an essential ingredient in that life which he shares with the community. "By his stripes we are healed." Death has lost its ultimacy. The act of dying for others has penetrated rather than sidestepped or merely reacted to the negative.

If the anointed of God has exposed himself to deprivation and oblivion, then men and women need fear no longer that the death and failure that they know in others or themselves can separate them from God. Those powers that they fear to be absolute have been rendered of no account as they appear either within or in their fellow creatures.

The question remains, of course, as to whether this vision undercuts the motive for works of mercy, relief, and reformation among people. I think not. The deflation of evil need not lead to quietism or complacency. It can be an enabling act. The negative has been deprived of its ultimacy. Hence men and women have been relieved of the burden of messianism. They need no longer repress the negative in themselves, or impose it on others, or be obsessed with it in their enemies, or protect themselves from it through the shield of the professional. They are free, therefore, to perform whatever acts of kindness and service they can and even to receive them from others, as a limited sign of a huge mercy that their own works have not produced.

Humility

One does not usually associate humility with professionals. Quite the contrary, long training and specialized knowledge set them apart and touch them with superiority. In popular literature, the professional often takes liberties denied to others as a sign of skill and hard work. We are treated to the reckless, swinging style of the surgeons in *M*A*S*H*, the final insouciance of the student lawyer in *The Paper Chase*, or the authoritarian law professor who presides over language like an accomplished hostess over her silver.

Clearly, the virtue of humility can have nothing to do with obsequiousness, or tentativeness, or ritual expressions of self-doubt over competence. No one needs to see his lawyer nervous before the trial or his surgeon shaky with doubt about his skill. Humility can only be understood as a necessary counterpart to the virtue of covenanted fidelity.

Idealistic members of the helping professions like to define themselves by their giving or serving alone—with others indebted to them. The young professional identifies himself with his competence; he pretends to be a relatively self-sufficient monad, unspecified by human need, while others appear before him in their distress, exposing to him their illness, their crimes, their secrets, or their ignorance, for which the professional as doctor, lawyer, priest, or teacher offers remedy.

A reciprocity, however, of giving and receiving is at work in the professional relationship that needs to be acknowledged. In the profession of teaching, to be sure, the student needs the services of the teacher to assist him in learning but so also the professor needs his students. They provide him with regular occasion and forum to work out what he has to say and to discover his subject afresh through the discipline of sharing it with others. The young rabbi or priest has more than once paused before the door of the sick room, wondering what to say to a member of his congregation, only to discover the dying patient ministering to his own needs. Likewise, the doctor needs her patients; the lawyer, her clients. No one can watch the professional nervously approach retirement without realizing how much she needs her clients to be herself.

The discipline of receiving is important in still further ways. The successful client interview requires addressing but also being addressed, giving but also taking in; it means both speaking and hearing, the tongue and the ear. The professional's debts, moreover, extend beyond his direct obligations to current clients; they also include public monies spent on education, the earlier contributions of clients upon whom he "practiced" while learning his craft, and the research traditions of his profession upon which he daily draws. Humility, finally, opens the door to professional self-renewal. No teacher stays alive if she does not remain a student. No preacher can preach the word if he no longer hears it. No physician can long dispense a range of professional services if not serviced herself by the research arm of her profession.

When the professional, of course, evinces some of the aforementioned virtues, she runs the danger of taking herself too seriously. Look what it took to get her where she is—perseverance, courage, integrity, compassion, candor, fidelity, prudence, public-spiritedness, and justice. So, at last, humility ought to let some of the air out of the other virtues; it ought to undercut the temptation to false posturing and heroics. It should remind us of the underground root system of receiving upon which professional life depends.

Notes

1.   Thomas L. Beauchamp and James F. Childress, *Principles of Biomedical Ethics* (New York: Oxford University Press, 1979), 235.

2.   Alasdair McIntyre, *After Virtue: A Study in Moral Theory*, 3rd ed. (Notre Dame, IN: University of Notre Dame Press, 1981), 178.

3.   Montesquieu, *The Spirit of the Laws*, Bk. III.

4.   John Stuart Mill, *Utilitarianism*, Library of the Liberal Arts, rev. ed., Oskar Piest, general ed. (Indianapolis: Bobbs-Merrill, 1957), 22.

5.   Helen Featherstone, *A Difference in the Family. Living with a Disabled Child* (New York: Penguin, 1981).

6. Virtue Ethics and Sexual Ethics

James F. Keenan

This chapter first appeared in *Louvain Studies* (2005).

In light of the recent controversies arising from the sexual abuse scandals that have broken out throughout the world, laity and clergy have been calling for a more urgent and credible articulation of Catholic sexual ethics. Presently intransigent debates occur throughout the church about the moral legitimacy of particular sexual actions.[1] Those of us in virtue ethics are more interested, however, in positing a theological agenda that primarily refers to the type of persons we ought to become. We do not avoid discussion about particular actions, but we believe that if we want to have a credible theological ethics in general and an equally credible sexual ethics in particular, then we need to begin where as the people of God we resonate with one another regarding commonly held truths and insights. We believe that there is much more that unites us than divides us.

Toward this end, I propose a virtue ethics for sexuality that goes beyond chastity. First, I briefly explore the virtue of chastity. Second, I explore virtue ethics and its relevance for moral education. Third, I propose a contemporary set of cardinal virtues in a specifically Catholic context. Fourth, I begin developing a sexual ethics on the foundation of these four virtues.

CHASTITY

When we think of Catholic sexual ethics, we think naturally of chastity. The *Catechism of the Catholic Church* places its discourse on chastity within the context of the sixth commandment (2331–2400), which specifically acknowledges chastity's reference to sexuality. In the *Catechism* chastity helps us to integrate the gift of sexuality. On the practical level, chastity functions in two ways: it invites us to understand ourselves as enhancing our lives whenever we seek to integrate our sexuality within ourselves as relational persons and it offers strong, regulatory norms of abstinence.

The first function is a positive appreciation of sexuality, embodiment, relationality, and maturing sexual intimacy. Appreciating sexuality as gift, chastity invites the Catholic to see the need for understanding the special ways that sexuality brings us together within the love of God. Chastity calls the Catholic to develop this positive appreciation incrementally throughout her or his life.

The latter function promotes an abstinence whether very narrowly in terms of a marital chastity that teaches that Catholic spouses should abstain from sexual relations outside of marriage, or for that matter any sexual activity that would in itself be antiprocreative, and more broadly in denying any sexual expressions that are genitally intimate outside of marriage.

Chastity promotes a considerable Christian realism about the challenges of sexuality in the modern world. Christian chastity is particularly important in engaging those who are growing to realize that the gift of sexuality requires a great deal of appreciation and prudential reflection and that the innate inclination to realize sexual desires needs to be checked by a realistic appraisal of one's own maturity and the willingness to commit to another. In short Christian chastity has always brought a sense of reality to much discussion on sexuality, though contrarily, Christians have sometimes not spent enough time considering how much of a gift sexuality actually is.[2] Thus, chastity helps draw a variety of basic lines about the moral liceity and nonmoral liceity of sexual expressions, a line drawing that the other virtues might not so easily attain. For this reason, it is always relevant for sexual ethics precisely because it provides basic moral guidelines especially in its ordinary propaedeutic function.

But is this enough to teach a sexual ethics? Do we need something more than chastity for a contemporary sexual ethics? I believe we do and I take my cue from the *Catechism* itself, which suggests we look to the virtues for further moral instruction.[3]

WHAT IS VIRTUE ETHICS?

Renewed interest in virtue ethics arises from a dissatisfaction with the way we do ethics today. Most discussions about contemporary ethics consider major controversial actions: abortion, nuclear war, gene therapy, and so on. These discussions basically dominate contemporary ethics.

Virtue ethicists have more extensive concerns.[4] We believe that the real discussion of ethics is not primarily the question about what actions are morally permissible, but rather who should we become? In fact, virtue ethicists expand that question into three key, related ones: Who are we? Who ought we to become? How are we to get there?[5] I now turn to each of these questions.

No question is more central for virtue ethics than the self-understanding or identity question, "Who are we?"[6] To virtue ethicists, the question is the same as "Are we virtuous?" To answer this first question we must focus on two major considerations. First, what standards are we to measure ourselves against? Second, how will we know whether we are measuring ourselves fairly?

Regarding the first point, two of the most important works in ethics attempt to assist us by naming the basic virtues. In the *Nicomachean Ethics*, Aristotle gives us eleven different virtues that are necessary for citizens to engage. Friendship, magnanimity, practical wisdom are some of these. In the *Summa Theologiae*, Thomas Aquinas takes from Plato, Cicero, Ambrose, Gregory, and Augustine the four cardinal virtues: prudence, justice, temperance, and fortitude. Together with these he adds the three theological virtues. He states that we can acquire the first four through deliberately willed and enjoyed habitual right action; the latter three are gifts from God. These virtues help us to answer the question of self-understanding: Are we just, prudent, temperate, and fortitudinous?

But how can we know whether we are answering the question objectively? How can we be sure that we are not simply deceiving ourselves regarding our self-understanding? Here Aristotle suggests that we can know ourselves by considering how we act in spontaneous situations: we "discover" ourselves when we act in the unplanned world of ordinary life. We may believe that we are particularly brave or cowardly, but that assessment is only correct if it conforms to how we actually behave in the unanticipated, concrete situation (*Nicomachean Ethics* II.3; III.6–9). Self-knowledge is key, therefore, but this is a self-knowledge that is critical and honest, not one based on wishful thinking.

The second question, "Who ought we to become?" embodies a vision of the type of persons we ought to become. Though we use Thomas's four cardinal virtues to learn how virtuous we presently are, we could use those same four virtues to determine our goals in life. Certainly, if we are honest in the first question, then some virtues are not as fully acquired by us as are others. In fact, for the honest person the virtues are not what we acquire in life; they are what we pursue.

We use the virtues, therefore, to set the personal goals that we encourage ourselves to seek. Thomas and others call this goal the "end." That is, the middle question sets the end that we should seek. That end is a type of person with the cardinal virtues. Setting this end means that the fundamental task of the moral life is to develop a vision and to strive to attain it. Inasmuch as that vision is who we ought to become, then, the key insight is that we should always aim to grow. As a person-oriented ethics, virtue ethics insists that without growth, we cannot become more moral.

Setting such an end describes then another way that virtue ethicists are different from other ethicists. Rather than first examining actions and asking whether we should perform them or not, virtue ethicists suggest that we ought to set ends for the type of people we believe we should become. Thus, to the extent that we are examining our lives and seeking ways of improving ourselves for the moral flourishing of our world, to that extent we are engaging virtue ethics.

Turning to the third question, in order to get to the end, we need prudence. For many years prudence has had a terrible reputation, being thought of as caution or self-interest. "Be prudent" meant "Don't get caught," "Be extra careful," "Watch out!"

For Aristotle and Thomas prudence is not simply caution. Prudence is rather the virtue of a person whose feet are on the ground and who thinks both practically and realistically. Prudence belongs to the person who not only sets realistic ends, but sets out to attain them. The prudent person is precisely the person who knows how to grow.[7]

Being prudent is no easy task. From the medieval period until today, we believe that it is easier to get something wrong than to get it right. For today we still assert if only one component of an action is wrong, the whole action is wrong.

Prudence is even more complicated when we try to figure out the appropriate ways of becoming more virtuous. It must be attentive to detail, anticipate difficulties, and measure rightly. Moreover, as anyone who has watched children knows, we are not born with prudence. Instead, we acquire it through a very long process.

Finding prudence is finding the middle point: all of prudence is precisely getting to the middle point or the "mean" between extremes. As Aristotle and Aquinas remind us repeatedly: "virtue is the mean" (*NE* II.6; *ST* Ia IIae, q. 64, aa.1–3). The mean is located where there is adequate tension for growth, neither too little nor too much. That mean is not fixed. The mean of virtue is not something set in stone: rather, it is the mean by which only specific persons or communities can grow. This is another reason why prudence is so difficult: no two means are the same.

Finding the mean of the right tension depends on who the persons or communities are. In a matter of speaking, a virtue ought to fit a person the way a glove fits one's hand. There is a certain tailor-made feel to a virtue, which prompts Aquinas to call virtue "one's second nature" (*ST* Ia IIae, q. 58, a. 1).

Virtue ethics is, therefore, a proactive system of ethics. It invites all people to see themselves as they really are, to assess themselves and see who they can actually become. In order both to estimate oneself and to set desired goals, it proffers the virtues for both. Moreover, it invites all people to see that they set the agenda not only of the end, but also of the means to accomplish that end. Virtuous actions, like temperate drinking or courageously facing our fears, are the prudential means for achieving the end of becoming more virtuous persons. Virtue ethics encompasses our entire lives. It sees every moment as the possibility for acquiring or developing a virtue. To underline this point, Aquinas held that every human action is a moral action. That is, any action that we knowingly perform is a moral action because it affects us as moral persons. Whatever we do makes us become what we do.

Thomas saw every human action as an "exercise" (*ST* Ia IIae, q. 65, a. 1, ad 1). Though some of us go through life never examining the habits we engage, Thomas suggests to us that we ought to examine our ways of acting and ask ourselves: are these ways making us more just, prudent, temperate, and brave? If they are, they are virtuous exercises.

When we think of exercise we think of athletics. The person who exercises herself by running eventually becomes a runner just as the one who dances becomes a dancer. From that insight Thomas like Aristotle before him sees that intended, habitual activity in the sports arena is no different from any other arena of life. If we can develop ourselves physically we can develop ourselves morally by intended, habitual activity.

Virtue ethics sees, therefore, the ordinary as the terrain on which the moral life moves. Thus, while most ethics make their considerations about rather controversial material, virtue ethics often engages the commonplace. It is concerned with what we teach our children and how; with the way we relate with friends, families, and neighbors; with the way we live our lives. Moreover, it is concerned not only with whether a physician maintains professional ethics, for instance, whether she keeps professional secrets or observes informed consent with her patients. It is equally concerned with her private life, with whether she knows how to respect her friends' confidences or whether she respects her family members' privacy. In a word, before the physician is a physician she is a person. It is her life as a person with which virtue ethics is specifically concerned.

Virtue ethics looks at the world from an entirely different vantage point, moving ahead with less glamour and drama, but always seeing the agent, not as re-actor, but as actor: knowing oneself and setting the agenda of personal and communal ends and means in both the ordinary and the professional life.

The virtues are therefore traditional teleological (that is, end-oriented) guides that collectively aim for the right realization of the human person. As teleological, they need to be continually realized and redefined; their final expression remains outstanding. The mature person is constantly growing in the virtues. This means that virtue is always at once looking for expression in action and when a virtue is realized in action it makes the person more virtuous. Thus the more we grow in virtue, the more we are able to recognize our need for further growth.

This type of growth ought not to be seen as a cycle or a circle but as a spiral moving us forward through history.[8] The nature of virtue is, then, historically dynamic; being in themselves goal-oriented, virtues require being continually considered, understood, acquired, developed, and reformulated.

Underlying the teleological nature of the virtues is then an implicit belief in the progress of ethical thought, both in the individual and in the community. This plays out in the lives of both individual persons and moral communities. For instance, as I age I consider how much I need to engage patience and reconciliation, when earlier I did not see these needed virtues in part because I lacked the prudence (and humility) to acknowledge them. Similarly, we see nation-states as they develop, continually redefining the meaning of justice so as to extend the circle of equality. We see this also in the language of "solidarity," which through religious leaders and social movements has become more and more relevant to people's lives though thirty-five years ago it was hardly known as a virtue.

Moreover, sometimes we try to replace the emphasis of one virtue over another, in part, to establish balance. For instance, Blessed John XXIII opened the Second Vatican Council on October 11, 1962, by calling the church to practice greater mercy in place of its severity. More recently Anne Patrick described virtuous shifts within society. She examined the canonization of Maria Goretti and suggested that it implicitly proposed a woman's chastity as a social virtue of greater importance than a woman's own life.[9] But then she noted how people's devotion turned to look for other heroines who upheld life, justice, and being a woman working through a full and robust life. Therein, among others, was Dorothy Day, a woman known for leadership, justice, and a long, generous life. Patrick presumes an ethical development in our insights in the shift from chastity as the signature virtue for women to a more egalitarian anthropology where justice is the hallmark virtue for both genders.

For this reason, ethicists and moralists have several tasks: to critically reflect on the contemporary situation to see whether existing anthropologies and the corresponding constellations of virtues inhibit or liberate members of our global community; to perceive new horizons of human possibility; to express the possible ways that virtue can attain those horizons; and to make politically possible the actual new self-understanding and self-realization. This final task is often overlooked: too often ethicists and moralists think that our work ends with written proposals, but inasmuch as ethical insight *to be ethical* must end in action, similarly the task of the ethicist must end in political action, an insight that Aristotle routinely affirmed. I hope in this paper to carry out these four tasks.

One final comment: virtue ethics intersects with natural law.[10] Natural law is the universally accessible study through human reason of a normative anthropology and of the attendant practices that realize that anthropology. Articulating that normative vision is problematic, however, since we each perceive the natural law from our own context. Despite the problematic, Christian ethicists try to perceive the *humanum* with the eyes of faith. Thus, we believe that our perception will be prompted by our faith and that what we see will have a particular urgency because of the narrative of salvation history. As Klaus Demmer puts it simply: "[G]enuine theology leads to a fundamental change in our way of thinking."[11] Thus virtue ethics is the attempt to articulate the normative anthropology of the natural law.

PROPOSING CATHOLIC CARDINAL VIRTUES

Our hermeneutical investigations into the nature of the human person, the horizon of our anthropological vision and the corresponding virtues, depend then where we are in history. That does not mean that we make up virtues. Rather we become more able to see what or rather who we should become. We are always being challenged to discover a more correct vision of human personhood and community.

The claim of moral objectivity is not then negated by the recognition of our historical context. Our right perception of that virtuous mean or what we today would call the anthropological goal of a particular character trait depends upon our ability to perceive it in the first place. This is why Aristotle recommended to us that we find the mean by seeing how a prudent person would determine it (*NE* II.6).

Yet Aristotle departed from Socrates on the point that prudence is sufficient for self-realization and self-determination. Prudence, Aristotle warned us, depended upon the other virtues and those virtues were dialectally dependent upon prudence (*NE* VI. 13). For this reason, the competency of prudence is deeply embedded in the historic nature of human beings such that human beings can only perceive well the horizon of their possibilities to the extent that they have rightly realized themselves through the virtues.

If we take the cardinal virtues as they are proposed in Thomas Aquinas (*ST* Ia IIae, q. 61), who built upon the insights of Cicero, Ambrose, Gregory, and Augustine, we find that the four cardinal virtues—prudence, justice, temperance, and fortitude—perfect four corresponding powers: the practical reason, the will, the concupiscible, and the irascible. These virtues inhere in a particular hierarchy. Temperance and fortitude are predominantly at the service of justice. Prudence determines the right choice of means for each of the virtues, but it especially looks to recommend the just action since justice governs all exterior principles. In a manner of speaking, the anthropological identity of the virtuous person is simply the just one.

But Thomas *developed* the patristic agenda on the virtues. For instance, Augustine held that all real virtues were rooted in charity without which there was no real virtue; Thomas modified Augustine's claim: while acknowledging that justice without charity is not perfect justice, for Thomas justice without charity is nonetheless virtue. This is why we often hear that Thomas used Aristotle to develop Augustine.

These classical cardinal virtues and their overarching structure are, however, no longer adequate and in fact endorse an anthropology that inhibits greatly the present theological agenda. As far as I see it, three reasons merit replacing them. First, contemporary writers repeatedly express dissatisfaction with the insufficiency of justice. For the most part, they offer hyphenated constructs, the most famous being "love-justice," which attempts to acknowledge that while working for the equality for all persons, we still maintain partial relationships that need to be nurtured and sustained.[12]

But the hyphen is distracting. Rather than reducing one to the other or eliding the two together, Paul Ricoeur places them in a "tension between two distinct and sometimes opposed claims."[13] Ricoeur's insight that the virtues are distinct and at times opposing stands in contrast with Aquinas's strategy of the cardinal virtues where justice is supported by fortitude and temperance, and neither shaped nor opposed by the two auxiliary virtues. Only when another virtue stands as a fully equal, heuristic guide can there be a dialectical tension wherein the virtues challenge and define one another, and, as Ricoeur suggests, "may even be the occasion for the invention of responsible forms of behavior."[14]

Second, the modern era insists that moral dilemmas are not based on the simple opposition of good and evil but, more frequently, on the clash of goods. Thus, a constellation of virtues acting as partial heuristic guides that already resolve the priority of one virtue over another by a preconceived hierarchal structure preempts realism. We cannot propose heuristic guides that prefabricate solutions when the concrete data is still forthcoming. Thus we need virtues that go beyond protecting the single good of justice and that allow us to interpret in each instance which of the primary virtues ought to be in play.

Third, the primary identity of being human is not an individual with powers needing perfection, but rather a relational rational being whose modes of relationality need to be rightly realized. On this last point we can begin proposing a set of cardinal virtues that allow us at once to try talking cross-culturally and that cover our main objections.[15]

Our identity is relational in three ways: generally, specifically, and uniquely. Each of these relational ways of being demands a cardinal virtue: as a relational being in general, we are called to justice; as a relational being specifically, we are called to fidelity; and, as a relational being uniquely, we are called to self-care. These three virtues are cardinal. Unlike Thomas's structure, none is ethically prior to the other; they have equally urgent claims and they should be pursued as ends in themselves: we are not called to be faithful and self-caring in order to be just, nor are we called to be self-caring and just in order to be faithful. None is auxiliary to the others. They are distinctive virtues with none being a subset or subcategory of the other. They are cardinal. The fourth cardinal virtue is prudence, which determines what constitutes the just, faithful, and self-caring way of life for an individual. The older two virtues, fortitude and temperance, remain auxiliary and exist to support the realization of the other four.

Let me explain how these four virtues work: our relationality generally is always directed by an ordered appreciation for the common good in which we treat all people as equal. As members of the human race, we are expected to respond to all members in general equally and impartially.[16]

If justice urges us to treat all people equally, then fidelity makes distinctively different claims. Fidelity is the virtue that nurtures and sustains the bonds of those special relationships that humans enjoy whether by blood, marriage, love, citizenship, or sacrament. If justice rests on impartiality and universality, then fidelity rests on partiality and particularity.

Fidelity here is like love in the "just-love" dialectic. It is also like the claim that Carol Gilligan made in her important work, *In a Different Voice*.[17] Gilligan criticized Lawrence Kohlberg for arguing that full moral development was found in the person who could reason well about justice as impartial and universal. She countered that the human must aim for both the impartiality of justice as well as the development of particular relational bonds.

Neither of these virtues, however, addresses the unique relationship that each person has with oneself. Care for self enjoys a considered role in our tradition, as for instance, the command to love God and one's neighbor as oneself. In his writings on the order of charity, Thomas Aquinas, among others, developed this love of self at length.[18]

Finally, prudence has the task of integrating the three virtues into our relationships, just as it did when it was among the classical list of the cardinal virtues. Thus, prudence is always vigilant looking to the future, trying not only to realize the claims of justice, fidelity, and self-care in the here and now, but also calling us to anticipate occasions when each of these virtues can be more fully acquired. In this way prudence is clearly a virtue that pursues ends and effectively establishes the moral agenda for the person growing in these virtues. But these ends are not in opposition to nor in isolation of one another. Rather, prudence helps each virtue to shape its end as more inclusive of the other two.

Inasmuch as all persons in every culture are constituted by these three ways of being related, by naming these virtues as cardinal, we have a device for talking cross-culturally. This device is based, however, on modest claims. The cardinal virtues do not purport to offer a picture of the ideal person, nor to exhaust the entire domain of virtue. Rather than being the last word on virtue, they are among the first, providing the bare essentials for right human living and specific action. As "hinges" (the

English for the word *cardo*), the cardinal virtues provide a skeleton of both what human persons should basically be and at what human action should basically aim. All other issues of virtue hang on the skeletal structures of both rightly integrated dispositions and right moral action.

I believe that these *thin* and skeletal virtues become *thickened* and enfleshed in different cultures in different ways.[19] For instance, some understanding of justice (the willingness to be impartial and to give to each their due) is presumably present in every culture. Justice in the United States, however, is affected considerably by the American esteem of personal autonomy and its respect of personal rights. Autonomy thickens justice inasmuch as we would not give "the due" to any persons without their consent. Our health-care system, for instance, so powerfully protects the rights of the individual that we could not imagine justice in a health-care system that did not privilege informed consent. This American understanding of justice differentiates itself from justice in the Philippines where an emphasis on "smooth interpersonal relationships" governs most social relationships. Similarly, through autonomy, American understandings of fidelity depend on the importance of mutual consent. In the Philippines, its strong emphasis on cohesion, unity, and peace clearly provides the yeast for translating fidelity into ordinary life.

Cultures give flesh to the skeletal cardinal virtues. This thickening differentiates, then, one virtue in one culture from a similar one in another. Justice, fidelity, and self-care in a Buddhist culture have somewhat similar and somewhat different meanings than they do in a liberal or Confucian context.[20]

When it comes to thickening in Catholic culture, we need to turn to the virtue of mercy, which, I have argued over the years, is the trademark of Catholicism.[21] In Catholic cultures, mercy thickens our understanding of the virtues. Inasmuch as mercy is, as I define it, the willingness to enter into the chaos of another so as to respond to their need, mercy thickens justice by taking into account the chaos of the most marginalized. Mercy does not temper justice as so many believe; rather, mercy prompts us to see that justice applies to all, especially those most frequently without justice, those abandoned to the chaos of the margins. In Catholic cultures, mercy prompts justice both to find the neglected, the persecuted, and the oppressed, and to bring them into the solidarity of humanity by assisting them in the pursuit of their rights.[22]

Similarly fidelity in the many relationships we enjoy is enfleshed by mercy. Mercy helps Catholics to see from the start that no relationship is without its chaos and that every relationship requires the merciful practice of reconciliation. In Catholic marriages, for instance, the balm of mercy prompts spouses to enter one another's chaos and to forgive each other not once or twice but seventy times seven times. Finally the Catholic practice of self-care urges each person, through mercy, to enter into the deep chaos of one's own distinctively complicated life. By the examination of conscience we believe that the loving, merciful light of Christ illuminates every dimension of the soul and helps us to see what we need to do in the care of ourselves.

DEVELOPING A SEXUAL ETHICS OUT OF THESE CARDINAL VIRTUES

When these virtues are applied to us as relational sexual beings we see how each has a very particular agenda relevant for sexual ethics. Together they offer a comprehensive sexual ethics. I saw this developed at length by one of my doctoral students, Ronaldo Zaccharias, SDB, from Brazil, who employed these virtues precisely for a Brazilian educational program of Christian sexual ethics. He took the four virtues that I have proposed and after seeing them as Catholic, that is, as thickened by mercy, he applied them to particular cases so as to elaborate a Catholic sexual ethics.[23]

In light of the conversations I had with him, I want to expand on some of the insights we shared. First, justice as it applies to sexual ethics is really about each of us learning to appreciate the other person with a dignity that belongs to being human and in the image of God. In sexual relations, justice always prompts us to see the other as subject and not as an object; justice leads us to recognize the importance of never taking advantage of another for the sake of fulfilling our own desires or needs. Justice requires therefore that we see the person whom we are attracted to, "in love with," "romantically involved with," or dating as a person with a dignity that cannot be compromised.

Justice in sexual ethics does not simply apply to the person we are dating or marrying. Justice informed by mercy makes us more sensitive to any sense of inequality or indignity that afflicts our neighbor. A justice informed by mercy is vigorously alert to those who are particularly vulnerable. The abuse of children by clergy is a violent violation of Catholic justice. It reminds us again and again why justice is so important in a sexual ethics. Thus, the sexual abuse of the vulnerable adult, long overlooked in the recent crisis, calls us to a sexual ethics that privileges justice: rape of anyone is seen as a flagrant act of injustice.[24]

In sexual ethics, this Catholic sense of justice calls us to recognize when others are denigrated, therefore, by the commercialization of sex, from prostitution to the kidnapping and transport of minors. Justice in a sexual ethics moves us to enter into the chaos of those whose dignity is compromised by sexual inequities as well. Here we especially think of the ongoing work of establishing the God-given equality of women. Justice in sexual ethics requires us to recognize, support, and promote the equality of the genders, with the understanding that such work still has much to accomplish.

Still, justice is particularly relevant in promoting more egalitarian understandings in heterosexual relationships where, as elsewhere, women still do not enjoy the status of equality in so many forms of life. But justice is not simply attentive to abuse and compromise in marriage. Clear-eyed justice ought to see the chaos of the lives of poor women and their lack of adequate power, this especially in a world where millions of people have HIV/AIDS and the rates of infection among women and particularly teenage girls continue to escalate unabatedly.

Moreover, because justice is a forward-looking virtue it prudently anticipates a way of seeing society more respectful of persons, their bodies, their expressions of sexuality. A justice informed by mercy looks to those who because of sexuality (histories of abuse, sexual dysfunction, orientation questions, and so on) cry out for protection, sanctuary, support, and hospitality. On the question of orientation, the beginning of justice would seem to be that church leaders could learn more about the experiences and self-understanding of gay and lesbian persons, especially those who are devoted members of the church, especially those in ministry.[25]

A Catholic justice informed by mercy in the context of sexual ethics can be taught in our classrooms, in our religious education programs, or from the pulpit. It helps us to see that our sexuality, where we are most capable of expressing, receiving, and mutually sharing love, is the embodiment of our most vulnerable dimensions. It is where through intimacy we leave ourselves open to the other. For this reason the church's long history of privileging justice easily extends its interest into the realm of sexual ethics.

Justice is not alone among the virtues. All societies call us to be faithful to the long-standing, particular relationships we have. Fidelity differs from justice in that the latter calls us to treat with impartiality all people, while fidelity recognizes that we each are constituted by a variety of specific interpersonal relationships. A fidelity informed by mercy then leads us toward approaching prudently and fearlessly those whom we love. It demands that we privilege the particular relationships that we enjoy.

Fidelity requires us not only not to end or walk out of loving relationships but more important to defend and sustain them. Fidelity requires that the entirety of each of our relationships must be embraced and that, informed by mercy, we are always called to stand with those whom we love, especially in their chaos.

Fidelity teaches us that in our sexual relationships we must consider the other in all his or her specificity. Therefore, fidelity demands an honesty to the sexual expression of the relationship. Fidelity calls us never to abandon our lover, to recognize rather that our sexual love must deepen, embrace, and extend through intimacy.

But by being informed by mercy Catholic fidelity anticipates the chaos of our sexuality and sexual relationships. Fidelity teaches us to be no fool in entering sexual relationships. It reminds us that entering into a sexual relationship with another means entering into an intimate complexity where we need to recognize the inevitable yet unpredictable moments of upheaval and confusion attendant to such intimacy.

Catholic fidelity therefore privileges dialogue. It seeks to make a couple capable of communicating as best they can their needs, hopes, fears, and desires. This fidelity helps the Christian to grow further in love and in humanity. It sees sex itself as a language that expresses in a variety of ways the human person in openness and in pursuit of the other.[26]

This fidelity becomes particularly relevant when children are born into the sexual relationship. Catholic fidelity does not simply mean no divorce or separation. It is not primarily defined by negatives. Rather, it seeks to convey the bond into which a child is born. For this reason

Catholics are intensely interested in the nature of marriage as the place where faithful love and procreativity concretely flourish.

Self-care is another virtue in which the person recognizes the call to be accountable for oneself. This brings with it a particular competency to not let oneself be taken advantage in any relationships, sexual or otherwise. Instead it calls for a recognition of knowing one's own capabilities, whether and when one can sustain a sexual relationship. It recognizes that while fidelity seeks to look to the other and to the relationship, self-care reminds us that we need to be responsible to ourselves in sexual relationships as well.

Often people enter sexual relationships before they are actually capable of being able to sustain one. They do harm to the other and to themselves. For this reason persons around the country and elsewhere constantly encourage younger people to delay sexual experiences and relationships, not because sex is bad but because sexual relationships are demanding and require a maturity that engages not just justice and fidelity, but self-care as well. Self-care also prompts people not to succumb to cultural disvalues that encourage casual sexual experiences.

Conversely, self-care might also lead us to acknowledge that we have long been inhibited and fearful of intimacy, touch, or sexual expression. Prudential self-care informed by mercy leads some people to delay as precipitous sexual intimacy, but for others it gently prods them to seek sexual love that has, for long, been an object of fear and dread.[27]

A self-care informed by mercy prompts us to attend to our own personal histories where areas of need or particular vulnerability need to be recognized rather than repressed. Interestingly, many of us are more willing to entertain and stand with another's chaos than with our own. Our pride basically keeps us from seeing the more messy side of ourselves where our hopes, needs, and vulnerabilities exist. Self-care invites us to be as patient with ourselves as we are with others and invites us to not look to sexual experiences as a way, for instance, of resolving problems of self-esteem. Self-care invites us to see sexuality and sexual relationships as goods to be pursued but precisely within a virtuous context.

Not only are sexuality and sexual relationships goods, but by self-care we are called to understand ourselves as embodied and alive with passion, which are goods as well. Virtue prompts us not to be indulgent but rather to take these goods seriously and to see whether we really appreciate these goods as such and whether we can develop the askesis or discipline to grow passionately, bodily, sexually to maturity.

CONCLUSION

The turn to virtue ethics gives us space as a community of faith to talk about basic character traits, dispositions, and stances that members of the community ought to develop to be faithful, loving Catholics. That space, when taken seriously, will inevitably lead to discussion on the particular practices attendant to the virtues that we believe need to be cultivated, and those practices will eventually be prescribed accordingly. But now we need at least to elaborate on who we ought to become as a community of faith, and from there develop an anthropology for a sexual ethics. I suggest that we start with being a people shaped by mercy in the pursuit of justice, fidelity, self-care, and prudence.

Notes

1. Thus, Joseph Selling urges us away from an act-centered sexual morality to a more positive, relational ethics of care and sees Lisa Sowle Cahill's *Sex, Gender, and Ethics* (Cambridge: Cambridge University Press, 1996) as illustrative of his proposal in his "The Development of Catholic Tradition and Sexual Morality," in *Embracing Sexuality: Authority and Experience in the Catholic Church*, ed. Joseph Selling (Aldershot: Ashgate, 2001), 149–62. See also Lisa Sowle Cahill, "Sexuality: Personal, Communal, Responsible," in *Embracing Sexuality*, 165–72; and her *Between the Sexes: Foundations for a Christian Ethics of Sexuality* (New York: Paulist Press, 1985). This is certainly foundational to the works of Jack Dominian (*Proposals for a New Sexual Ethic* [London: Darton, Longman and Todd, 1977]), Christine Gudorf (*The Body, Sex and Pleasure: Reconstructing Christian Sexual Ethics* [Cleveland, OH: Pilgrim Press, 1994]), and Kevin T. Kelly (*New Directions in Sexual Ethics: Moral Theology and the Challenge of AIDS* [London: Geoffrey Chapman, 1998]).

2. This is of course being rectified by the theology of the body by Pope John Paul II; see Pope John Paul II, *The Theology of the Body* (Boston, MA: Daughters of St. Paul, 1997). For other developments, see Charles Curran and

Richard McCormick (eds.), *Dialogue about Catholic Sexual Teaching* (Mahwah, NJ: Paulist Press, 1993).

3. John Grabowski also offers virtue for sexual education and begins with chastity but augments the virtue as well in his *Sex and Virtue: An Introduction to Sexual Ethics* (Washington, DC: Catholic University of America, 2004).

4. James Keenan, *Virtues for Ordinary Christians* (Kansas City, MO: Sheed and Ward, 1996), and his "Virtue Ethics," in *Basic Christian Ethics: An Introduction*, ed. Bernard Hoose (London: Chapman, 1997) 84–94; Joseph Kotva, Jr., *The Christian Case for Virtue Ethics* (Washington, DC: Georgetown University Press, 1996); Gilbert Meilaender, *The Theory and Practice of Virtue* (Notre Dame, IN: University of Notre Dame Press, 1984); Jean Porter, *The Recovery of Virtue: The Relevance of Aquinas for Christian Ethics* (Louisville, KY: Westminster Press, 1990); William Spohn, "The Return of the Virtues," *Theological Studies* 53 (1992): 60–75.

5. Alasdair MacIntyre, *After Virtue: A Study in Moral Theory* (Notre Dame, IN: University of Notre Dame Press, 1981).

6. John Kekes, *The Examined Life* (Lewisburg, PA: Bucknell University Press, 1988).

7. Daniel Mark Nelson, *The Priority of Prudence* (University Park, PA: Pennsylvania State University, 1992).

8. Thomas R. Kopfensteiner, "The Metaphorical Structure of Normativity," *Theological Studies* 58 (1997): 331–46.

9. Anne Patrick, "Narrative and the Social Dynamics of Virtue," in *Changing Values and Virtues*, ed. Dietmar Mieth and Jacques Pohier (Edinburgh: T. and T. Clark, 1987), 69–80.

10. On natural law see Jean Porter, *Natural and Divine Law: Claiming the Tradition for Christian Ethics* (Grand Rapids, MI: Eerdmans, 1999); *Nature as Reason: A Thomistic Theory of the Natural Law* (Grand Rapids, MI: Eerdmans, 2005).

11. Klaus Demmer, "Die autonome Moral—eine Anfrage an die Denkform," in *Fundamente der theologischen Ethik*, ed. Adrian Holderegger (Freiburg: Herder, 1996), 262.

12. James Keenan, "Proposing Cardinal Virtues," *Theological Studies* 56 (1995): 709–29; reprinted in *The Historical Development of Fundamental Moral Theology in the United States*, ed. Charles Curran and Richard McCormick, Readings in Moral Theology 11 (Mahwah, NJ: Paulist Press, 1999), 281–306. Also, James Keenan, "Virtue and Identity," in *Creating Identity: Biographical, Moral, Religious*, ed. Hermann Haring, Maureen Junker-Kenny, and Dietmar Mieth [*Concilium* 2000/2] (London: SCM Press, 2000), 69–77.

13. Paul Ricoeur, "Love and Justice," in *Radical Pluralism and Truth: David Tracy and the Hermeneutics of Religion*, ed. Werner G. Jeanrond and Jennifer L. Rike (New York: Crossroad, 1991), 196.

14. Ibid., 197.

15. This important point is repeatedly made by Cahill, Selling, and others.

16. Ricoeur, "Love and Justice," 195.

17. Carol Gilligan, *In a Different Voice: Psychological Theory and Women's Development* (Cambridge, MA: Harvard University Press, 1982).

18. Stephen Pope, "Expressive Individualism and True Self-Love: A Thomistic Perspective," *Journal of Religion* 71 (1991): 384–99; Edward Vacek, *Love, Human and Divine* (Washington, DC: Georgetown University Press, 1995), 239–73.

19. Michael Walzer, *Thick and Thin: Moral Argument at Home and Abroad* (Notre Dame, IN: University of Notre Dame Press, 1996). See also Martha Nussbaum, "Non-Relative Virtues: An Aristotelian Approach," in *Ethical Theory: Character and Virtue*, ed. Peter A. French et al., Midwest Studies in Philosophy 13 (Notre Dame, IN: University of Notre Dame Press, 1988), 32–53.

20. Lee H. Yearley, *Mencius and Aquinas: Theories of Virtue and Conceptions of Courage* (Albany: State University of New York Press, 1990).

21. Daniel Harrington and James Keenan, *Jesus and Virtue Ethics: Building Bridges between New Testament Studies and Moral Theology* (Lanham, MD: Sheed and Ward, 2002); James Keenan, *Moral Wisdom: Lessons and Texts from the Catholic Tradition* (Lanham, MD: Sheed and Ward, 2004); *The Works of Mercy* (Lanham, MD: Sheed and Ward, 2005). See also Roger Burggraeve, "Une éthique de miséricorde," *Lumen Vitae* 49 (1994): 281–96; and his "From Responsible to Meaningful Sexuality: An Ethics of Growth as an Ethics of Mercy for Young People in This Era of AIDS," in *Catholic Ethicists on HIV/AIDS Prevention*, ed. James Keenan, assisted by Lisa Sowle Cahill, Jon Fuller, and Kevin Kelly (New York: Continuum, 2000), 303–16; William Spohn, *Go and Do Likewise: Jesus and Ethics* (New York: Continuum, 1999).

22. Despite some attempts to argue that rights language is inimical to virtue or even theological language, see Brian Tierney, *The Idea of Natural Rights: Studies on Natural Rights, Natural Law and Church Law 1150–1625* (Atlanta, GA: Scholars Press, 1997).

23. Ronaldo Zaccharias, *Virtue Ethics as a Framework for Catholic Sexual Education: Towards the Integration between Being and Acting in Sexual Education*, STD Dissertation, Weston Jesuit School of Theology, Cambridge, MA, 2003.

24. On the sexual abuse crisis, see Regina Ammicht-Quinn, Hille Haker, and Maureen Junker-Kenny (eds.), *The Structural Betrayal of Trust* [*Concilium*

2004/3] (London: SCM, 2004). Also James Keenan, "Ethics and the Crisis in the Church," *Theological Studies* 66 (2005).

    25. See James Alison, *Faith Beyond Resentment* (New York: Crossroads, 1999).

    26. André Guidon, *The Sexual Language: An Essay in Moral Theology* (Ottawa: University of Ottawa Press, 1976).

    27. Michael Hartwig, *The Problem of Abstinence and the Poetics of Sexual Intimacy* (New York: Peter Lang, 2000).

7. Virtue, Feminism, and Ecology

Louke van Wensveen

This chapter first appeared in Louke van Wensveen, *Dirty Virtues: The Emergence of Ecological Virtue Ethics* (Amherst, NY: Humanity Books, 2000).

   Tradition functions as a source for critical reflection on ecological virtue discourse. Another source that can provide a whole new range of critical insights is experience. This is particularly true for human experiences of oppression, because these stand as a record of concrete and easily recognizable instances in which the good (of human flourishing in this case) has been violated. In this chapter I therefore pursue the practical questions: What do the hard lessons of experience teach us as we seek to cultivate ecological virtues, and how can we avoid some of the mistakes from the past? My focus is on the oppression of women, whereby I want to heed the ecofeminist suggestion that, if we are serious about our efforts to end the oppression of nature, we should pay attention to what has happened to women in our patriarchal societies.[1]

   Unfortunately, virtue discourse has a less attractive side. Building on recent feminist writings, I will show how for centuries it has subtly contributed to the oppression of women in the Western world. If we follow an ecofeminist line of thought, this means that when it comes to the task of creating a truly liberating ecological ethic, virtue discourse is suspect. Yet can it be retrieved? Much depends, I believe, on how we deal with what I call the gender construction of virtue language. If ecological virtues are to be part of a widespread, public ethic, then we must first face the experiences of women within this heritage of gender construction.

Gender-constructed virtue language divides the life of virtue into four categories, rather than simply the two categories of virtue and vice. There are virtues for women and virtues for men, as well as "typically feminine" vices and "typically masculine" vices. Gender-constructed virtue language occurs in many languages and contexts. Yet it is not always immediately obvious whether four categories rather than two determine the moral life of a particular time or people, because hypocrisy commonly accompanies the multiplication of categories. For example, a virtue may in theory be claimed to apply to all, whereas in practice one sex may be held exempt from the risks and burdens of its cultivation (for example, sexual fidelity). Thus the identification of gender-constructed virtue language often requires detective work.

Several feminist scholars have engaged in such critical work, motivated by the suspicion that we are dealing with an ideology that has served to oppress women and that needs to be unmasked.[2] Mary Daly voices the suspicion as follows:

> Much of the traditional theory of Christian virtue appears to be the product of reactions on the part of men—perhaps guilty reactions—to the behavioral excesses of the stereotypic male. There has been theoretical emphasis upon charity, meekness, obedience, humility, self-abnegation, sacrifice, service. Part of the problem with this moral ideology is that it became generally accepted not by men but by women, who have hardly been helped by an ethic which reinforced their abject situation. This emphasis upon passive virtues, of course, has not challenged exploitativeness but supported it.[3]

As a result of feminist detective work, it is now possible to sketch the historical development of gender-constructed virtue language in the West. It is beyond the scope of this chapter to provide a full account of this development, but a few highlights will help provide a context for the ensuing argument.

The origin of gender-constructed virtue language must be sought in the belief, held throughout much of Western history, that women are not particularly capable of developing those virtues that are most valued (by the men who do the valuing). Hence the "need" for a separate moral standard for women—a standard commonly tied to their prescribed social functions. As Susan Moller Okin points out in her book, *Women in Western Political Thought*, pre-Socratic Greeks associated the concept of *areté* (excellence or virtue) with the kind of life that was only possible for elite men. Consequently, "woman's *areté*" was a relative term, consisting of a set of qualities entirely different from those expected of men, who alone could achieve absolute excellence.[4] Following a similar assumption, Aristotle subsequently argued that women could not develop the virtues of justice and friendship to the extent that men could, due to their inferior position in relation to men.[5] Aristotle also associated lack of perseverance, and especially the cowardly act of seeking death to escape from pain, with *malakía* (softness, effeminacy).[6] Women, then, were not only incapable of exhibiting virtuous perfection, but they were also more prone than men to exhibit certain vices.

Christian virtue language has also been marked by gender constructions. The influential virtue theory of Thomas Aquinas provides a good example. As the great synthesizer of Christian and pagan traditions, Aquinas borrows from and expands on the gender-constructed virtue language belonging to these traditions. He approvingly cites Augustine's assumption that "thou shouldst excel thy wife in virtue"[7] and, like Gregory the Great before him, uses the image of "daughters" to discuss the consequences of the capital vices. Aquinas also shares Aristotle's assumption that women are more prone to cowardice and lack of perseverance. To this he adds the opinions of other classical philosophers, who had argued that the Aristotelian virtues of confidence and magnificence are particularly "manly" virtues.[8] Aquinas goes to some length explaining the gender connections in even greater detail than his predecessors had done.

With the political philosophy of Machiavelli, the gender construction of virtue language takes a subtle turn. The idea of moral virtue becomes associated primarily with the "gentler" Christian virtues, which conveniently get relegated to the private realm of the home—the realm of women—where they will not interfere with the power politics of the public world, the realm of men.[9] Morality becomes synonymous with chastity, obedience, self-sacrifice, patience, meekness, and charity: qualities increasingly perceived as "feminine"—that is, as natural characteristics of the ideal image of middle-class and aristocratic women. Courage, magnificence, and other traditionally "masculine" virtues continue to be valued in the public realm, but are no longer considered marks of *moral* virtue—rather, they become simply marks of virility,[10] along with other more questionable traits such as aggression, toughness, domination, ambition, cynicism, and emotional control.

From the time of Machiavelli to the present, much lip service has been paid to the "feminine" virtues of the private realm. Yet in the overall scheme of values, they are actually held in low esteem. Riane Eisler's claim that "soft" or "feminine" values get devalued when masculinity is associated with domination and conquest may offer an explanation of this curious cultural lapse of integrity.[11] At any rate, the association of "virtue" with femininity has not, as might be expected, improved the status of women in Western society. On the contrary, this Machiavellian development in the gender construction of virtue language has contributed to the isolation of women from social structures of power.

Moreover, the Machiavellian association of women with private virtue has resulted in women's alienation from the power of their own embodiment. As Catharina Halkes has observed, "At first, women were perceived as more animal and corporeal, features that simultaneously scared and fascinated men. Yet in the 18th and 19th centuries a change occurs: women are now seen as mistresses of home and family, and they are released from their sexuality."[12] If Halkes is correct, we see that women are increasingly held up as models of virtue, but the ideal of femininity has been purged of sexual connotations. This purging was made necessary by the ancient, but still operative, belief that virtue and sexual passion are mutually exclusive.[13] Thus only when relieved of the curse of Eve and remade in the image of the Virgin Mary do women gain the privilege of being closer to perfection than men. Yet the privilege comes at the price of having to renounce, deny, and suppress embodiment and sexuality as sources of identity, community, and power.

Finally, the Machiavellian association of women with private virtue has also contributed to class and race segregation between women, leaving some women in a doubly or even triply disadvantaged position. As Catharina Halkes continues to observe, the women who during the eighteenth and nineteenth centuries were praised for their domestic qualities belonged either to the middle class or to the aristocracy. Working-class women—and, I would add, women of color—were still viewed with contempt.[14] The portrayal of these women as never within reach of perfection continued more ancient traditions of gender-constructed virtue language. Yet even in ancient times, the imperfect female had had a place in the social order and hence a degree of value. The working-class woman and the woman of color, however, did not fit in the newly conceived private realm. Without spatial legitimation, she had no positive value. Only the so-called "feminine vices" defined her being: if she was dark, or worked in a sweatshop, she was presumably also loose, lazy, or even a lunatic. Thus, the gender construction of virtue language resulted in the segregation of women into two groups, split along class and racial lines: virtuous, "high" women and vicious, "low" women.

This, in a nutshell, is the legacy of gender-constructed virtue language. Rather than improve the life of virtue, as it was ostensibly designed to do, it has contributed to many problems, including the segmentation and privatization of ethics, the hypocrisy of moral ambivalence, the disembodiment of ethics, and moral elitism. All of these have been factors in the oppression of women. In the remainder of this chapter I will show why the heritage of gender-constructed virtue language gives reason for caution as newly emerging ecological virtue language becomes part of a wider public discourse.

"FEMININE" ECOLOGICAL VIRTUES

When we examine ecological virtue language in light of the Western heritage of gender-constructed virtue language, one thing immediately stands out: many core ecological virtues would traditionally have been considered "feminine" virtues. For example, ecowriters widely and consistently advocate love, caring, compassion, gentleness, harmonizing, humility, healing, intuitiveness, listening, modesty, nurturing, sensitivity, tenderness, openness, adaptability, and cooperation.[15] Especially since Machiavelli, these virtues have primarily been associated with women.

This historically embedded association invites critical questions. As ecological virtue language gains a wider popular following, will it be construed according to old patriarchal patterns? How can ecologically minded people prevent a repeat of the harms that have accompanied gender construction, a repeat that might extend to the nonhuman world as well? Ecoliterature currently displays four different approaches in dealing with the "feminine" image of key ecological virtues. I will label them the "Go-on Option," the "Head-on Option," the "Dream-on Option," and the "Hands-on Option."[16] As my titles already suggest, I see only the last one as viable in preventing a repeat of patriarchal problems.

One approach is to accept the assumption that certain traits are "feminine," but to deny that these are genuine virtues. In other words, the "Go-on Option" continues the patriarchal tradition of holding that "feminine" traits do not lead to flourishing, or perhaps even form an impediment. According to Josephine Donovan, this is the position taken by animal rights activists Peter Singer and Tom Regan. Singer, she writes, "fears that to associate the animal rights cause with 'womanish' sentiment is to trivialize it."[17] And in *The Case for Animal Rights*, Regan suggests that "since all who work on behalf of the interests of animals are…familiar with the tired charge of being 'irrational,' 'sentimental,' 'emotional,' or worse, we can give the lie to these accusations only by making a concerted effort not to indulge our emotions or parade our sentiments. And that requires making a sustained commitment to rational inquiry."[18] Regan's words suggest that a "feminine" image must be avoided, and this can be done by building an ecological virtue ethic around "masculine" traits, such as rationality.

This approach has various problems. First of all, the feminine image of certain traits is rather uncritically accepted. One misses an analysis of how this image got constructed in patriarchal societies, and especially how it acquired such negative connotations. After all, it is not self-evident why being "emotional" should be a liability in social interactions between persons who all have emotions. Second, even from a "masculine" perspective not all traditionally "feminine" virtues can be so easily dismissed. Although it may be possible and sometimes strategically desirable in a patriarchal context to control one's emotions and not come across as "sensitive," how could it ever be advisable to suppress one's ability to feel compassion, to care, to listen? Or worse, who, in the name of ethics, would ever want to pride themselves on not having such abilities at all?[19] An ethic without these virtues would be a heartless monstrosity, something we would have reason to fear (and I do not think Singer and Regan have this in mind). Finally, the "masculine" traits on whose shoulders the entire weight of ecological virtue discourse would come to rest may turn out to be not reliable enough for the task at hand. Control and rationalism—these very traits have been widely implicated in creating our problematic relationships with the nonhuman world.

A second approach is to face the history of gender construction head-on and to affirm that virtues such as caring, healing, sensitivity, and cooperation are indeed "feminine," even quintessentially so, but then to draw the opposite conclusion: that these virtues are key assets in the effort to build better ecological relationships. Central to this "Head-on Option" is the idea that women and nature are integrated in many ways, including through physical cycles, production, and reproduction. Because of this close association, women know how to sustain a flourishing network of human and nonhuman relationships.[20] Many radical and spiritual feminists, including Susan Griffin, Charlene Spretnak, and Vandana Shiva, follow this path.[21]

There are several problems with this approach also. Many ecofeminists have objected to the essentialism inherent in the radical feminist position. How do we know that traditionally "feminine" virtues are indeed "natural" for women, and not rather the result of socialization?[22] Being the mother of both a son and a daughter, I personally have become less skeptical about essentialism than I used to be—at least I cannot attribute all the traditional gender differences I see in my children to "nurture," nor to the uniqueness of their characters. Yet I do pose questions at the combination of essentialist reasoning with hierarchical reasoning when specifically "feminine" virtues are seen as superior to all other traits. I agree with Lori Gruen that "by establishing superiority in theory, the groundwork is laid for oppression of the inferior in practice."[23] More specifically, if essentialism implies that only women can adequately cultivate the key ecological virtues,[24] then we would be faced with reverse discrimination in the environmental movement, since men could by virtue of their gender only be second-class participants. Even though women who are currently sidestreamed in the movement[25] may, with justified anger, wish for such a reversal, the implied exclusivism would ultimately undercut our efforts for more inclusive relations with the nonhuman world.[26] Finally, the "Head-on Option" is also likely to have counterproductive results in circles beyond the core of the environmental movement. In the hands of the public media, a strong praise of green femininity will be turned into a praise of pink folly, matched by a reactionary affirmation of blue masculine values. Of course we may choose not to care; but then we have also written off prospects for a wider socioecological transformation.[27]

A third approach involves striving to change the image of feminine ecological virtues so that they can be incorporated into a "gender-blind" ethic that could be followed equally by everyone. This option depends on a commonplace line of "proof": that men can be caring and sensitive, just as women can be rational and courageous. In other words, there are no substantive moral differences between the sexes, and in order to avoid past discrimination we must make our moral discourse as gender-neutral as possible. If necessary, this may involve redefining and renaming some traditionally "feminine" virtues. For example, we may have to clarify that cooperation has nothing to do with "selling out," but that it is rather a form of solidarity. With the exception of some ecofeminists, most ecowriters who value traditionally "feminine" ecological virtues already treat them as gender-neutral. Thus, de facto, this option reflects a majority position, even though few authors would see it as a choice they consciously made.

The approach, though popular, is not quite problem-free either. As Janis Birkeland observes, "A gender-blind prism hides problems centering on power, dominance, and masculinity, and consequently backgrounds certain realities with an impact upon the environment."[28] To be "gender-blind" is nowadays politically correct, just like it is to be "color-blind." It is part of a well-intentioned dream of inclusivity. But in our blindness we ignore the persistence of old injustices, as well as the existence of real differences.[29] That is why I call this the "Dream-on Option." Moreover, if we simply gloss over the long history of gender construction by systematically silencing the adjective "feminine" and fabricating redefinitions of "womanish" virtues, we are not solving problems but rather creating new taboos. And taboos tend to create their own spirals of denial and suppression. This surely cannot be a liberatory route.

A fourth approach involves critically dealing with the historically grown "feminine" image of key ecological virtues. I call this the "Hands-on Option," an option already practiced by many ecofeminists. It implies a permanent awareness of the heritage of gender construction and its victims, lest the old harmful patterns repeat themselves.[30] It implies a relentless effort to change the patriarchal institutions that support harmful gender construction. It implies an honest appreciation of the value of traditionally "feminine" virtues in an ecological age, so we can build wholesome relational networks. It implies that the question of a genetic basis for these virtues in women and men be left open for inquiry rather than dogmatically decided, so we can steer between the extremes of biological reductionism and genetic denial. It implies that we move beyond limiting conceptions of femininity and masculinity, including the related concepts of private and public,[31] so we can avoid the harmful habits of stereotyping and dualistic thinking.[32] And this does not imply gender blindness.

Of course no option is perfect, and I must admit that the "Hands-on Option" suffers from involving too much work. But at least we will know that we are not just chasing a fantasy through smiles and denials, as in the "Dream-on Option." Nor will we suffer from lack of guidance in going about the task of building a gender-conscious ecological virtue ethic. By paying close attention to women's experiences of oppression within a long heritage of gender-constructed virtue language, we can at least learn to avoid the mistakes of the past. In the remainder of this chapter I will infer five boundary conditions from these experiences, criteria that can be used to guide the retrieval of traditionally feminine virtues for an ecological ethic.

LESSONS FROM EXPERIENCE

(1) *The Inequity Test.* In patriarchal societies, most of the burden of cultivating the "feminine" virtues that are now being reclaimed for an ecological age has fallen on women, exactly because of the perception that this is "women's territory" (nurturing, caring, supporting, and so on). This role diversification has often led to inequity, since women have been expected to do many other work tasks as well. What lessons can we learn here?

First of all, obviously, we should make sure that the cultivation of "feminine" ecological virtues is fairly distributed between women and men. For example, we should not accept any situation in which women do most of the "support" work—that is, as Linda Vance points out, the "actual" work—in the environmental movement while men "are disproportionately valued as spokespersons, theorists, and leaders."[33] If the hierarchical mind-set that puts male above female has been an enabling factor in the exploitation of nonhuman nature, then such exploitation is unlikely to stop as long as, de facto, the mind-set remains alive.

Second, we should be on the alert for parallel inequities between private and public efforts to work for environmental change. As long as "feminine" virtues are perceived as "private," we can expect popular concern for the environment to translate primarily into efforts to change the consumption patterns of the home.[34] But we should not be satisfied with high-visibility recycling and energy-saving campaigns aimed at consumers and schoolchildren, while production and distribution patterns are only marginally altered.[35] Such an imbalance obviously shortchanges the Earth and its life-forms.[36]

(2) *The Trade-off Test.* In patriarchal societies women are often expected to cultivate "feminine" virtues in order to compensate for acknowledged "masculine" vices. Catharina Halkes has, for example, highlighted the traditional assumption that women will caringly keep hot-tempered and beleaguered men on the right moral path.[37] The idea was not that women would fundamentally reform men, but that they would avert the worst male excesses and clean up the broken pieces. Thus the good works of one would cancel out the evil works of another.

Given this legacy of hypocritical and oppressive trade-offs, we should take special care that the cultivation of "feminine" ecological virtues not be abused as an excuse to continue other harmful habits. No matter how well intended the virtue ethic, its effects will surely be nullified. For example, when a chemical company takes certain "soft" (read: "feminine") measures, such as adopting an environmental ethics committee or initiating a tree-planting program, while leaving its "hardcore" (read: "masculine") production program unaltered, the ecological balance sheet will still not show a gain in clean air. Moreover, such calculated compensation strategies enhance moral hypocrisy and cynicism, which are dangerous attitudes in an ecological age.

(3) *The Escapism Test.* The cultivation of feminine virtues has also traditionally been encouraged to ensure the creation of pleasant escapes from the hardness of the world. Love, beauty, and understanding, cultivated by women, would enable tired men to recuperate at the end of an

ugly workday.[38] While women were forcibly pushed into romantic roles, their very effectiveness in fulfilling these roles made it possible for the hardness of the world to continue—a hardness that not only played havoc with people, but also with the nonhuman world.

Such a romantic line of thinking forms another trap that must be avoided as we cultivate feminine ecological virtues. While ecoactivists may not be liable to fall into this trap, ordinary concerned citizens are. For example, in my native country, the Netherlands, a growing popular desire to care for nature has recently been combined with a growing need to seek respite from the stresses of modern life, producing a veritable national gardening craze.[39] Yet while shuffling in the backyard calms the uneasy consciences and re-energizes the bodies and souls of millions of citizens, the mushrooming "garden centers" make inordinate profits and the spirit of capitalism smiles once again. Except that Holland now has a lot fewer plain lawns and a lot more exotic plants that get replaced according to the latest fashion in garden color, not much has changed. Romantic escapism ultimately supports the status quo.[40] Again we see how easily the cultivation of feminine virtues such as caring and nurturing can be co-opted to serve reactionary ends. And this is still a benign example. As Chaia Heller reminds us, during the Nazi period, "Germans were encouraged to recover their close tie to nature, to the German wilderness, in order to purge themselves of the poison of foreign, decadent influences such as Leftists and Jews."[41] Love of nature lies dangerously close to love of nation. We should permanently guard against such escapist distortions of "feminine" virtue.

(4) *The Pedestal Test.* Many women have experienced the curious phenomenon of variably being praised and despised for the cultivation of feminine virtues, of alternately being placed on a pedestal and being dragged through the mud. This experience results from the schizophrenia of a patriarchal value system in which male alienation is expressed through both idolization and fear of females.[42] An article by ecofeminist Sharon Doubiago nicely illustrates the situation. At one point Doubiago describes a typical pedestal, consisting of traditionally feminine virtues. The pedestal also reflects the desires for compensation and escape mentioned above:

> Women have had the role of, have been loved and valued for
> being, the Other—that is, the Voice of the heart, love, con-

science, unconsciousness, compassion, sensitivity, sensual-
ity, nature, nonlinear intuitive perception—the Other that
men have demanded and greatly needed to turn back to, to
return home to, from their ruthless world-making, their
bloody battlefields.[43]

Elsewhere in the article, Doubiago shows how one of these "feminine" virtues, intuitive perception, is also regularly devalued in our society. She writes, "Woman traditionally listens to her inner voice. The habit
is considered symptomatic; indeed, hormonal, anatomic."[44] The moral
ambivalence expressed by these two passages is paradigmatic for the
double standard operative in gender-constructed virtue language.

The persistence of patriarchal pedestals undercuts the effectiveness of any ethic in which "feminine" virtues play an important role.
This is especially true for an ecological ethic, which is additionally ham-
pered by the fact that nature tends to be put on the same pedestal as
women. In order to be effective, an ethic needs to be wholeheartedly
respected. This does not mean that we should surround "feminine" ecological virtues with artificial pomp and propaganda. (If mud is not dirty,
then pedestals are unnecessary!) But it does mean that we should consistently expose any contempt that gets expressed for so-called "soft"
ecovirtues,[45] and that we should continue to chip away at the patriarchal
roots of this contempt.[46]

(5) *The Counterfeit Test.* Not all traditionally feminine virtues are
genuine virtues; some are merely counterfeits, since they categorically
block the flourishing of women (which surely cannot be reckoned as
part of "the good"— whichever good!). Purity, for example, is an ideal
of questionable value. As Catharina Halkes points out, feminine purity
must be interpreted as the projection of a romantic, androcentric desire
for escape.[47] In their attempts to cater to this desire, many women have
ended up denying their own bodies, characters, and power. Similarly,
obedience, as a "feminine" virtue, has meant little more than blind obedience to male commands (see Eph 5:22–23!),[48] again an ideal of questionable value that has effectively oppressed many women in the past.

As ecologically minded people, we can learn from the widespread
suffering caused by the cultivation of counterfeit "feminine" virtues.
Although we may, with good reason, advocate caring for wetlands, com-

passion for animals, or sensitivity to the limits of ecological systems, we may want to think twice about advocating "back-to-nature purity" or "obedience to Nature." If historically the ideals of purity and obedience have been so consistently linked to the oppression of women, then it is quite possible that, even in ecological garb, these "virtues" are more likely to oppress people than to liberate nature.[49] A viable ecological virtue ethic should be clearly distinguishable from ecofascism, and listening to the voices of the oppressed is one way to do that.

CONCLUSION

At this point we may well raise a critical question: If the retrieval of traditionally feminine virtues for an ecological virtue ethic requires so much work, and if traditionally masculine virtues present even greater problems, given that they have been implicated in contributing to the current crisis, why should we bother with virtue language at all? Could we not do without virtue language altogether and just build an ethic around rights, duties, rules, or principles?

I do not think this is a realistic option. Any viable ethic must have a practical base, that is, roots in the ordinary language of people committed to causes other than devising ethical theories. If a theory ignores its base, it will itself be ignored. The practical base of a viable ecological ethic is the environmental movement. Here we find traditionally feminine virtues already well established, including in the language of ecofeminists. To dream of constructing an ecological ethic without terms such as *love*, *care*, *compassion*, *humility*, and *sensitivity* has at this point in time little practical value. We have no realistic alternative, then, but to proceed with these "feminine" virtues. However, we do have the option to proceed with caution. Historically speaking, the cultivation of "feminine" virtues has not improved the lot of women in Western society. The cultivation of these virtues in the context of an ecological ethic may, for parallel reasons, not improve the lot of nonhuman nature either.[50] Yet the predicaments of the past can also show opportunities for the future. If we are willing to learn from women's experiences of oppression, we will come closer to building a fully liberating ecological virtue ethic.

Notes

1. Ecofeminists explore the symbolic and historical connections between the oppression of women and nature while seeking avenues toward the liberation and flourishing of everything within the web of life. Ecofeminist thought has multiple roots and these are a matter of some debate. Rosemary Ruether has described ecofeminism as a merger between feminism and certain schools of ecology, particularly deep ecology in the United States ("Ecofeminism: Symbolic and Social Connections of the Oppression of Women and the Domination of Nature," in *Ecofeminism and the Sacred*, ed. Carol Adams [Maryknoll, NY: Orbis Press, 1992]). Others see it simply as a logical outgrowth of feminism, particularly mediated through feminist pacifism (see Ynestra King, "The Ecology of Feminism and the Feminism of Ecology," in *Healing the Wounds: The Promise of Ecofeminism*, ed. Judith Plant [Philadelphia, PA: New Society, 1989], 18–28).

In what respect the method of this chapter can be characterized as ecofeminist is best indicated by Deborah Slicer's observation that "ecofeminists, as other feminists, trust the empirical facts of women's historical experience in order to formulate and to verify their theoretical work, and their theoretical work is not carried out simply to satisfy their intellectual curiosity, but to change the concrete empirical realities of life for those who suffer the oppression of 'patriarchal hell'" ("Is There an Ecofeminism-Deep Ecology 'Debate'?" *Environmental Ethics* 17 [1995]: 163).

2. See, for example, Mary Daly, *Pure Lust: Elemental Feminist Philosophy* (San Francisco: Harper, 1984), 197–226; Anne Patrick, "Narrative and the Social Dynamics of Virtue," in *Changing Values and Virtues*, ed. Dictmar Mieth and Jacques Pohier, *Concilium* 191 Special Column (Edinburgh: T. & T. Clark, 1987), 69–80; Sharon D. Welch, *A Feminist Ethic of Risk* (Minneapolis: Fortress Press, 1990), 125–26 (Welch follows Michel Foucault here).

3. Mary Daly, "After the Death of God the Father: Women's Liberation and the Transformation of Christian Consciousness," in *Womanspirit Rising: A Feminist Reader in Religion*, ed. Carol P. Christ and Judith Plaskow (San Francisco: Harper & Row, 1979), 60.

4. Susan Moller Okin, *Women in Western Political Thought* (Princeton: Princeton University Press, 1979), 88.

5. Aristotle, *Nicomachean Ethics*, trans. W. D. Ross (Oxford: Oxford University Press, 1925), 1161a20–25; see also Okin, *Women in Western Political Thought*, chap. 4.

6. Aristotle, *Nicomachean Ethics*, 1116a10–15, 1150b1–5.

7. Thomas Aquinas, *Summa Theologiae* IIa IIae, q. 151, a. 1, trans. the Fathers of the English Dominican Province (New York: Benziger Brothers, 1948).

Interestingly, this assumption occurs in a passage criticizing the hypocrisy of husbands who expect their wives to be chaste while they themselves yield "to the first onslaughts of lust." Augustine and Aquinas thus criticize one double standard on the basis of another double standard. Their criticism contributes to the internal consistency of gender-constructed virtue language; it must not be mistaken for a criticism of this language itself.

8. Ibid., IIa IIae, q. 128, ad 6.

9. See Jean Bethke Elshtain, *Public Man, Private Woman: Women in Social and Political Thought* (Princeton: Princeton University Press, 1981), 91–99.

10. The term *virile* for Machiavelli simply means "manliness" (he thereby stays close to the etymological root of the term, which is derived from the Latin *vir*, man). For further analysis, see Hanna Fenichel Pitkin, *Fortune Is a Woman: Gender and Politics in the Thought of Niccolò Machiavelli* (Berkeley: University of California Press, 1984).

11. Riane Eisler, "The Gaia Tradition and the Partnership Future: An Ecofeminist Manifesto," in *Reweaving the World: The Emergence of Ecofeminism*, ed. Irene Diamond and Gloria Orenstein (San Francisco: Sierra Club Books, 1990), 30.

12. Catharina Halkes, *En Alles Zal Worden Herschapen: Gedachten over de Heelwording van de Schepping in het Spanningsveld tussen Natuur en Cultuur* (Baarn, The Netherlands: Ten Have, 1989), 60 (my own translation). See also the English-language edition: Catharina J. M. Halkes, *New Creation: Christian Feminism and the Renewal of the Earth* (Louisville, KY: Westminster/John Knox Press, 1991), 48.

13. See, for example, Aristotle, *Nicomachean Ethics*, 1140b10–20; see also Thomas Aquinas, *Summa Theologiae* IIa IIae, q. 47, a. 16, IIa IIae, q. 53, a. 6.

14. Halkes, *En Alles Zal Worden Herschapen*, 60.

15. Ecowriters also advocate traditionally "masculine" virtues, such as competence, courage, critical reflection, determination, discipline, efficiency, humor, justice, leadership, managing/stewardship, perseverance, prudence, realism, responsibility, self-confidence, self-reliance, and vigilance.

16. The first, second, and fourth options parallel Ynestra King's typology for conceiving the woman-nature connection. See King, "The Ecology of Feminism and the Feminism of Ecology," 22–23.

17. Josephine Donovan, "Animal Rights and Feminist Theory," in *Ecofeminism: Women, Animals, Nature*, ed. Greta Gaard (Philadelphia, PA: Temple University Press, 1993), 167.

18. Tom Regan, *The Case for Animal Rights* (Berkeley and Los Angeles: University of California Press, 1983), xii (cited in Donovan, "Animal Rights and Feminist Theory," 167–68).

19. As Linda Vance argues, "Identification and empathy may be dismissed by rationalists as sentimental—as feminine—but passionate convictions, beliefs from the heart, can always get us through the hard times when reason and argument fail" ("Ecofeminism and the Politics of Reality," in *Ecofeminism: Women, Animals, Nature*, ed. Gaard, 136).

20. On the symbolic connection between woman/nature as contrasted to man/culture see, for example, Sherry B. Ortner, "Is Female to Male as Nature Is to Culture?" in *Woman, Culture, and Society*, ed. Michelle Rosaldo and Louise Lamphere (Stanford: Stanford University Press, 1974), 67–87.

21. As Lon Gruen observes, radical feminists "embrace the connection (between woman and animals/nature) and attempt to strengthen it by denying the value of its opposite. In other words, radical feminists see women as closer to nature and men as closer to culture and thereby reject the cultural in favor of the natural. They elevate what they consider to be women's virtues—caring, nurturing, interdependence—and reject the individualist, rationalist, and destructive values typically associated with men" ("Dismantling Oppression: An Analysis of the Connection Between Women and Animals," in *Ecofeminism: Women, Animals, Nature*, ed. Gaard, 77). For a concrete example of women redefining and affirming the woman-nature connection, see Vandana Shiva, *Staying Alive: Women, Ecology and Development* (London: Zed Books, 1989), 47.

22. Ynestra King, Janis Birkeland, and others make the additional argument that "since all life is interconnected, one group of persons cannot be closer to nature" (Janis Birkeland, "Ecofeminism: Linking Theory and Practice," in *Ecofeminism: Women, Animals, Nature*, ed. Gaard, 22). Along the same lines, Joan Griscom suggests, "Only the nature/history split allows us even to formulate the question of whether women are closer to nature than men. The very idea of one group of persons being 'closer to nature' than another is a 'construct of culture'" (ibid., 22). I do not find these arguments particularly helpful, since they obscure the question of the quality of one's connection with the nonhuman world. While I agree that we are all connected to nonhuman nature, some of us are better attuned than others.

23. Gruen, "Dismantling Oppression," 80. In general, Gruen highlights several of the same problems addressed in this paragraph (see esp. 77–78).

24. This is not a necessary implication, since one may hold that virtues are *cultivated* qualities that require no natural affinity.

25. Some ecofeminists have pointed out that the environmental movement is currently segregated, with women being the second-class citizens. See, for example, Linda Vance, "Ecofeminism and the Politics of Reality," 124.

26. This argument is a mirror image of the common ecofeminist claim that male exclusivism toward women has spilled over into their attitudes toward the nonhuman world. Personally, I see support for the argument insofar as I

believe that the virtue of inclusivism cannot be fully cultivated if one practices exclusivism with respect to any particular party. Exclusivism implies that judgmentalism is part of one's character. Thus one's inclusivism toward certain parties is by definition *conditional*. The possibility of rejection always lurks closely under the surface. Such selective inclusivism is only a semblance of the true virtue, which is based on compassionate understanding. (Incidentally, compassionate understanding can be critical of what is harmful, but that would never cause it to *reject* another party.)

27. The "Head-on Option" may also create hypocrisy if it is not accompanied by sufficient self-examination. Josephine Donovan warns that "one cannot simply turn uncritically to women as a group or to a female value system as a source for a human relationship ethic with animals," because women "have been complicit in that abuse, largely in their use of luxury items that entail animal pain and destruction (such as furs) and in their consumption of meat" ("Animal Rights and Feminist Theory," 168). Such hypocrisy will surely not be missed by the media either.

28. Birkeland, "Ecofeminism: Linking Theory and Practice," 26.

29. On the inappropriateness of "color blindness" in business, see Lennie Copeland, "Learning to Manage a Multicultural Workforce," *Training* 25 (May 1988): 48–49, 51, 55–56.

30. Phyllis Trible proposes a similar approach in dealing with patriarchal texts in the Bible. See *Texts of Terror* (Philadelphia: Fortress Press, 1984).

31. Birkeland, "Ecofeminism: Linking Theory and Practice," 17, 20.

32. This implies that we take another look at so-called "masculine" ecological virtues as well. The field of men's studies could help in sifting the more helpful from the more harmful elements in these virtues. I also think we should more critically examine the commonplace rejection of "masculine" vices such as aggression and rationalism. It would be helpful if we saw these along the same lines as Aristotle sees ambition: harmful if too extreme, but helpful in the right amount for a particular context. Here too I think it is important to keep the question of a genetic basis open for inquiry rather than dogmatically decided.

33. Vance, "Ecofeminism and the Politics of Reality," 124.

34. For a related argument, see Rosemary Ruether, *New Woman/New Earth: Sexist Ideologies and Human Liberation* (New York: Seabury Press, 1975), 200–204.

35. When businesses adopt recycling and ride-share programs without substantially altering their production and distribution patterns, this does not change the situation of inequity. Such businesses simply bring the private/public split within their own walls, creating a hypocrisy that is very obvious to employees and the general public. Still, even limited efforts such as recycling should be commended; they may have subversive effects. My business students tell me

stories of employers who find that the daily recycling of office paper has caused a mushrooming environmental concern among their employees, accompanied by demands for further changes.

36. Consider, for example, that municipal solid waste, upon which homemakers and cottage industry owners can have an impact, constitutes only 1 percent of U.S. annual solid waste production (see Walter H. Corson, ed., *The Global Ecology Handbook* [Boston: Beacon Press, 1990], 267).

37. Halkes, *En Alles Zal Worden Herschapen*, 60.

38. Cf. Ruether, *New Woman/New Earth*, 196–200.

39. Annegreet van Bergen and Marijke Hilhorst, "De Lusthof Nederland," *Elsevier* 25 (22 June 1996): 64–70.

40. Along the same lines Janis Birkeland observes: "Mainstream emphasis on the individual 'at one with nature' distracts attention from structural and systemic issues. Institutions embody values, so they must be changed as well" ("Ecofeminism: Linking Theory and Practice," 45).

41. Chaia Heller, "For the Love of Nature: Ecology and the Cult of the Romantic," in *Ecofeminism: Women, Animals, Nature*, ed. Greta Gaard, 237.

42. For a nice visual representation of the pedestal treatment, see *Tussen Heks en Heilige [Between Witch and Saint]: Het Vrouwbeeld op de Drempel van de Moderne Tijd, 15de/16de Eeuw* (Nijmegen: Uitgeverij SUN, 1985).

43. Sharon Doubiago, "Mama Coyote," in *Healing the Wounds: The Promise of Ecofeminism*, ed. Judith Plant and Petra Kelly (Honolulu: University of Hawaii Press, 1992), 41 (inspired by Dorothy Dinnerstein, *The Mermaid and the Minotaur*).

44. Ibid., 40.

45. Just as, when push comes to shove, the EPA is not taken as seriously as the Pentagon in policy formation, so many people still do not take caring for the environment as seriously as, say, being a "tough" manager at work, much lip service to the contrary.

46. Janis Birkeland suggests, for example, that "we must expose the assumptions that support Patriarchy and disconnect our concept of masculinity from that of 'power over' others and the rejection and denigration of the 'feminine'" ("Ecofeminism: Linking Theory and Practice," 19).

47. Halkes writes, "Women are always evaluated from an androcentric point of view: be it as inferior, as a mere body with emotions and passions, or as an instrument for procreation and for the care of daily household life; or be it as exalted, as Muse, as guardian angel, as the Virgin Mary, pure and chaste, as 'The Lady,' as the poetry in the daily prose, and thus also as a means of escape" (*New Creation*, 48). Both the trade-off mentality and the pedestal idea shine through in this passage.

48. Susan Griffin cites this example in *Woman and Nature: The Roaring Inside Her* (New York: Harper & Row, 1978), 10.

49. Note, in this context, the parallel between instrumentalist, anthropocentric attempts to keep natural wilderness "pure" as a place of retreat for humans, and attempts to con women into providing retreats for men (see Halkes, *En Alles Zal Worden Herschapen*, 59–60).

50. An even stronger claim can be made if one takes as a starting point the thesis, supported by many ecofeminists, that human domination of nature is rooted in male domination of women (see, for example, King, "The Ecology of Feminism," 24). If this is true, then gender-constructed virtue language, which has sustained the oppression of women, must itself be considered a contributing factor in the network of causes underlying the ecological crisis. The implication is that retrieval of gender-constructed virtue language for an ecological age will ipso facto be counterproductive, unless all gender constructions can be undone.

Personally, I prefer to take an inductive approach that looks at individual gender-constructed virtues and makes projections on the basis of concrete problems associated with these virtues in the past. I present my conclusions as the sum of such projections. This approach has the benefit of circumventing problems associated with demonstrating the thesis that the domination of nature is rooted in the domination of women.

Part Three

SPECIFIC VIRTUES

8. The Fundamental Option, Grace, and the Virtue of Charity

Jean Porter

This chapter first appeared in *Philosophy & Theology* 10 (1997).

From the standpoint of the moral theologian, perhaps the most influential aspect of Karl Rahner's theology is the thesis of the fundamental option, that is, the claim that the individual's status before God is determined by a basic, freely chosen, and prethematic orientation of openness toward or rejection of God that takes place at the level of core or transcendental freedom. According to Joseph Fuchs, Rahner developed this thesis from ideas that he found in the writings of Jacques Maritain and Joseph Marechal, and he preferred to speak of "the human person's disposition of his self as a whole," rather than of a "fundamental option."[1] Moreover, this thesis has been developed in moral theology by others, including preeminently Fuchs himself. Nonetheless, for most Catholic theologians, the thesis of the fundamental option is understood in terms of Rahner's transcendental analysis.

This thesis has won widespread acceptance among moral theologians. However, recent statements of the magisterium, culminating with the encyclical *Veritatis splendor*, have called the idea of the fundamental option into question.[2] According to *Veritatis splendor*, the Catholic tradition is unalterably committed to the idea that there are mortal sins, that is, acts that have the effect of definitively separating the individual from God.[3]

Fuchs responds that the pope and his advisors do not seem to realize that the fundamental option and specific acts take place on different

159

levels of freedom.[4] Moreover, he insists that defenders of this thesis do take the theological significance of human actions seriously, even though on their view there can be no one criterion for determining whether a particular action, even a morally wrong action, is indeed a mortal sin or not.[5] In fact, as we will see, there is indeed less distance between the doctrine of the fundamental option and the traditional account of sin and grace than might be assumed from reading *Veritatis splendor*.

Nonetheless, there is a grain of truth in the objection that the thesis of the fundamental option does not offer an adequate account of the theological significance of human action. Yet this lacuna cannot be addressed through reviving the traditional account of mortal and venial sins, as the encyclical tries to do. We need to develop a third option for addressing these issues.

In this paper, I will try to indicate what is problematic about the Rahnerian conception of the fundamental option, and to suggest an alternative way of thinking about some of the issues that this thesis raises. Before attempting a critique or exploring alternative approaches, however, it will be necessary to have the main lines of this thesis before us.

THE FUNDAMENTAL OPTION: THE MAIN LINES OF THE THEORY

Of course, the main lines of Rahner's account of transcendental freedom are well known among Catholic theologians; nonetheless, it will be helpful to focus our reflections through a brief review of this account.[6]

According to Rahner, the human person, considered as a spiritual being, is constituted by an infinite openness to reality through knowledge and love. No categorical object can satisfy the human spirit, which is always capable of knowing more and loving more fully, and this infinite openness to reality is inescapably present to the spiritual creature in and through its awareness of itself as knowing or willing some finite object. Thus, this infinite openness is a fundamental datum of all human experience, even though it is not generally articulated as such. Through one's self-awareness as a being whose capacities are never satisfied by categorical objects, the human person is likewise aware at a prethematic level of an infinitely satisfying object of knowledge and love, which forms the necessary horizon for every categorical act of knowledge or will. From the standpoint of Christian theology, this Object is identified as God, and yet it is present to all persons, whether they are conscious of it as such, indeed whether they believe explicitly in God or not.

If the human spirit were left to itself, so to speak, this horizon would be perceived as Mystery, but it would not be felt as a personal claim. However, God has in fact offered Godself to every human being, in and through this prethematic experience of the infinite horizon of knowledge and will. This offer, which Rahner describes as a supernatural existential, is a wholly free gift of grace, and yet it is offered to every woman and man.[7]

Just as the awareness of God as Mystery is a prethematic datum of human self-awareness as a spiritual creature, so God's offer invites a response at the same level of core or transcendental freedom. That is, the human person is invited to respond to God's self-offer through a free gift of her- or himself. Since this involves a disposal of the person experienced as subject, this response cannot be reduced to any one human action in the ordinary sense, because the latter are directed toward categorical objects and do not involve a disposition of the person as a whole. That is to say, it is a fundamental option, either to constitute oneself as open to God's self-offer, or to say no to that offer in sinful refusal of God's gracious gift.[8]

For Rahner and his followers, the particular actions of the human person take their theological significance from their relationship to this fundamental option. Normally, most human acts will reflect the individual's fundamental option, but since these acts are expressions of categorical freedom, they will not exhaust that option. Moreover, it is always possible that a particular act at the categorical level may be inconsistent with the individual's fundamental option, without thereby changing it.[9]

This suggests four possibilities: First, the morally good actions of someone whose fundamental option is positive are straightforwardly expressions and acts of grace, and in that sense meritorious, although of course they do not earn the reward of union with God. Second, a morally evil act committed by someone whose fundamental option is good is construed as an expression of categorical freedom that is inconsistent with the direction of her or his transcendental freedom. As such, this act is not a mortal sin, that is to say, a sin that cuts the individual off from God, even though it may be gravely immoral. Third, a morally evil act committed by someone whose fundamental option is likewise bad would be an expression of her or his refusal of God's grace, and as such, would be mortally sinful. Finally, a morally good act committed by someone whose fundamental option is bad would be an inconsistent exercise of the individual's categorical freedom. As such, it could not be described as an act of grace, but presumably it would not be sinful either. We may hope that it expresses a process of repentance and conversion to God that is taking place at the level of the individual's transcendental freedom.

Thus, defenders of the thesis of a fundamental option do preserve the traditional distinction between mortal and venial sins. Any act that expresses a fundamental option of refusal of God's grace is mortally sinful, since it embodies a stance that is deadly to the spiritual life of the person. However, acts that are morally wrong, but that do not express a negative fundamental option, are not similarly expressive of the individual's spiritual death. It might be said that they are venially sinful, although admittedly this label would be incongruous in some cases.[10]

In two respects, the account of sin implied by the fundamental option diverges from the traditional view, as reaffirmed by *Veritatis splendor*. On the latter view, the gravity of sins as moral failures is correlated with their theological significance; that is, acts of a kind judged to be seriously wrong are at least presumed to be mortal sins, although it was acknowledged that in some circumstances, an act of a kind which is generically neutral or trivially wrong might nonetheless be mortally sinful. The Rahnerian account is not prepared to assume this link, since even a gravely wrong action may coexist with an individual's positive fundamental option. Furthermore, the traditional view held that a mortally sinful act changed the individual's status before God, cutting the person off from the divine life. On the more recent view, however, even mortally sinful acts do not themselves determine the individual's status; they merely express a reality that is grounded in the individual's self-disposal at the level of transcendental freedom.

The break between older and more recent accounts, however, is not as sharp as is sometimes assumed. The traditional doctrine also modified the link between the moral gravity of the individual's act and the degree of its sinfulness. On that view, an act of a kind that is gravely wrong may not be mortally sinful, because it is not fully voluntary, or not the product of complete deliberation.[11] This qualification should not be identified straightforwardly with the view that a gravely wrong act may not express the individual's fundamental option. Seen from within the categories of Rahnerian theology, deficiencies of voluntariness would presumably be seen as breakdowns within the realm of categorical freedom, rather than as (necessarily) evidences of a mismatch between the individual's categorical choices and her or his fundamental option. Nonetheless, the fact that so many exponents of the traditional view found it necessary to qualify it in this way suggests that they too were uneasy with the straightforward identification of serious moral wrongdoing and mortal sin.

This brings us to a point that must be appreciated if we are fully to assess the significance of the Rahnerian thesis of the fundamental option. That is, this thesis has won such widespread acceptance because it addresses serious and widely felt difficulties in the traditional account of grace and sin. Not to put too fine a point on it, the traditional account is too horrible to be believed. For Catholics in the earlier decades of the twentieth century (and earlier), the moral life was a scene of high drama, in which one action could have eternal and unspeakable consequences. On this view, no matter how praiseworthy and even holy an individual's past life may have been, the commission of one mortal sin, if not repented, will result in eternal damnation. When we add that the standard lists of mortal sins included such items as bad (that is, sexual) thoughts, it is easy to see why so many Catholics lived their lives in a state of neurotic anxiety, and why theologians felt pressured to modify this view.

Hence, the Rahnerian account of the fundamental option addresses a deep difficulty with the more traditional view of sin and grace. The rejection of this thesis in *Veritatis splendor* does not address this difficulty, and for this reason, it will not be persuasive to many theologians who have adopted the Rahnerian account. Yet the Rahnerian account does raise problems of its own; at least, that will be the argument of the next section.

A CRITIQUE OF THE THESIS OF THE FUNDAMENTAL OPTION

The thesis of a fundamental option follows naturally from Rahner's overall account of transcendental freedom. At the same time, much of the attractiveness of this thesis, seen from the standpoint of the moral theologian, lies in the fact that it offers an alternative to the traditional account of sin. From this perspective, the thesis of the fundamental option is attractive precisely because it weakens the link between the individual's standing before God and the moral life of the individual, by means of distinguishing between the person's particular actions, and her or his self-disposition at the level of core or transcendental freedom. Once this link is weakened, it is possible to acknowledge that a person might be fundamentally united with God, even while engaged in morally reprehensible behavior, and this in turn provides a way of acknowledging the complexity and brokenness that are to be found in even the most admirable lives.

This is an important gain, but it comes at a high cost. Rahner's account of transcendental freedom is constructed in such a way that there is no necessary connection between the person's observable actions, and her or his self-disposition at the level of the fundamental option. Indeed as we have seen, Rahner insists on the point that the exercise of transcendental freedom is not to be understood in terms of the exercises of categorical freedom, and moral theologians who have developed the idea of the fundamental option have concentrated on just this point. Yet this is where the difficulty arises. The problem is not just that Rahner sees no necessary link between the individual's fundamental option and any particular categorical action; more basically, Rahner's account is constructed in such a way that the individual's fundamental option has no normal or paradigmatic connection to any particular kind of categorical acts. His theology severs the conceptual links between freedom and action that could alone give concrete meaning to the concept of freedom.

Why is this problematic? The language of freedom, which is so central to Rahner's theology, finds its immediate and natural context in a wider discourse about human action, the ways in which people are restrained or prevented from acting, the extent and the limits of accountability, and other related issues. This discourse, in turn, takes its meaning and its point from reflection on specific human acts and recurrent kinds of actions. We speak in terms of freedom and restrictions on freedom because these concepts express our sense of what is going on when people successfully pursue a goal through what they do, or fail to achieve the end that they are seeking. We draw distinctions among different degrees of voluntariness, because we need them to do justice to the different degrees of accountability to which we hold one another. And so on....

The central difficulty with Rahner's account of transcendental freedom is that it employs the language of freedom, while at the same time systematically stripping that language of the context that alone could give it meaning and point. Transcendental freedom, as he understands it, is a capacity that is exercised apart from any categorical act, and that furthermore has no object, since it concerns the agent's self-disposition as subject. Yet how are we to understand an exercise of freedom that has no necessary connection to any observable action or object of choice at all? In order to make sense of this language, we must appeal to other terms and claims within Rahner's overall metaphysics: transcendental freedom is exercised in the context of the agent's experience of herself or himself as subject; it has to do with the Holy Mystery that is the Horizon of all knowing; transcendental knowing, in turn, is the agent's self-awareness as subject, capable of infinite self-transcendence in knowledge and love; and so forth. In other words, the language by which Rahner speaks of transcendental freedom takes its meaning from its place in a highly self-referential system, which has very little grounding in actual observations or concrete experiences.

What is true of Rahner's notion of transcendental freedom is likewise true of the Rahnerian notion of the fundamental option, and of the other concepts that are central to his doctrine of grace. That is, all of these notions draw on the language of human actions and dispositions, and yet Rahner consistently denies that any of them can be understood in terms of paradigmatic relationships to specific, recognizable kinds of actions. Rather, these notions are said to be appropriate to the realm of transcendental freedom and knowledge, and one part of what characterizes this realm is precisely that it does not have any essential relationship to any specific kind of action in the categorical realm.

Admittedly, Rahner's accounts of transcendental freedom and self-disposal in response to God's self-offer are internally consistent. However, they offer very little in the way of a usable language of human action, through which we can interpret and reflect on our own experiences and what we observe in the behavior of those around us. Interpreted in Rahnerian terms, the classical Christian doctrines of sin and grace lose their existential relevance and their power to provide compelling interpretations of human life, because they do not attach to concrete experience anywhere. Correlatively, these doctrines themselves lose the dimension of concrete meaning, and the self-corrective resources, which a different sort of analysis might provide.

At this point, it might be objected that Catholic teaching has traditionally held that we cannot know for certain whether we are in a state of grace. That is true, but what is at issue here is not the epistemic question of how someone might know that she is in a state of grace; what is at issue is rather the conceptual question of what it means to be in a state of grace, or alternatively, to have a disposition of openness to God. If openness to God means anything at all, apart from an extrinsic juridical status, it must be understood, in part, as a disposition to act in certain ways. This is a general point, which does not depend on the theological character of the language of grace. In order to be fully meaningful, any language concerning human dispositions must be linked to the specific kinds of actions that manifest those dispositions; that is, in order to understand what it means for someone to have a certain disposition, we must be able to recognize kinds of actions that manifest that disposition. At the same time, this does not mean that someone who has a particular disposition will necessarily always act in accordance with it, or conversely that someone who acts in the characteristic way will necessarily have the disposition.

To take a morally neutral example, we would not know what it means to have a disposition to speak fluently, unless we also had some idea of what fluent speech is, at least sufficient to recognize it when we hear it. That does not mean that a fluent speaker can never stammer, nor does it mean that one fluent speech is enough to reassure us that someone actually possesses the disposition of fluency. However, it does mean that unless we can at least recognize fluent speech, the disposition of fluency will have no meaning for us; similarly, we could not make sense of the claim that someone who never speaks, or who always stammers, is actually a fluent speaker (as opposed to *potentially* a fluent speaker).

Another objection may arise at this point. As John Sachs points out, Rahner does in fact offer concrete examples of categorical actions that might offer a locus of encounter with God.[12] Moreover, as Mary Maher reminds us, Rahner insists that the human person can only come to knowledge and experience love in and through categorical experiences.[13]

To consider the more general objection first: it is true that according to Rahner, transcendental knowledge and freedom are only actualized, as it were, in and through categorical acts of knowledge and desire. The locus of transcendental knowledge and freedom is found in the agent's self-awareness as agent, and this self-awareness presupposes that the agent is actually exercising her or his spiritual capacities. This is an important aspect of Rahner's overall theory, and it should not be overlooked. Nonetheless, it does not provide the kind of conceptual link that we need between transcendental freedom and specific kinds of categorical acts. There is no such link and there can be no link, on Rahner's account, precisely because for him, the agent's transcendental capacities are actualized in each and every specific action:

> But since in every act of freedom which is concerned on the categorical level with a quite definite object, a quite definite person, there is always present, as the condition of possibility for such an act, transcendence toward the absolute term and source of all of our intellectual and spiritual acts, and hence toward God, there can and must be present in every such act an *unthematic "yes" or "no"* to this God of original transcendental experience.[14]

What about the connections that Rahner draws between specific kinds of experiences and the encounter with God? In his earlier writings, Rahner does indeed speak of concrete experiences of grace, although without attempting to interpret these experiences in the wider context of his overall theology.[15] However, in his later writings, Rahner at his most concrete sounds a great deal like Rahner at his most abstract:

> The form in which [the experience of God] impinges upon us is extremely concrete, even though it manifests itself as the element of the ineffable in the concrete experience of our everyday life. While it is present unacknowledged and unexpressed in *every* exercise of our spiritual faculties, it nevertheless manifests itself more clearly and in some sense as an

object of enquiry in those episodes in which the individual, normally lost amid the individual affairs and tasks of his daily life, is to some extent thrown back upon himself and brought to a position in which he can no longer overlook those factors in his life which he customarily evades. Thus it is when man is suddenly reduced to a state of *aloneness*, as it were, when every individual thing recedes, as it were, into remoteness and silence and disappears in this....Thus it is when man suddenly experiences that he is inescapably brought face to face with his own freedom and *responsibility*, feeling this as a single and total factor embracing the whole of his life and leaving him no further refuge....Thus it is when man suddenly makes the experience of personal *love* and encounter, suddenly notices, startled and blessed in this both at once, the fact that he has been accepted with a love which is absolute and unconditional even though, when he considers himself alone in all his finitude and frailty, he can assign no reason whatever, find no adequate justification, for this unconditional love that reaches out to him from the other side.[16]

This is very far from the kind of reflection that could alone provide Rahner's account of grace with concrete meaning. These kinds of examples simply push the problem back a stage; how can we determine what counts as confronting aloneness, as being under an absolute moral demand of responsibility, or as being loved and loving unconditionally, without further reflection on the kinds of actions that are characteristic of these experiences?

Perhaps it is unfair to take Rahner to task for these generalities, because of course every theologian must generalize at some points. The difficulty, however, is that Rahner hesitates ever to move to a level of specificity, in terms of which these generalities could have meaning. And given the logic of his transcendental analysis, it is difficult to see how he could do so. The point of identifying a condition for freedom as transcendental is of course to claim that it is necessarily present in every action whatever. Thus, by claiming that openness to God is a transcendental condition for human action, Rahner is committed to saying that this quality is present in every particular action, but by the same token, he is also committed to denying that it is characteristic of any particular *kind* of action.

Yet, even if the force of these criticisms is granted, it is still true that we cannot simply return to the traditional way of conceiving of sin and grace. The traditional schema did have the advantage of associating one's status before God with specific kinds of actions, but it did so in a horrific and implausible way. More important, from our standpoint, the traditional schema is *so* schematic that it also offers very little in the way of real interpretative power. On this earlier view, specific kinds of actions are indeed correlated with theologically significant descriptions, but the criteria for these correlations are set forth in such a way as to flatten out, or simply to ignore, the complexities of actual human experience. Efforts to mitigate the rigidity of this view only introduced further distortions in our understanding of the theological significance of human action. I have not emphasized this point because it is not the primary focus of this paper, but I believe that it will be clear to anyone who is at all familiar with the earlier account of sin and grace.

What we need is a more adequate *language* of grace, that is to say, a conceptual framework that will provide us with a way of interpreting and speaking about our actual experiences from a theological perspective. In developing this language, we may well find that there are questions that we cannot answer, situations about which we literally have nothing to say. Yet it is important nonetheless to attempt to develop an account of these matters, if Christian doctrine is to continue to provide us with a way of interpreting and speaking about our experiences.

Seen from this perspective, the Rahnerian account of the fundamental option and the earlier account of sin and grace are almost equally problematic, and problematic for the same reason. Rahner's account offers very little in the way of concrete concepts with explanatory power. The earlier account does attach to the world, so to speak, through its detailed descriptions of the kinds of actions that are to be considered to be mortal sins. Yet the theological evaluation attached to these descriptions is inflexible and overly simplistic. Within such a framework, there is little room for interpreting the ambiguities of actual human experience, and even less for allowing our experiences to modify the theological framework that we bring to them.

AN ALTERNATIVE: AQUINAS ON CHARITY

In the second half of this essay, I would like to suggest an alternative way of developing an experientially adequate language of grace. The alternative that I shall suggest is not new. That is, I will argue that Aquinas's theology of grace, developed as it is through a well-developed account of charity and the other virtues, does provide us with a theological framework that is rich enough to have real interpretative power, and yet flexible enough to respond to the ambiguities of actual experience and to correct itself in the light of what they reveal.[17] It may seem strange to appeal to Aquinas for an alternative to the Rahnerian account of the fundamental option. For one thing, Rahner understood himself to be reformulating Aquinas's thought in terms of contemporary thought. It would take us too far afield to explore the merits of transcendental Thomism as an interpretation of Aquinas's theology, but whatever may be said on that score, there are naturally some aspects of Aquinas's thought that are not central to Rahner's own work. This is hardly surprising, since any effort to reformulate an earlier system of thought for contemporary use is bound to be selective. Nonetheless, one of the aspects of Aquinas's thought that Rahner does not address in any detail does in fact offer an alternative way of thinking about sin and grace, namely, his account of charity as a virtue, understood in relation to other virtues, beliefs, and disposition of the agent.

Of course, the Thomistic idea of charity is central to Rahner's thought in one way; that is, Rahner, like Aquinas, emphasizes the centrality of love as a way to God. However, in his treatment of love of neighbor, what Rahner emphasizes are precisely the transcendental aspects of love. The act of love is not seen by him as being tied to any specific kinds of actions; rather, it consists in an absolute openness to the Other, which in its embrace of created finitude is simultaneously an act of openness to God.

For Aquinas, on the other hand, charity is a virtue, whatever else it may be, and as such, the concept of charity is inextricably tied up with an account of the kinds of actions, the background beliefs and characteristic affective dispositions that give content to the virtue. In other words, for Aquinas, charity is a moral concept; that is, it serves both to interpret and to provide a normative criterion for human actions. At the same time, it is of course one of the central conceptions of his doctrine of grace. While

Aquinas is careful not to identify charity and the other infused virtues with grace, he does claim that they provide the stable capacities for acting in accordance with grace (IIa IIae, q. 23, a. 2 and q. 24, a. 2).[18]

The disposition to act is the point at which the theological and the moral come together in this system, because for Aquinas, a capacity for self-directed action is the defining characteristic of the human being.[19] If grace were not able to be expressed in actions that reflect stable dispositions of the agent, it would not *be* grace, that is, it would not be a salvific transformation of the human person. Hence, Aquinas argues at IIa IIae, q. 23, a. 1 that the view of charity as the Holy Spirit dwelling in the soul is actually a derogation of charity, since it implies that the actions of the charitable person are not really expressions of the agent's own character and will. Yet for this very reason, for Aquinas, the language of grace must be a moral language (cf. IIa IIae, q. 23, a. 8). And because it is such, his doctrine of grace has a concreteness and richness of meaning that many later accounts, including Rahner's, lack.

Of course, Aquinas is well aware that grace involves an irreducible element of mystery because it places us in a direct relation to God, whose reality is inconceivable and who can only be spoken of indirectly and imperfectly (cf. I, q. 13, aa. 5 and 12). Thus, for Aquinas, charity involves the love of an object who is known imperfectly and incompletely, even while being loved (IIa IIae, q. 23, a. 6, ad 1, q. 27, a. 4; cf. I, q. 12, a. 7). Nonetheless, the virtue of charity has another dimension for Aquinas, and that is the congeries of human actions and dispositions in which it consists. Precisely because charity is a moral concept, it has a concrete existential meaning, which is bound up with the kinds of actions, beliefs, and feelings that express it, even though the meaning of charity cannot be reduced to this existential dimension.

It is important to note that the actions and dispositions that we identify as being characteristic of charity are not simply given through experience. In this respect, charity is like any other virtue. In order to identify some act or disposition as characteristic of a virtue, we must already have some conception of the virtue, which provides an interpretative framework that we then bring to bear on experience. At the same time, a concept of a particular virtue is itself subject to modification through this very process of application. We may find, for example, that some persons exhibit characteristic acts and dispositions of a virtue in ways, or under circumstances, in which we would have thought that this virtue could not be developed or displayed. If such discrepancies are serious enough, they may lead us to revise our idea of the virtue in question. In a very real sense, therefore, concepts of virtues are empirical concepts; they provide us with a way to understand and to speak of an aspect of our experience, and like any other empirical concepts, they are open to correction and reformulation in the light of further experience.

It is important to note that Aquinas's account of charity, considered as a virtue, does incorporate an openness to revision in the light of experience, because as we will see, there are difficulties with some aspects of that account. Consider this objection: Doesn't an appeal to Aquinas's account of charity reintroduce the very problems that made the thesis of the fundamental option so attractive in the first place? For example, he asserts that charity is lost with any act of mortal sin (IIa IIae, q. 24, a. 12). Thus, he undermines the richness of his own account by tying the presence of God's grace in a mechanical way to the commission of specific actions. In so doing, he helps to prepare for what later became the traditional understanding of grace and mortal and venial sin.

All this is true. Yet what it suggests is that Aquinas's account of charity must be appropriated through a critical reformulation, not that its problematic aspects rob it of all value. The essential strength of this account is reflected in its capacity for self-correction, and if we are to build on what Aquinas has done, we must take full advantage of that capacity. We will return later to this point, in order to see that while Aquinas does indeed claim that charity is lost through every mortal sin, it is possible to reclaim the essentials of his account of charity without committing ourselves to that specific view. First, however, it is necessary to examine in more detail what it means for Aquinas to speak of charity as a virtue. What is implied by this, given Aquinas's overall account of virtue, and what can we learn from the specifics of his account of charity as such? We now turn to both of those questions.

Charity as a Virtue

As is well known, Aquinas's account of the virtues is developed out of a synthesis of neo-Platonic and Aristotelian elements, with

Aristotle's doctrines of the mean of virtue and the connection of the virtues playing central roles in his overall theory. However, the key to understanding Aquinas's account of the virtues is provided in a little-noticed passage that occurs in his discussion of justice. There, he remarks that every virtue must be characterized in terms of its characteristic acts (IIa IIae, q. 58, a. 1). For charity, as for every other virtue, we cannot understand the disposition to act without taking note of the kinds of acts to which the disposition is directed.

The significance of this point is often overlooked, because of a widespread tendency to think of the virtues as if they provided a sharp contrast with moral rules. On this view, the virtues are ideals of character that can be understood and developed without any reference at all to the kinds of behavior that manifest them, in contrast to the moral rules, which call for the performance or (more typically) the avoidance of specific kinds of actions.

This contrast overlooks the fact that ideals of virtue can only be understood in terms of the kinds of actions that exemplify those virtues. This does not mean that the virtues should be understood reductively, as sheer capacities for performing certain kinds of actions. Nonetheless, a virtue is a stable disposition (that is to say, a habit) to act in a certain way, although that is not all that it is.

Hence, what was said above about dispositions generally is likewise true of the virtues; we cannot be said to have a real understanding of what it means to have a virtue, unless we can recognize some kinds of actions as being paradigmatically acts of this virtue. We would have no conception of generosity, for example, if we had no idea at all of the kinds of actions that count as generous acts, no way of offering examples of generous acts or of recognizing them when we see them.

Moreover, Aquinas himself identifies charity with specific kinds of actions that he takes to be paradigmatic of the virtue. Of course, the principal act of charity is to love (IIa IIae, q. 27), and in addition, it is also exemplified by more specific external actions, including beneficence, the works of mercy, and fraternal correction (IIa IIae, qq. 31–33). The point of identifying these acts is not to provide an infallible test for determining whether an individual has charity; apart from the theological problems that this would raise, Aquinas is aware that any action that is typical of a virtue can be performed by someone who lacks the virtue

(Ia IIae, q. 63, a. 2). Nor does he claim that charity can only be expressed through these kinds of actions. Nonetheless, he does identify certain kinds of actions as being paradigmatically acts of charity, because these kinds of actions provide a picture, so to speak, of what is distinctive about the charitable person and the way of life that she or he enjoys.

At the same time, charity, like any other virtue, cannot be reduced to the performance of certain kinds of actions. Rather, like all other virtues, charity is an enduring disposition in the agent's soul, by means of which she or he is able to act in certain characteristic ways. Because the ultimate effect of a life of charitable activity is direct union with God in the beatific vision, an end that exceeds the capacities of any created nature, God must bring it about through direct action on the soul (Ia IIae, q. 62, a. 1 and q. 63, a. 1; IIa IIae, q. 24, a. 2). In this way, charity is like the infused moral virtues and the other theological virtues, but unlike the acquired virtues, which, as the name suggests, are acquired by the agent's own efforts (Ia IIae, q. 63, a. 2).

Furthermore, charity, like all the other virtues, must be understood in terms of the faculty of the soul that it transforms. Prudence, which is strictly speaking an intellectual virtue, transforms the intellect, and the affective virtues, temperance and fortitude, transform the passions (Ia IIae, q. 56, aa.3–4). Faith, too, is a virtue of the intellect (IIa IIae, q. 4, a. 2).

Charity, like justice and the other theological virtue of hope, is a virtue of the will (Ia IIae, q. 56, a. 6). This claim is especially significant from our point of view, because it represents the most direct point of contact between Aquinas's account of charity and the Rahnerian thesis of the fundamental option.

The will, for Aquinas, is the distinctively human faculty for desiring the good. Of course, like all other animals, we naturally desire what is good and shun what is harmful or unpleasant, as these are mediated to us through our senses; the faculties through which we do so are the passions (Ia IIae, q. 23, a. 1). Unlike the animals, however, we are also capable of grasping the good rationally under some conception of what is good (or correlatively, bad), and this rationally perceived good is desired by the will (Ia IIae, q. 8, a .1 and q. 9, a. 1). Because it is directed toward the good as mediated through the intellect, the will is capable of being directed toward indefinitely many objects (Ia IIae, q. 10, a .2). At the same time, because the will is the distinctively human expression of a general tendency toward the good to be found in all creatures, it would be misleading to construe the will as an open-ended tendency toward goodness, *tout court*; rather, like the analogous inclinations of other kinds of creatures, the will is naturally directed toward the agent's own good, her or his fulfillment as a specific kind of creature (Ia IIae, q. 56, a. 6). For Aquinas, this is equivalent to saying that all persons naturally desire happiness, which is nothing other than the distinctively rational or intellectual form of the fulfillment as a creature of a specific kind that is sought in some form by all creatures (Ia IIae, q. 1, a .8 and q. 5, a. 4, ad 2, q. 5, a. 8).

Unlike Rahner, Aquinas does not believe that the human person's natural desire for the good involves any implicit or prethematic desire for or awareness of God (I, q. 12, a. 1; Ia IIae, q. 5, a. 8, ad 2). The fulfillment as a specific kind of creature that the human person naturally seeks is in fact a kind of union with God, but in this sense, every creature, including inanimate creatures, can be said to seek union with God, simply in virtue of its natural inclination toward its own specific kind of perfection and toward the overall perfection of the universe (Ia IIae, q. 109, a. 3). The human person is also capable of a higher and more direct form of union with God as a personal reality; however, Aquinas denies that everyone does in fact desire this personal union with God (again, see Ia IIae, q. 5, a. 8, ad 2).

At the same time, the fact that the human person is oriented toward the good as mediated through the intellect creates a logical space, as it were, for the human person to love God as a personal reality, and not merely as the first principle of all created goods. This possibility is transformed through charity, working in tandem with the other infused theological and moral virtues, into an actual love of, and desire for, God in Godself, that is, not merely as First Cause (IIa IIae, q. 27, a. 3). Hence, charity, seen as a transformation of the will, directs the person's overall orientation toward the good in such a way as to direct the agent toward God as the unmediated object of love. In this sense, charity is similar to the Rahnerian fundamental option; that is, it consists in an overall personal orientation toward the ultimate Good that is God.

This effect is distinctive to charity, but there is another sense in which the transformation brought about by charity is similar to the transformation brought about by another virtue of the will, namely, justice. That is, both charity and justice transform the will in such a way that the agent no longer desires her or his own individual good alone (which is the natural orientation of the will), but now desires above all some wider and more universal good (Ia IIae, q. 56, a. 6). The remaining difference is that justice, in itself, is still directed toward created goods, that is, the community and the norms of fairness that govern its common life; charity, on the other hand, directs the agent to the Uncreated Good that is God.

Because charity is a virtue of the will, it presupposes that the intellect has been transformed in such a way as to present the Good that is its object to it. That is why charity presupposes faith, the virtue of the intellect through which the agent is capable of apprehending God's existence and God's invitation to personal union through Christ (Ia IIae, q. 65, a. 5). At the same time, the relation of charity to faith remains ambiguous, since charity loves more fully than faith can ever know (IIa IIae, q. 23, a. 6, ad 1; cf. Ia IIae, q. 67, aa. 3 and 6). Moreover, while the love of God proper to charity is not itself a passion, it generates characteristic passions and emotional dispositions, including joy, peace, and mercifulness (IIa IIae, qq. 28–30).

The fact that charity is a virtue of the will is also critical to understanding Aquinas's claim that it is the form of all the other virtues, both the other theological virtues and the infused cardinal virtues (IIa IIae, q. 23, a. 8). In Aquinas's view, the orientation of the will determines the orientation of the whole person toward a narrow self-love or toward the wider good of the human community or of God. This being so, the transformative effect of charity must necessarily express itself in all the person's desires for, and efforts toward, whatever is perceived as being in any way good. This is what it means to say that charity is the form of the virtues; that is, charity informs the operations of the other virtues, in order to direct them all toward the ultimate good of union with God, which orients the whole life of the charitable person.

Aquinas does not hold that every finite good is subsumed in the infinite goodness that is God; created goods retain their integrity and desirability, even from the perspective of charity. Correlatively, the virtues that take their identity from their orientation toward the various finite categories of the good in human life are not swallowed up in charity. To the contrary, the individual who possesses charity must necessarily possess the infused cardinal virtues as well, precisely in order that each faculty have its own proper virtue (Ia IIae, q. 65, a. 3). Thus, charity's formative effect should not be understood as if the whole moral life of the charitable person were an expression of charity *tout court*. All the good acts of the charitable person are indeed acts of charity, but many of them are also simultaneously acts of one or more of the other virtues, depending on the particular goods at stake and the appetites or intellectual judgments brought into play. The same thing may be said of the operation of the acquired cardinal virtues, which may be attained without grace; for example, acts of chastity are expressions of both temperance and justice, and every truly moral act is an expression of prudence as well as of one or more of the moral virtues (IIa IIae, q. 154, a. 1; Ia IIae, q. 65, a. 1, IIa IIae, q. 47, a. 7).

Because Aquinas holds that charity brings with it, so to speak, infused analogues of all the cardinal virtues, much of the concrete content of his account of charity is provided by his analyses of these other virtues. Yet it would be misleading to conclude that for Aquinas, the life of grace is practically equivalent to a life of moral goodness. To the contrary, Aquinas sets up more than one contrast between the life of a person who acquires virtue through her or his own efforts, and the virtuous life as lived by one whose moral virtues have been infused together with charity.[20]

The most obvious of these contrasts has to do with differences in content between the acquired and the infused cardinal virtues. As Aquinas explains at Ia IIae, q. 63, a. 4, the infused cardinal virtues are specifically different from their acquired counterparts, because they are directed toward different ends; the acquired virtues are directed toward the attainment of natural human flourishing, which consists in a life lived in accordance with reason, whereas the infused virtues are directed toward the attainment of personal union with God. For example, he continues, acquired temperance is expressed through a healthful moderation in food and drink, whereas infused temperance practices moderation and even fasting in obedience to the divine law, which enjoins us to discipline our bodies for God's service.

Even more important, Aquinas also points to contrasts between the acquired and infused moral virtues at the level of acquisition and experience. For example, he notes that because the infused moral virtues, unlike the acquired virtues, are not formed through the repeated performance of the appropriate kinds of actions, the former, unlike the latter, can exist in the presence of vices that render their operation difficult and unpleasant (Ia IIae, q. 65, a. 3, ad 2). It follows that the life of virtue may actually involve more struggle and imperfection for someone whose virtues are expressions of grace than for someone who has acquired the virtues through his or her own efforts (Ia IIae, q. 58, a. 3, ad 2)!

Another example of this sort of contrast, and perhaps the most significant, is found in Aquinas's treatment of the gifts of the Holy Spirit, that is, understanding, counsel, wisdom, knowledge, piety, courage, and fear (Ia IIae, q. 68, a. 1).[21] He takes the gifts to be dispositions within the soul to respond to God's direct promptings, in such a way as to act in accordance with the divine will (Ia IIae, q. 68, a. 2). These dispositions are distinct from the infused virtues and are bestowed as additional gifts, because without God's direct prompting at the moment of action, even the infused virtues cannot consistently give rise to actions that express the grace made operative through charity (Ia IIae, q. 68, a. 1). Those who possess the acquired virtues only do not need, and do not have, any similar superadded inspiration, since for them the judgment of human reason is sufficient (ibid.).

Thus, Aquinas sets up a further contrast between the person who practices the virtues through grace and one who has acquired virtues through human effort. That is, the charitable person possesses specific capacities for insight and judgment that the person of acquired virtue does not have. It is also noteworthy that the gift most closely associated with charity is wisdom (IIa IIae, q. 45). Hence, the charitable person is able to discern God's will in specific situations by a kind of intuitive insight, which expresses the agent's connaturality with God through grace (IIa IIae, q. 45, aa. 1 and 5).

When we examine a particular article of the *Summa*, "concrete" and "experientially rich" are not adjectives that are likely to come to mind. Yet when we consider Aquinas's overall discussion of charity, including not only the questions specifically focused on that topic but also those that consider related matters, what emerges, perhaps surprisingly, is a richly detailed account of what it means to be a charitable person, and what the life of charity practically involves. The charitable person is someone with specific beliefs and affective dispositions; her or his life is characterized by certain kinds of distinctive actions, including acts of kindness, mercy, and fraternal correction; and even those actions of the charitable individual that are not distinctive to charity nonetheless reflect the overarching orientation toward union with God that charity generates. Finally, the charitable person's specific choices reflect not only charity and the other virtues, but a set of dispositions through which those virtues are effectively brought to bear in action, namely, the gifts of the Holy Spirit.

Yet the very concreteness of Aquinas's account also renders it problematic for us, in more than one way. To mention only one: as was noted above, Aquinas claims that charity is lost through one mortal sin (Ia IIae, q. 63, a. 2, ad 2; IIa IIae, q. 24, a. 12). Since charity is generated by God's direct action on the soul, rather than emerging through repeated acts, as do the acquired virtues, it is lost whenever one makes a choice that is contrary to charity. Such a choice severs the connection, as it were, between God's grace and the will of the individual, and once that connection is broken, there is nothing to sustain the *habitus* of charity in the soul. This reasoning seems on the face of it to be unassailable, but from it follow all the unacceptable consequences that we noted above.

For these reasons, it is not sufficient simply to appropriate Aquinas's account of charity as it stands. The insights and concerns that informed the work of Rahner and those who have accepted his thesis of the fundamental option must still be addressed. Indeed, these concerns provide a critical test of the overall soundness of Aquinas's account of charity. Does this account have the inner resources that would allow for its own transformation, in such a way as to address the questions of our own day? If so, then a further question arises: Would a revised version of Aquinas's account of charity still retain the concreteness that is lacking in contemporary accounts of God's love as appropriated in a fundamental option?

In my view, both of these questions should be answered in the affirmative. However, it would call for another essay, or more than one, to address them adequately. In this paper, I will limit myself to indicating how I think these questions could be addressed, thus suggesting further avenues for reflection.

Virtue and Sin: Toward a Revised Account of Charity as a Virtue

Aquinas's theology of grace, spelled out as it is through a well-developed account of the virtues, provides us with a theological framework that is rich enough to have real interpretative power, and yet flexible enough to respond to the ambiguities of actual experience and to correct itself in the light of what they reveal. Yet this power and flexibility have often been obscured, because Aquinas's accounts of grace and the virtues have often been taken to be closed to further revision and development, and applied in such a way as to foreclose any criticism based on actual human experience. This sort of defense of Aquinas's thought actually fails to do him justice, because it does not take the depth of his analysis with full seriousness. And it has the effect of depriving us of one of the most powerful frameworks for interpreting our experience in a theological light.

In view of this, what are we to make of Aquinas's assertion that charity is lost through every act of mortal sin? Even though the logic of Aquinas's account may seem on first reading to be compelling, given his distinction between infused and acquired virtues, it grates on modern sensibilities, especially since we know that it contributed to the worst excesses of later theologies of sin. Yet if our reaction to Aquinas's account were simply a matter of registering its incongruity in the light of our own beliefs and sensibilities, there would be nothing more of theological interest to say about this account. We might embrace it as a kind of nostalgic alternative to our own intellectual world, or else regard it as being of "merely" historical interest, but we would no longer consider it as a system of thought with which we might fruitfully be engaged in open-ended dialogue.

Yet Aquinas's theology of grace cannot be so easily dismissed, or petrified, because the incongruities that we feel in considering his views on mortal sin are to some extent incongruities within the system itself. That is, it is possible to offer counterexamples to Aquinas's claim that charity is lost through one mortal sin, which he could recognize as problematic on the terms of his own system; there are persons whose lives exhibit charity by Aquinas's own showing, yet who do commit actions that he would consider to be mortal sins, either unrepentantly or at least repeatedly. In other words, Aquinas's judgment that charity is lost by one mortal sin may turn out to be too hasty on his own terms, as well as being repugnant to us. For this reason, this claim may offer us a way into Aquinas's moral theology, which allows us to preserve its insights, while drawing on the resources of that theology to correct and expand it. That, at least, is what I will try to show, in a tentative and exploratory way, in what follows.

The first point to note is that the summary sketch of the sort of incongruity in question could apply to at least two importantly different kinds of cases. On the one hand, we have the case of someone whose life reflects charity by Aquinas's terms, and yet also includes practices that Aquinas would characterize as sinful, but that the person her- or himself does not regard as such. For example, someone may display the characteristic dispositions and actions of charity, while at the same time maintaining a sexually active homosexual relationship or regularly using contraceptives. On the other hand, there is the case of someone whose life apparently displays genuine and perhaps even heroic charity, together with a pattern of actions that the individual considers to be problematic or sinful.

Graham Greene's "whiskey priest," and Martin Luther King, whose life combined repeated marital infidelities with a willingness to die in pursuit of justice and peace, offer literary and actual examples of this latter sort of case.[22]

At the risk of oversimplifying, I would suggest that these two sorts of cases offer two sorts of lessons, about the moral quality of certain kinds of actions, on the one hand, and about the operations of grace, on the other. To consider the former example first, what this kind of case suggests is that Aquinas was just mistaken in considering some kinds of actions to be sinful. If our collective experience has really convinced us that it is possible to combine a sexually active homosexual relationship or the use of contraceptives with a life of kindness, Christian joy, and concern for and service to others, then on Aquinas's own terms, not to mention ours, this counts as very strong evidence that homosexual acts and the use of contraceptives are not necessarily sinful.

These claims invite the response that one is simply substituting one's own cultural prejudices for Aquinas's prejudices, or perhaps, his insights. And of course, cultural blindness is a pervasive danger, which we must always resist but which will probably always infect our judgments to some degree. After all, we have no choice but to live in our own time and to form judgments in the context of our own culture. Yet it should be emphasized that on Aquinas's *own* terms, it is very difficult to see how repeated performance of a vicious action could be integrated into a life that is virtuous in other respects. For him, the virtues must operate in tandem if they are to operate at all; that is why he insists that even the acquired cardinal virtues are connected, in such a way that anyone who truly possesses one necessarily has them all (Ia IIae, q. 65, a. 1). Hence, when we consider revising Aquinas's specific judgments on what constitutes sinful behavior, on the grounds that persons who engage in that behavior often seem to live otherwise virtuous lives, then we are not simply judging him by our own cultural standards; we are posing a challenge to his theology in terms drawn from that theology itself, as we apply it to the evidences of our lives.

It is also significant that when we think of counterexamples to Aquinas's claim that charity is lost through one mortal sin, the situations that come to mind are likely to involve sexual acts and relationships of one sort or another. This is not surprising, since sexual ethics is probably the one area of moral theology in which our convictions are most at odds with those of Aquinas and his contemporaries.

Yet there is another and deeper reason why we tend to think of sexual "sins" as counterexamples to the claim that charity is lost through one mortal sin. That is, it is not obvious that all sexual acts that fall outside the traditional norms are contrary to charity, because it is not obvious that they harm anyone. That is why it is easier to think of someone who is engaged in a gay sexual relationship or the use of contraceptives as living a life of charity, than it is to form the same judgment about someone who is consistently cruel or callous or who makes a living through acts of violence and exploitation.

At this point, it would seem that we are certainly substituting our own cultural sensibilities for those of Aquinas and his peers, rather than engaging in a critical reappropriation of his theory. There is some truth in this judgment; Aquinas does consider unnatural sexual sins to be offenses against God, rather than against the just claims of other persons, and they are more grave than other kinds of sexual sins precisely for that reason. Yet he also claims that since we cannot harm God, every sinful act is ultimately such because it involves some kind of harm of the agent or of someone else.[23] Moreover, he also claims that actions involving other persons are wrong insofar as they involve some kind of harm of the other (Ia IIae, q. 100, a. 1, a. 3, ad 1 and a. 5). Hence, even here, where the cultural distance between Aquinas and ourselves would seem to be greatest, there are points of contact that allow us to offer revisions of his views on grounds that he himself could have accepted.

At the same time, it is clear that sexual relationships, like most other forms of human relationships, run along a spectrum from the most loving and morally admirable, through a whole gamut of compromised, ambiguous, or problematic arrangements, to relationships that are self-ish, unfree, callous, or downright inhumane. While almost any kind of sexual relationship can fall anywhere along this spectrum, there are some kinds of relationships that by their nature are almost inevitably ambiguous and problematic, although not necessarily reprehensible in every situation, extramarital relationships being the most obvious example of these. Furthermore, the ambiguities that we observe in sexual relationships are also prevalent, although generally not so obvious, in most other kinds of human relationships. It would seem that the more a relationship offers possibilities for personal intimacy and the pursuit of shared goods, the more vulnerable it is to corruption.

What these observations suggest is that the traditional categories of sinfulness, and even the more fundamental categories of moral wrongdoing, are overly simplistic, at least in some areas of our lives. We stand in need of a more nuanced vocabulary of moral and religious judgment than our religious and secular traditions provide us, in order to think and speak adequately of these matters. Here we do stand in need of a new departure, not only from Aquinas, but from much of the rest of the Catholic moral tradition.

There is another kind of case that seems to present a counterexample to Aquinas's claim that charity is lost through every mortal sin. That is the situation in which someone combines repeated actions of a kind that both the agent himself and most observers consider to be seriously sinful or wrong, with persistent and even heroic acts of love of God and neighbor, within one lifetime. Greene's "whiskey priest" and Martin Luther King offer extreme examples of this sort of person; both fell repeatedly into patterns of behavior, mostly involving sexual transgressions, that they themselves considered to be wrong, and yet both also persevered in fulfilling the demands of justice and charity, up to the point of willingly accepting death. There are two ways of responding to these sorts of examples that would save Aquinas's doctrine that charity is lost by every mortal sin; one would be to deny that the actions in question were subjectively sinful, the other would be to deny that persons such as these truly have charity. Neither approach is fully persuasive. Although Greene suggests that his protagonist is an alcoholic, and King's sexual behavior may well have been compulsive to some degree, it is difficult to explain away their morally problematic acts as pathological and unfree without remainder. On the other hand, it would be logically possible to say that, regardless of the evidence to the contrary, someone like Greene's character or King simply cannot have true charity; and so what looks like charitable behavior must express a similitude of charity. But the cost of saving Aquinas's system in this way is very high indeed. Greene's character offers a fictional example, and King offers a real example, of someone who knowingly risks and undergoes death in order to be faithful to the demands of love of the neighbor. If that is not to count as true charity, on Aquinas's terms or ours, then what does?

Moreover, when we consider the actual example that King offers us, it is striking that not only did he consider himself to be a sinner, he also claimed that his work on behalf of social justice was grounded in a strength not his own. In his own account of the Montgomery campaign, he describes a moment of crisis in 1956 when, tormented by fear, he experienced the presence of Jesus in a new and personal way: "And it seemed at that moment that I could hear an inner voice saying to me, 'Martin Luther, stand up for righteousness. Stand up for justice. Stand up for truth. And I will be with you, even until the end of the world.'"[24] This is exactly how Aquinas says grace should work, that is, by providing the agent with a power that both strengthens the individual's natural capacities, and brings her or him to a new level of love for God and neighbor.

These sorts of examples lead us to the conclusion that Aquinas was simply wrong on this point: genuine sin, even serious sin, can coexist with a life that expresses what he himself would acknowledge to be charity. Yet on reflection, it is perhaps not so surprising that Aquinas's moral theology would call for revision at this point. When Aquinas makes the claim that he does, he argues on the basis of a judgment about the way in which God's power works through the infused virtues. In the last analysis, however, we have no direct knowledge of how God works. Whatever indirect knowledge we may have on this score can only be drawn from a theologically based interpretation of those of our experiences that we take to be experiences of God's transforming and sustaining activity. Because Aquinas offers a framework by which to interpret certain experiences as experiences of grace, he also provides us with the necessary framework within which to revise our assumptions about how God's power can work in human lives.

This brings me to one final point. Perhaps I have given the impression that my aim in this last section has been to vindicate Aquinas's moral theology at all costs. I do happen to believe that Aquinas is right, on fundamentals if not in every essential, about the character of the Christian moral life. Yet the vindication of Aquinas has not been my chief aim. What I have attempted to do, rather, is to indicate what it means to have an account of grace and the moral life that is sufficiently rich to interpret our actual experience, and to admit of correction by that experience. Rahner's theory of transcendental freedom, and the accounts of the fundamental option developed from that theory, are not in my view sufficiently rich to offer such an account. Aquinas does offer us such an account, but I do not claim that he is the only Christian theologian to do so.

Notes

1. Joseph Fuchs, "Good Acts and Good Persons," in *Understanding Veritatis Splendor*, ed. John Wilkins (Cleveland: Pilgrim Press, 1994), 22.

2. Pope John Paul II, *Veritatis splendor*, promulgated August 6, 1993. English translation in *Origins* 23.18 (1993): 297–334, paragraphs 65–70 (all references to the encyclical are given by paragraph number).

3. Ibid., paras. 69–70.

4. Fuchs, "Good Acts and Good Persons," 23–24.

5. Ibid., 24–25.

6. Karl Rahner, *Foundations of Christian Faith: An Introduction to the Idea of Christianity,* English translation originally published in 1978 (New York: Crossroad, 1985), 24–43 and 90–106, offers a good summary discussion of the meaning of transcendental freedom. This is of course a central theme in all of Rahner's work.

7. Ibid., 126–33.

8. Ibid., 96–99; also see Rahner, "Reflections of the Unity of the Love of Neighbor and the Love of God," in *Theological Investigations* 6 (New York: Crossroad, 1969), 231–52; "The Experience of God Today," in *Theological Investigations* 11 (New York: Crossroad, 1974), 122–32; "Experience of Self

and Experience of God," in *Theological Investigations* 13 (New York: Crossroad, 1975).

9. See Rahner, *Foundations of Christian Faith*, 96–99, and Fuchs, "Basic Freedom and Morality," in *Introduction to Christian Ethics: A Reader*, ed. Ronald P. Hamel and Kenneth R. Himes (New York: Paulist Press, 1989), 187–98. Originally published in *Human Values and Christian Morality* (Dublin: Gill and Macmillan Ltd., 1970).

10. Rahner, *Foundations of Christian Faith*, 97–105.

11. *Veritatis splendor* para. 70; for one example, out of many, from among earlier moral theologians, see John C. Ford and Gerald Kelly, *Contemporary Moral Theology, Volume I* (Westminster, MD: Newman Press, 1964), 205–14.

12. John R. Sachs, "Transcendental Method in Theology and the Normativity of Human Experience," *Philosophy & Theology* 7.2 (1992): 221.

13. Mary V. Maher, "Rahner on the Human Experience of God: Idealist Tautology or Christian Theology?" *Philosophy & Theology* 7.2 (1992): 153.

14. Rahner, *Foundations of Christian Faith*, 98; emphasis in the original.

15. See in particular Rahner, "Reflections on the Experience of Grace," in *Theological Investigations* 3 (New York: Crossroad, 1967), 86–90.

16. Rahner "The Experience of God Today," 157–58; emphasis in the original.

17. A similar argument is developed by Romanus Cessario, *The Moral Virtues and Theological Ethics* (Notre Dame, IN: University of Notre Dame Press, 1991). While I find this book to be illuminating in many ways, however, he does seem to me to assume too quickly that Aquinas's moral theory is closed to any further development, and this, as I argue below, actually undercuts the strength of Aquinas's analysis.

18. Thomas Aquinas, *Summa theologiae* (Madrid: Bibliotheca de Autores Cristianos, 1961. Originally 1266–73). Hereafter, references to the *Summa* will be in parentheses.

19. See the preface to the *Prima secundae* on this point.

20. Apparently, the former is a real, and not merely an abstract possibility for Aquinas, even though the kind of virtue in question, which takes human reason as its highest norm, cannot lead ultimately to direct union with God; see Ia IIae, q. 63, a. 2, ad 2; Ia IIae, q. 63, a. 4.

21. Ultimately, this list derives from Isaiah 11:2–3.

22. See Graham Greene, *The Power and the Glory* (London: W. Heinemann, 1940); my main source for information on King's life is David J. Garrow, *Bearing the Cross: Martin Luther King, Jr., and the Southern Christian Leadership Conference* (New York: William Morrow, 1986). I have discussed the implications of King's example in more detail elsewhere (Jean Porter,

"Virtue and Sin: The Connection of the Virtues and the Case of the Flawed Saint," *The Journal of Religion* 75.4 ([1995]: 521–39), which may partially excuse the sketchiness of what follows.

23. Thomas Aquinas, *Summa contra gentiles. Book three: Providence, Part II*, translated by Vernon J. Bourke (Notre Dame, IN: University of Notre Dame Press, 1975; original date of translation, 1956; original work, 1259–64). (III II, 122; cf. *ST* IIa IIae, q. 154, a. 2).

24. Martin Luther King, *Stride toward Freedom: The Montgomery Story* (New York: Harper and Brothers, 1958).

9. Reimagining the World: Justice

Paul J. Wadell

This chapter first appeared in Paul J. Wadell, *Happiness and the Christian Moral Life: An Introduction to Christian Ethics* (Lanham, MD: Rowman & Littlefield, 2008).

"The world is sick."[1]

It's my favorite line from *Populorum Progressio* ("On the Development of Peoples"), Pope Paul VI's 1967 social encyclical on justice and human development, because it doesn't dance around the point. The world is sick, and the disease eating away at it is the cancer of injustice. It is not that things are only slightly amiss—a weak flu that just a little rest can overcome. No, the cancer of injustice runs deep, so much so that without radical personal and social transformation the survival of the world is in question. Injustice is a terminal disease because each day it brings destitution and diminishment to millions—and death to thousands of others. Too, left untreated it creates a world characterized by fear, instability, and violence. Alarm, urgency, desperation, and even anger are the tone of *Populorum Progressio* because Paul is convinced that we cannot wait to undo the webs of injustice in which so many lives are painfully trapped. "We must make haste: too many are suffering, and the distance is growing that separates the progress of some and the stagnation, not to say the regression, of others,"[2] the pope writes. When Paul looked around the world in 1967 he saw "situations whose injustice cries to heaven."[3] Is it really any different today? If justice is postponed, Paul warns, there is no hope for the future. The world is at a crisis point, and if individuals, communities, and nations do not

188

work together on behalf of justice, the social order will crumble. As the pope lamented in *Populorum Progressio*, "Would that those in authority listened to our words before it is too late!"[4]

Injustice is a scandal, but one that we have learned to tolerate pretty well, especially if we profit from it. Justice means "we are all in this together," but the truth is we live as if we are not. As Patricia McAuliffe writes, "*Disorder, disharmony, and the already damaged humanum are not exceptions to the rule; they represent the rule.*"[5] Take a look around the world, and it is not hard to conclude that what we see would more accurately be described as a "rule of injustice" rather than of justice.[6] The hundreds of thousands of persons who face starvation, the millions of people without adequate shelter or health care, the never-ending litany of victims of war and violence: this is the world we have grown so accustomed to that it is hard for us to imagine it any other way. Injustice is the air we breathe, and for the privileged of the world it may seem to be clean, healthy air even if for millions of others it is toxic. But the fact is that not only are its victims sickened by injustice, but those who perpetrate and profit from it are too because they have lost the moral vision needed to recognize that something is horribly wrong.

Injustice is a failure of moral imagination. In order to move from injustice to justice, we must be able to reimagine the world. The conversion to justice demands that we be able to see, think, and imagine differently. But for those who may be profiting from injustice, it equally demands radical and unsettling changes in our attitudes and values, and especially in the ways we live. Something like a conversion to justice occurred for Pope Paul VI when he was drawn into the world of the poor. Near the beginning of *Populorum Progressio* he mentions trips he took that changed his life. A few years before he was elected pope he traveled first to Latin America and then to Africa, and wrote that those journeys brought him "into direct contact with the acute problems pressing on continents full of life and hope."[7] After his election as pope in 1963, Paul "made further journeys, to the Holy Land and India," and in both places was "able to see and virtually touch the very serious difficulties besetting peoples with long-standing civilizations who are at grips with the problem of development."[8] There are certain memories we do not want to leave behind, memories we want to continue to shape and guide our lives, because they brought us to a very different way of looking at and understanding the world. Pope Paul VI's travels to Latin America, Africa, India, and the Holy Land left him with such memories and explain why when he wrote *Populorum Progressio* he was looking at the world through the eyes of the poor. This is the moral and spiritual challenge for those who have never known the ravages of injustice firsthand.

In many respects, a book on Christian ethics should begin, not conclude, with a chapter on justice because at its core the Christian moral life is about responding to persons in need. "If we ask ourselves, Why be ethical; why ought we, why must we, be ethical?" Patricia McAuliffe writes, "it seems our response must be because there is need. Ethics is a response to need. And the overwhelming need in our world is that massive excessive deprivation, suffering, and oppression be alleviated."[9] Justice is not an afterthought to Christian morality because none of us can claim to be moral if we ignore or remain indifferent to the marginal, forgotten persons of the world. As Jesus' famous parable of the Last Judgment (Matt 25:31–46) indicates, the final assessment of our lives will be made in terms of the justice we either extended to or withheld from those most in need. It is through justice and compassion that we gain entry to the kingdom of God, while it is through greed, selfishness, and indifference that we are excluded. If the Christian moral life is an ongoing training in the nature of happiness, we must discover not only that no true happiness can be gained through injustice, but also that our happiness cannot be had apart from the well-being of others. For Christians, happiness is a communal enterprise; it is something we share in together. Thus, any one person's happiness is lessened in the measure that any other person is shunned, ignored, or excluded. In the Christian moral life, justice is the linchpin to happiness because it opens our eyes to the persons we need to recognize and respond to in order for all of us to be complete. Put bluntly, if there is any group we need to make connections with in order "to get ahead in life," it is the poor and the oppressed, not the wealthy, for the Bible suggests they are the ones with the inside track to God. In this chapter, then, we will look at this core virtue in the Christian life by first exploring the meaning and foundations of justice, as well as the different types of justice. We will then consider a more explicitly Christian theology of justice, and conclude with some considerations of how a conversion to justice might occur. That last step is crucial because it is only when our hearts are turned to the poor that we discover, oddly enough, what happiness really is.

WHAT JUSTICE IS AND WHERE IT BEGINS

The virtue of human togetherness, justice governs our relations with others by ensuring that we respect their dignity as persons and give them their due. But it is important to note that justice does not create a bond between ourselves and others, but recognizes and honors a bond that is already there.[10] It is precisely because of the deep connections that exist between us and everything else that lives—the web of relations we are born into—that we need to learn to live in a way that respects and strengthens those bonds instead of ignoring, denying, or violating them. A just person is the man or woman who knows how to live in right relationship with God, with friends and family, with co-workers or community members, with anyone he or she may come in contact with, and with the natural world. Such persons see the bonds that link all of life together and recognize the obligations and responsibilities those bonds create. They know we cannot be indifferent to the well-being of others who are connected to us and, therefore, family members. They know that every act of injustice is an attempt to deny what is irrefutably true: we are all members one of another. Justice is relevant to every relationship, to every situation and circumstance of life, because there is no setting in which we do not have to take into account our responsibilities to others. What justice requires will differ depending on the nature of those relationships, but it will always be pertinent and can never be dismissed without the fundamental fact of our moral existence being ignored. Viewed through the lens of justice, the principal moral question is always the same: What needs to be done here to honor a bond that always exists?

St. Thomas Aquinas defined justice as "the habit whereby a person with a lasting and constant will renders to each his due."[11] Aquinas's definition suggests that justice comes second—it is a response to something more fundamental—because we would be under no obligation to give anything to anybody if there did not already exist a relationship that created obligations and responsibilities.[12] "To be just means, then, to owe something and to pay the debt,"[13] Josef Pieper notes. But we owe something to others (and they owe something to us) because our lives are always enmeshed in relationships that carry inescapable moral demands. This is why, as Aquinas noted, our willingness to respond to the claims of justice must be "lasting and constant," not occasional or haphazard. A person of justice is *habitually* disposed to take the needs and well-being of others into account because he or she recognizes there is never a moment in which the claims of others, including God and other species, do not impinge on us. This does not mean that the needs and rights of others are absolute, but it does mean that they always matter and cannot be casually ignored. Thus, justice is both an abiding quality of character and a principle of action. It is, more precisely, a virtue because a person of justice is habitually attuned to the needs of others and characteristically attentive to their good. In this respect, justice can be described as *"fidelity to the demands of a relationship,"*[14] including those relationships we did not choose, but which nonetheless exert claims on us.

A just person lives with others in mind. But that so much of the world is not in "right relationship" reveals that many persons do not live with others in mind. Ideally, justice bolsters connections that are already there by ensuring that the rights of all persons are honored. Ideally, justice holds relationships, communities, and societies together by insisting that each person or group is given its due and that no person or group takes more than its share. That's the way it ought to be; but unfortunately injustice may be more common than not because we live in a world where greed, egotism, selfishness, and indifference bust the connections justice is meant to preserve. If God created a world that was "originally just," a world where all things lived in harmony and right relationship, it didn't take long for human beings to throw things out of balance and to invest a lot of their ingenuity to keeping it that way. Thus, because "injustice is the prevalent condition"[15] of the world, justice typically aims to restore or renew connections that should never have been broken. More pointedly, if justice means to give another person or group what is its due, justice commonly takes the form of *restitution* exactly because so many persons and groups are regularly denied what they rightly deserve.

Injustice is thievery because it is to take what belongs to others, whether basic human rights, economic resources, respect for their dignity, or truthfulness. As an act of restitution, justice works to return to others what was rightly theirs in the first place. It sets things right by correcting a wrong, by restoring balance and equity, by making amends. This is true whether we are talking about a lie that violates a person's right to the truth, gossip that destroys one's right to a good reputation, or economic policies that unduly favor the rich over the poor. In each case something is "stolen" from another and needs to be returned. In each case, the right relationships achieved by justice are undermined and demand to be addressed and remedied. This is why justice regularly takes the form of recompense and restoration.[16] It is why justice is so often about repairing what is broken, whether that be ruptures in a relationship, ruptures in a church, or the abiding rupture between the rich and the poor. As Karen Lebacqz notes, "Because the world is permeated with injustice, justice is corrective or reparative—it is dominated by the principle of redress or setting things right."[17]

Three Types of Justice

Justice is the virtue that orders the various relationships of our lives. In general, justice moves between three fundamental sets of relationships. It guides our relationships with other individuals, the relationship between societies and their individual members, and the relationships of individuals to the larger society or community.[18] The justice that regulates our relationships with other persons is *commutative justice*. Commutative justice oversees contracts, transactions, agreements, or promises between individuals to ensure that each person is treated fairly or to address transgressions when they are not. Theft would be a violation of commutative justice because to take what legitimately belongs to another upsets the order that ought to characterize relationships between persons in society. More broadly, lying violates commutative justice because it denies another person her right to know the truth and destroys the trust that is essential for good relationships. Anyone who has ever watched a friendship or marriage deteriorate because lying destroyed persons' trust in one another can testify to the importance of commutative justice. In the classroom, the dishonesty of plagiarism attacks commutative justice because it undermines the respect and honesty that ought to characterize students' relationships with their teachers and with one another. To unfairly attack another person's reputation (the injustice of slander) is a clear transgression of commutative justice not only because it robs him of his right to a good reputation, but also because it negatively impacts how others will see him and relate to him.

The second type of justice, *distributive justice*, oversees the relationship between societies or communities and their individual members by ensuring that each person receives an equitable share of the common goods of a society. Distributive justice recognizes that all persons have a right to some share in the basic goods and services of a society, goods such as adequate food and housing, education, medical care, employment and a fair wage, and opportunities for advancement. And they have a right to these goods that are essential for human beings even if they are unable to directly contribute to them.

For example, neither children nor the extremely infirm or elderly may be able to add anything to the economic goods of a society, but they nonetheless have a right to those goods because they are members of the community and share in the bond that connects all persons in a community and makes them responsible for one another.[19] More generally, distributive justice also maintains fairness and right order in society by ensuring that every person can participate in the political, cultural, religious, and social institutions of a society. The government is the primary agent of distributive justice because ordinarily it is best suited to guarantee a fair allocation of the goods, resources, and benefits of a society to all of its members.[20] As David Hollenbach summarizes, distributive justice "establishes the equal right of all to share in all those goods and opportunities that are necessary for genuine participation in the human community. It establishes a strict duty of society as a whole to guarantee these rights."[21]

But because not every member of society always has fair access to the fundamental goods that are necessary for life, the main task of distributive justice is often to *redistribute* those essential goods, benefits, and services so that the "disorder" wrought by their unjust allocation might be overcome. The purpose of distributive justice is to give every person his or her fair share of the common good. A fair share does not necessarily mean an equal share (although in some cases it might); but it does mean that it is unjust for certain persons or groups to have such disproportionate access to the goods and benefits of a society that others have little or none. When this is the case, distributive justice must work to protect the rights of those who are regularly shut out of the common good by limiting those who grab much more than their fair share of it. This is the corrective function of distributive justice. If any one person or group gains too much power and privilege at the expense of other persons and groups, distributive justice is violated. If this occurs, the policies and patterns that enable the unjust distribution of the community's goods must be changed. Practically, this means there are times when the needs and rights of the poor and powerless members of society have priority over the claims of the rich and privileged.[22] If patterns of privilege regularly deny persons and groups just access to the fundamental goods and opportunities of a society, then those patterns must be corrected. That the poor and the powerless are so regularly excluded from the common good is why David Hollenbach argues that distributive justice will be achieved only when societies adopt "three strategic moral priorities: (1) The needs of the poor take priority over the wants of the rich. (2) The freedom of the dominated takes priority over the liberty of the powerful. (3) The participation of marginalized groups takes priority over the preservation of an order that excludes them."[23]

Finally, the justice that guides the relationship between individuals and the larger society is *social justice*, sometimes called *contributive justice*, because it focuses on the obligation every member of society has to contribute to the common good of that society.[24] If distributive justice focuses on what we receive from the common good, the focus of social justice is on what we owe the common good; it is the debt we owe to society.[25] Creating and sustaining a just society depends on the commitment and investment of each of its members to the overall well-being of that society. Social justice is a "political virtue" because it underscores the obligation every citizen has to work for a social, political, and economic order in which the basic rights of every person are respected and the fundamental needs of every person are met.[26] We fulfill the obligations of social justice through paying taxes, by serving on juries, by being politically informed, and by voting. We fulfill them when we work on behalf of those regularly shut out of the common good, whether by protesting patterns of discrimination and exclusion, lobbying on behalf of more jobs, seeking better education and health care, or advocating fairer tax laws or more just economic policies.[27] Social justice reminds us that justice does not end when our personal rights are secured and our own good is honored, but only when the good of all persons is secured. And it especially reminds us that just societies depend on just persons, persons who see beyond their own needs, security, and comfort to the welfare of all citizens of the world.

This is why a fundamental work of social justice is to create the structures, institutions, and policies necessary for a truly just society, one that respects and serves the common good not only in our local communities, but also throughout the world. There is a close connection between distributive justice and social justice because social justice makes distributive justice possible. And it does so through a concerted effort to create institutions, structures, and policies that give every member of society (including global society) equitable access to the goods, benefits, and services of that society. It is through social justice that the demands of distributive justice are met.[28] By contrast, if the political and economic institutions of society create (rather than remove) barriers between those who are able to participate in the life of society and those who are not, then social justice is lacking and those institutions need to be transformed. There is no social justice in any community where people are homeless, hungry, chronically unemployed, or simply deemed expendable, because pushed to the sidelines of society they cannot share in its goods. Injustice denies the poor access to the common good by creating impermeable barriers between them and the privileged. We see these barriers today not only in our local communities, but across the world, barriers that divide the insiders from the outsiders, one ethnic group from another ethnic group, democracies from tyrannies, and the wealthy countries of the world from the destitute ones. Social justice works to remove these barriers wherever they exist, whether they are in our communities, between our country and other countries, or stretched across the world.[29]

The Foundation of Justice

There are two principal foundations for justice. The first is the *value and dignity of persons*, and indeed the value and dignity of all of God's creation. Justice calls us out of ourselves on behalf of others because every person and every creature has a dignity and a value that demands our respect, and to which we must fittingly attend. Justice begins in, and is sustained by, the discovery of the value of other persons (and species) because we will never feel we owe anything to someone we judge to be without value. The virtue of justice is born from a moral vision that apprises every person and every creature as valuable and, therefore, worthy of our attention. It is easy to be unjust if we convince ourselves that another person, group, race, or society lacks worth and dignity. It is easy to be unconcerned about the plight of any persons or creatures if we believe they are without value and, therefore, expendable. Injustice thrives when we persuade ourselves that some persons have value and others do not, that some racial groups are clearly superior to other racial groups, or that some nations ought to prosper even if that means other nations must be deprived. Inequities abound when we divide the world between people who matter and people who do not, between people who are clearly human and people we decide can never be. As Daniel Maguire writes in *A New American Justice*, "Justice is thus founded upon a perception of the worth of persons. We show what we think persons are worth by what we ultimately concede is due to them."[30]

For Christians, human beings have intrinsic value and dignity because they are created in the image and likeness of God. For Christians, justice hinges upon being able (and willing) to discern the presence of God in another human being, and on being able to see traces of God's goodness in other species, and indeed in all of nature. But such an essential moral skill cannot be assumed and can be easily lost. It is something we have to work at, something we must commit ourselves to deepening and refining every day. Injustice takes hold when our vision becomes overly selective, when it is skewed by self-interest or twisted by prejudice. Or injustice takes hold whenever we tire of trying to find God in the persons and groups we would rather dismiss. One reason it is easy to overlook the plight of the poor is that we are not able (or perhaps refuse) to see the beauty of God in them. The same is true with any person or group we are convinced cannot be God's presence in the world. In this respect, injustice "defaces and obscures" the image of God in others to the point that we may believe it is not really there.[31]

This is one way to explain the absolute indifference of the rich man to the beggar Lazarus, the two characters recounted in Jesus' parable in the sixteenth chapter of the Gospel of Luke. The rich man "dressed in purple garments and fine linen and dined sumptuously each day" (16:19), while ignoring the beggar Lazarus, who sat outside his door and "who would gladly have eaten his fill of the scraps that fell from the rich man's table" (16:21). The rich man had taught himself not to see the poor man right outside his door because as long as he did not see him, he did not have to care for him. It is hard to see God's image in everyone; in fact, like the rich man, it is much easier to obscure and deface that image lest in seeing it we are budged from our complacency. As Enda McDonagh writes, recognizing the image of God in others "constitutes a way of life…and is constantly in danger of being obscured by the false beauties of gods created in our own image."[32] God's presence in Lazarus was obscured by the idols of wealth and possessions in the rich man's life; in fact, the rich man's way of life was the antithesis of justice because it prevented him from seeing the poor man at all. But it is also true that if the rich man had reached out to Lazarus, perhaps the poor beggar could have taught him to see. In the gospel story, Lazarus is not the only one in desperate straits. The rich man, who felt completely comfortable with himself, secure and unassailable in his wealth, was in a moral and spiritual crisis he could not recognize. He needed to be awakened from his blindness and his selfishness, but the person who could liberate him was the man he consistently ignored. That is why Jesus said the abyss the rich man had created between Lazarus and himself on Earth had become absolutely unbridgeable in the afterlife, the only difference being that then Lazarus is the one who is consoled and the rich man the one who is in desperate need (16:24–26). This is a disturbing parable because it suggests that the person most in peril is not Lazarus, the victim of injustice, but the rich man who thinks he has not a worry in the world.

The second foundation of justice is a *vision of interdependence and solidarity*. Solidarity means that all of humanity—and indeed the whole of creation—constitutes one body, a true fellowship of being. And interdependence suggests not only that we need and depend on one another, but also that the unity that exists between us is so penetrating and extensive that there is no way anyone of us can exist apart from everyone else. In his 1961 encyclical on social justice, *Mater et Magistra* ("Christianity and Social Progress"), Pope John XXIII captured the essence of interdependence and solidarity when he wrote that we are all "members of one and the same household."[33] Instead of envisioning us as isolated and utterly disparate individuals who have little connection to each other besides the connections we choose or are willing to accept, John saw that human beings are morally and spiritually connected to one another and, therefore, responsible for one another. Solidarity makes justice both intelligible and imperative because it recognizes that human life, from first to last, is shared life; as Daniel Maguire wrote, "Everything about us is social."[34]

Solidarity was an even more prominent theme in the social encyclicals of Pope John Paul II, particularly his letter *Sollicitudo Rei Socialis* ("On Social Concern"). There John Paul described solidarity as "a *firm and persevering determination* to commit oneself to the *common good*; that is to say to the good of all and of each individual, because we are *all* really responsible *for all*."[35] The virtue of solidarity teaches us to think beyond our own individual good to the common good. It forms us into persons who commit themselves to watching after the good of others, particularly the poor. Moreover, as John Paul II realized, solidarity is a virtue that needs to be cultivated not only by individuals, but by communities and societies as well. The only way to create a just social order is for societies to embrace a vision of solidarity and interdependence.

Otherwise, social life easily degenerates to the survival of the fittest or, perhaps more accurately, the luckiest. Regarding solidarity, David Hollenbach writes that it is "not only a virtue to be enacted by individual persons one at a time. It must also be expressed in the economic, cultural, political, and religious institutions that shape society."[36]

These two foundations of justice are continually eroded by the excesses of individualism. At its worst, individualism teaches that we are beholden to no one and can pursue our interests and desires with little consideration of their impact on others. Viewed through the lens of individualism, justice is reduced to protecting individual rights and liberties. Obviously, that is an important component to justice, but it is hardly all that justice involves. Overlooked in such an understanding of justice are the ties that bind us to others and the responsibilities that derive from them. When guaranteeing individual rights and liberties is seen as the almost singular business of justice, injustice always results because there is no way the poor and powerless can claim their rights and liberties to the degree that the wealthy and privileged can. Without a strong foundation in the value and dignity of persons and the interdependence and solidarity of peoples, justice is impotent because it cannot do what justice should always do, namely, seek the common good by attending to the needs of all persons. As Russell Connors and Patrick McCormick stress,

> [W]e have slipped into this corrupted vision of justice because the blinders of individualism screen out the social ties that bind us to our neighbors, to the social structures required to create and sustain a just community, and to the special duties we have toward the weakest in our societies. As long as we think that we are, first and foremost, individuals, and that our social obligations are weak, secondary ties, then the heart of justice will always be about defending our personal freedoms and punishing those who harm us. But such a stripped down view of either ourselves or the concept of justice lacks an adequate grasp of the common good, the need for social justice and the importance of compassion and love. Such skeletal justice can define the minimal standards of individual behavior in exchanges between persons, but it cannot construct truly good communities. It pays insufficient attention to the social systems and structures required for a good community and ignores the social obligations we have to all our neighbors, particularly the weakest and poorest in society.[37]

Similarly, solidarity vanishes and the rights of the poor of the world are trampled when greed is no longer viewed as a vice, but instead is esteemed and celebrated. This is not just a modern phenomenon. In their essay "Patristic Social Consciousness—the Church and the Poor," William J. Walsh and John P. Langan show that a consistent theme of the earliest Christian writings was the dangers of greed because greed destroys the moral sensitivity necessary for justice. For example, the author of the *Didache* argues that greed makes the wealthy callous and ruthless. The greedy are "bent only on their own advantage, without pity for the poor or feeling for the distressed."[38] Another early Christian writing, *The Shepherd of Hermas*, warns that wealth weakens the sympathy and imagination necessary to understand the plight of the poor, and thus leaves the rich "untouched by the excruciating sufferings of the poor."[39] Both writings suggest that greed cultivates indifference and hardness of heart. Likewise, in the fourth century Basil of Caesarea described greed as an enslaving addiction that weakens compassion because the greedy are so completely absorbed by wealth that they see and care for little else, especially those most in need.[40] These early Christian writers were astute. They railed against greed not only because it was utterly incompatible with the teaching and example of Jesus, but also because they recognized that greed produced a social order that was glaringly inhumane. Injustice excludes—it is designed to exclude—but for many of the world's citizens that exclusion is fatal. The most excluded members of our global society are denied throughout the whole of their brief lifetimes what anyone needs to survive. Each day their existence is threatened because what injustice allows and justice could alleviate is ignored.[41] To allow such injustice to continue is viciously inhumane. At its extreme, injustice so thoroughly violates the dignity of persons that it makes them nonpersons. At its extreme, injustice says to the poor and the oppressed: we would be better off without you. In her analysis of the dehumanizing effects of injustice, Karen Lebacqz stresses that the "net result of the web of injustice is the humiliated human being."[42] Injustice victimizes persons, but it also degrades them because it tells them they are expendable, that their survival is not important, and that their premature deaths are no loss. As the U.S. Catholic bishops wrote in their 1986 letter "Economic Justice for All," "The ultimate injustice is for a person or group to be treated actively or abandoned passively as if they were nonmembers of the human race. To treat people this way is effectively to say that they simply do not count as human beings."[43]

A CHRISTIAN THEOLOGY OF JUSTICE

How then do we move from the "rule of injustice" to a "reign of justice"? If injustice is a failure of moral imagination, how do we need to reimagine the world? To begin to see, think, and act differently so that all persons can share in the world's goods?

A hopeful response to each of these questions may be found in a Christian theology of justice. What Christians think about justice comes not from theories about justice, but from a story. It is a story learned in a faith community called church.[44] Through the scriptures Christians not only hear, but are also formed in stories of a God who is passionate about justice, and especially passionate about justice to the poor and oppressed. The Bible abounds with passages about God's commitment to justice, about the importance of doing justice for those who claim to know God, and about the call to be instruments of God's compassionate justice in the world. The writer of Psalm 103 praises God, for "The LORD does righteous deeds, / brings justice to all the oppressed" (v. 6). The prophet Amos tells Israel that if they want to be pleasing to God they must "let justice surge like water, / and goodness like an unfailing stream" (5:24). Probably the most succinct summary of moral conduct given in the Old Testament is the oft quoted declaration of Micah 6:8: "You have been told, O man, what is good, / and what the LORD requires of you: / Only to do the right and to love goodness, / and to walk humbly with your God."

The Bible reveals God as a lover of justice and a doer of justice (Isa 61:8), so much so that God is not only committed to justice, but defined by it.[45] In the Old Testament, justice is the chief attribute of God.[46] God is patient, God is faithful, God is compassionate, and God is merciful, but it is justice that most clearly expresses the very being of God, justice that most accurately *names* God.[47] The prominence of justice continues in the New Testament. Justice is the cornerstone of the reign of God, the central focus of Jesus' preaching. Jesus begins his Sermon on the Mount, the core of his moral teaching, with the memorable declaration that in the reign of God the prevailing order of the world will be turned upside down. In that new social order everything is reversed: the poor will be blessed, the lowly will inherit the land, the hungry will be filled, while those who laugh and prosper now "will grieve and weep" (Luke 6:25).

The paradigmatic event for confirming this understanding of God was God's deliverance of the Israelites while they were slaves in Egypt. Israel's decisive revelation about God came in God's response to the brutal suffering and affliction caused by the pharaoh's injustice. This was so pivotal for the Israelites that they interpreted their history, identity, and purpose in light of it, and certainly their thinking about God. The story begins in Exodus 3:7–8 where the oppression suffered by the

Israelites rouses God to act on their behalf. Having "witnessed the affliction of my people in Egypt" and having "heard their cry of complaint against their slave drivers" (3:7), God enters into history to free them. What is striking about this story, Bernard Brady notes, is that God acts not because the Israelites were particularly religious and not because they had necessarily done anything praiseworthy to merit God's intervention; rather, God acts because God is moved by human suffering and angered by injustice.[48] For Israel, this is who God is, a God who does not remain silent or indifferent in the face of human suffering, but responds to it in an act of liberation and deliverance.

This story is the cornerstone in Israel's theology of God and indicates what set their God apart from other gods. A God who knows their suffering will not let pharaoh's tyranny prevail. Their God sides not with the rulers of the world, but with the oppressed and afflicted. Liberation from the bondage of injustice is what identifies Israel's God from other gods. Their knowledge of God began in the rescue of slaves, in the liberation of an oppressed and exploited people; that act, more than anything else, unlocked the mystery of God for them. As Karen Lebacqz writes, "The God known to the Israelites and the early Christians was a God who hears and responds to the suffering of the people. It was this that distinguished YHWH from other gods."[49]

From this key revelatory event in the history of Israel, certain conclusions can be made about a Christian theology of justice. First, like their Jewish ancestors, a Christian theology of justice is grounded in, is shaped by, and depends on remembrance. What Christians believe about justice is rooted in a memory they cannot afford to forget or forsake, the memory not only of Israel's deliverance from slavery, but also of their own deliverance from sin by the death and resurrection of Jesus. Christians, like Jews, are a remembering people.[50] They know who they are and what they are called to do by continually remembering what God has done for them. It is by recalling God's saving deeds to them that Christians glean some understanding of the kind of people they are called to be and the mission entrusted to them. Like their Jewish sisters and brothers, Christians' justice in the world is done in memory of God's gracious justice toward them. It is justice shaped not through the lens of a philosophical theory, but from a memory that bequeaths gratitude. For Jews and Christians both, "Recollection is the root of justice."[51]

Second, if God sides with the poor and oppressed peoples of the world, Christians should "remember God" by doing the same. When trying to discern the demands of justice, Christians take a cue from the justice of God. If anything is demonstrably clear about God's justice, it is that God takes sides. God's justice is absolutely partial because God takes the side of the poor, God stands with the victims of the world, with the suffering and forgotten, and as followers of God Christians must do the same. As Daniel Maguire notes, if we popularly think of justice as blind and impartial, biblical justice is unabashedly "biased in favor of the poor and critical of the rich."[52] Therefore, if for Christians it is God's actions that determine the meaning and goal of justice, then "the poor become the litmus test of justice,"[53] not the powerful and the rich. Whether a community or society is just—as with any economic, political, or social order— must be measured by "the plight of the poor and oppressed."[54] As liberation theologians have rightly argued, a biblically informed understanding of justice will always privilege the poor because "they know better than the rich what justice requires, what it would take to have 'right relationship.'"[55] Practically, for Christians this means that conversations about justice and what justice requires must begin with the poor. To be faithful to the justice of God, they must be the first to speak.

Third, Israel was liberated from justice for the sake of justice. They who had known God's justice in their deliverance from slavery were to be agents of that justice to others. They were to show to others the same compassion and concern God had shown to them.[56] In other words, they understood who God called them to be and what God called them to do only by faithfully remembering their own rescue from slavery and oppression. Memory and vocation were intimately linked for Israel because it was their memory of God's intervention on their behalf that gave them the mission of being a people who sought liberation and justice for the oppressed in their midst. The same is true for Christians. Memory and vocation are intimately linked for them as well. The deliverance that gives Christians freedom and life in Christ also gives them a communal identity and an unmistakable responsibility. They are to be a sacrament of God's justice in the world, a people who vividly embody and practice God's special concern for the poor and forgotten. When churches fail to do so, when they turn in on themselves and become more concerned about their own status and security than they are about the needs of the poor, they betray the Christ who is their hope. For both Jews and Christians, faithfulness to God is measured in justice to the poor.

Fourth, if for Israel God was revealed through acts of justice on their behalf, then real knowledge of God comes only through lives spent doing justice for others.[57] Apart from doing justice, authentic knowledge of God is impossible. One knows God only when he or she lives justly and seeks justice for others (Jer 22:16). It is not, then, that one first knows God and then does justice, but that one comes rightly to know God only in and through the practice of justice. As the prophets of the Old Testament declared, justice precedes knowledge of God and makes it possible; indeed, *justice is knowledge of God.* In this respect, justice is more important than worship if worship is not preceded by and followed by acts of justice on behalf of the poor. The Bible does not allow people to separate religion from their everyday lives, thus worshipping God one day a week and feeling comfortable with ignoring others the rest of the week. The prophets made it very clear that all sacrifices, prayers, and worship were not only worthless, but scandalously offensive to God if they were not accompanied by justice on behalf of the poor.[58] Worship without social responsibility is a sham, an arrogant affront to a God who cares much more about the well-being of the poor and oppressed than about the chants and burnt offerings of a people gathered for worship (Amos 5:21–24; Mic 6:6–8; Isa 1:10–17). This is why people who meet their liturgical obligations but neglect justice are religious failures, not religious exemplars.[59]

It is no different with Jesus' mission in the New Testament. The central element of Jesus' preaching and ministry is the "reign of God" or "kingdom of God," language that envisions a reordering of the world according to the justice and peace of God. In his inaugural sermon in the synagogue at Nazareth, Jesus identifies himself with the poor, imprisoned, and forgotten members of society and announces that his ministry will be especially directed to them. He will "bring glad tidings to the poor," "liberty to captives," "recovery of sight to the blind," and release to prisoners (Luke 4:18). And Jesus brings the reign of God to life through his table fellowship with those who have no place in the community. By taking his place at table with the misbegotten of society—the sinners and the sick, the lawbreakers and the poor, the wayward and the needy—Jesus shows that the reign of God begins when justice is shown to these neglected and forgotten ones. Those who are regularly last in the eyes of the world shall be first in the new social order that is the reign of God. And those who enter the reign of God are only those who have fed the hungry, given drink to the thirsty, clothed the naked, welcomed the stranger, visited the imprisoned, and comforted the ill (Matt 25:31–46). Everyone else is excluded. As the metaphors of the "reign of God" and the "kingdom of God" attest, for Jesus, salvation entails deliverance from sin, but it is also inherently social and political because at its core salvation is the restoration of the justice and peace of God. As Daniel Maguire states, "Beyond any doubt *justice* is the primary distinguishing theme and hallmark of the new order envisioned by the reign."[60]

Furthermore, the Gospels make clear that the reign of God is not a religious idea, a concept or a theory, but a new way of life and a new kind of community organized and guided by the justice of God. It is, as Stephen Charles Mott says, a "social reversal" that is meant to impact the institutions, structures, and practices of a community.[61] The temptation is to limit and reduce the reign of God either by identifying it exclusively with the eternal world of heaven or by restricting it to a purely private, interior, or spiritual state so that the kingdom of God lives within us, but nowhere else. But that is obviously not what Jesus had in mind. As Jesus' miracle of the multiplication of the loaves and fishes suggests, the reign of God is a new social and economic order characterized not by greed and hoarding, but by sharing and generosity. It is a new social and political order marked by radically different attitudes toward wealth and possessions, radically different attitudes about revenge and retaliation, about power, and especially about our obligations to those most in need. We pervert the kingdom of God when we interpret it in overly spiritual ways. We honor it when we answer its challenge to re-envision and reconstruct the world so that God's *shalom* can be experienced by all. Jesus never envisioned the reign of God as an unreachable social utopia. No, Jesus declared that the reign of God was a call to a new community and a new way of life that was to begin in him and be carried forward by his followers. As John Donahue summarizes, "Jesus as the eschatological proclaimer of God's Kingdom and God's justice shows that this Kingdom is to have effect in the everyday events of life. The Kingdom is the power of God active in the world, transforming it and confronting the powers of the world."[62]

We see one effect of this understanding of Jesus' preaching of the reign of God in the early church's attitude to wealth, property, and possessions. A prominent theme in the writings of the early church, and one that should guide a Christian understanding of justice, is that God intended the goods of creation to be for all persons, not just the rich. As Ambrose, bishop of Milan and mentor of Augustine, wrote, "God has ordered all things to be produced so that there should be food in common for all, and that the earth should be the common possession of all."[63] If the goods of the Earth belong by right to all, one should see himself not as an "owner" of his wealth and possessions, but as a "steward" who is entrusted by God to use what he has to serve those most in need.[64] Beginning with the *Didache*, patristic literature lightens one's hold on property by asserting that "sharing material goods is to replace possessing them as a value for Christians."[65] While not denying the right to private property, these early Christian theologians consistently proclaimed that the right to private property must always yield "to the demands of one's fellow human beings" because "rich and poor are all of the same stock," all members of the one family of God.[66]

A Christian should be concerned not with amassing wealth and possessions, but with how best to share them. And since the resources of the Earth are meant for all persons, if the wealthy and powerful grab more than their share, they are thieves who take what rightly belongs to the poor. Similarly, when from their excess wealth they give to those in need, they are not practicing charity but restitution, because they are returning to the poor what was rightly theirs in the first place. Far from consoling the rich, Ambrose bluntly tells them: "You are not making a gift of your possessions to the poor person. You are handing over to him what is his."[67] John Chrysostom puts it even more strongly: "'The rich are in possession of the goods of the poor, even if they have acquired them honestly or inherited them legally.' If they do not share, 'the wealthy are a species of bandit.'"[68]

Notes

1. Pope Paul VI, "*Populorum Progressio*: On the Development of Peoples," in *Catholic Social Thought: The Documentary Heritage*, ed. David J. O'Brien and Thomas A. Shannon (Maryknoll, NY: Orbis Books, 1992), #66.

2. Ibid.,#29.

3. Ibid., #30.

4. Ibid., #53.

5. Patricia McAuliffe, *Fundamental Ethics: A Liberationist Approach* (Washington, DC: Georgetown University Press, 1993), 66.

6. Karen Lebacqz, *Justice in an Unjust World: Foundations for a Christian Approach to Justice* (Minneapolis: Augsburg Publishing House, 1987), 11.

7. Paul VI, *Populorum Progressio*, #4.

8. Ibid.

9. McAuliffe, *Fundamental Ethics*, 2.

10. Bernard V. Brady, *The Moral Bond of Community: Justice and Discourse in Christian Morality* (Washington, DC: Georgetown University Press, 1998), 101.

11. Thomas Aquinas, *Summa Theologiae* (New York: McGraw-Hill, 1966), IIa IIae, q. 58, a. 1.

12. Josef Pieper, *The Four Cardinal Virtues* (Notre Dame, IN: University of Notre Dame Press, 1966).

13. Ibid., 57.

14. John R. Donahue, SJ, "Biblical Perspectives on Justice," in *The Faith That Does Justice: Examining the Christian Sources for Social Change*, ed. John C. Haughey (New York: Paulist Press, 1977), 69.

15. Pieper, *The Four Cardinal Virtues*, 79.

16. Ibid., 78.

17. Karen Lebacqz, "Justice," in *Christian Ethics: An Introduction*, ed. Bernard Hoose (Collegeville, MN: The Liturgical Press, 1998), 167.

18. Daniel C. Maguire and A. Nicholas Fargnoli, *On Moral Grounds: The Art/Science of Ethics* (New York: The Crossroad Publishing Co., 1991), 31.

19. David Hollenbach, *Justice, Peace, and Human Rights: American Catholic Social Ethics in a Pluralistic Context* (New York: The Crossroad Publishing Co., 1988), 26.

20. Brady, *The Moral Bond of Community*, 114.

21. Hollenbach, *Justice, Peace, and Human Rights*, 27.

22. David Hollenbach, *Claims in Conflict: Retrieving and Renewing the Catholic Human Rights Tradition* (New York: Paulist Press, 1979), 151.

23. Ibid., 204.

24. David Hollenbach, *The Common Good and Christian Ethics* (Cambridge: Cambridge University Press, 2002), 195.

25. Maguire and Fargnoli, *On Moral Grounds*, 30.

26. Hollenbach, *Justice, Peace, and Human Rights*, 27.

27. Hollenbach, *The Common Good and Christian Ethics*, 196.

28. Hollenbach, *Claims in Conflict*, 152. "Social justice is a measure or ordering principle which seeks to bring into existence those social relationships which will guarantee the possibility of realizing the demands of distributive justice. This means that it calls for the creation of those social, economic and political conditions which are necessary to assure that the minimum human needs of all will be met and which will make possible social and political participation for all."

29. Hollenbach, *The Common Good and Christian Ethics*, 202–3.

30. Daniel C. Maguire, *A New American Justice* (Minneapolis: Winston Press, 1980), 58.

31. Enda McDonagh, *The Making of Disciples: Tasks of Moral Theology* (Wilmington, DE: Michael Glazier, 1982), 128.

32. McDonagh, *The Making of Disciples*, 130.

33. John XXIII, "*Mater et Magistra*: Christianity and Social Progress," in *Catholic Social Thought: The Documentary Heritage*, ed. David J. O'Brien and Thomas A. Shannon (Maryknoll, NY: Orbis Books, 1992), #157.

34. Maguire, *A New American Justice*, 77.

35. John Paul II, "*Sollicitudo Rei Socialis*: On Social Concern," in *Catholic Social Thought: The Documentary Heritage*, ed. David J. O'Brien and Thomas A. Shannon (Maryknoll, NY: Orbis Books, 1992), #38.

36. Hollenbach, *The Common Good and Christian Ethics*, 189.

37. Russell B. Connors Jr. and Patrick T. McCormick, *Character, Choices and Community: The Three Faces of Christian Ethics* (New York: Paulist Press, 1998), 67.

38. William J. Walsh, SJ, and John P. Langan, SJ, "Patristic Social Consciousness—The Church and the Poor," in *The Faith That Does Justice: Examining the Christian Sources for Social Change*, ed. John C. Haughey (New York: Paulist Press, 1977), 119.

39. Ibid.

40. Ibid., 124. In a scathing passage, Basil of Caesarea says about the greedy: "The bright gleam of gold delights you....Everything is gold to your eyes and fancy; gold is your dream at night and your waking care. As a raving madman does not see things themselves but imagines things in his diseased fancy, so your greed-possessed soul sees gold and silver everywhere. Sight of gold is dearer to you than sight of the sun. Your prayer is that everything may be changed to gold, and your schemes are set on bringing it about" (Homily on Luke 12:18).

41. McAuliffe, *Fundamental Ethics*, 56.

42. Lebacqz, *Justice in an Unjust World*, 35.

43. U.S. Catholic Bishops, "Economic Justice for All," in *Catholic Social Thought: The Documentary Heritage*, ed. David J. O'Brien and Thomas A. Shannon (Maryknoll, NY: Orbis Books, 1992), #77.

44. Lebacqz, "Justice," 170.

45. Daniel C. Maguire, *The Moral Core of Judaism and Christianity: Reclaiming the Revolution* (Minneapolis: Fortress Press, 1993), 128.

46. Stephen Charles Mott, *Biblical Ethics and Social Change* (New York: Oxford University Press, 1982), 60.

47. Lebacqz, *Justice in an Unjust World*, 72.

48. Brady, *The Moral Bond of Community*, 25.

49. Lebacqz, *Justice in an Unjust World*, 71.

50. Charles R. Pinches, *A Gathering of Memories: Family, Nation, and Church in a Forgetful World* (Grand Rapids, MI: Brazos Press, 2006), 123–38.

51. Lebacqz, *Justice in an Unjust World*, 63.

52. Maguire, *The Moral Core of Judaism and Christianity*, 131.

53. Lebacqz, "Justice," 168.

54. Ibid.

55. Ibid.

56. Mott, *Biblical Ethics and Social Change*, 72.

57. Maguire, *The Moral Core of Judaism and Christianity*, 104.

58. Mott, *Biblical Ethics and Social Change*, 75.

59. Brady, *The Moral Bond of Community*, 33.

60. Maguire, *The Moral Core of Judaism and Christianity*, 126.

61. Mott, *Biblical Ethics and Social Change*, 98.

62. Donahue, "Biblical Perspectives on Justice," 87.

63. Walsh and Langan, "Patristic Social Consciousness," 127.

64. Ibid., 128.

65. Ibid., 114.

66. Ibid., 127.

67. Ibid., 128.

68. Ibid., 129.

10. Prudence

Romanus Cessario

This chapter first appeared in Romanus Cessario, *The Moral Virtues and Theological Ethics*, 2nd ed. (Notre Dame, IN: University of Notre Dame Press, 2009).

When contemporary students of moral theology talk about Christian freedom, they expect that the discussion will also address personal responsibility. For example, Charles Curran emphasizes responsibility as a principal consideration in moral decision making.[1] Debate in theological ethics about what constitutes a responsible Christian, however, frequently ignores the role that the intellectual virtues play in achieving this stage of maturity. As a result, fewer theologians emphasize the position of Christian wisdom in the structure and development of moral responsibility.[2] Despite this lack of emphasis, the intellectual virtues do occupy an indispensable place in the mature Christian life and their function surpasses the mere informing of conscience.

The relationship between the intellectual and moral virtues principally involves one virtue of the practical intellect, the cardinal virtue of prudence. The role of prudence in Christian morals reflects the importance that the New Testament and the tradition that follows it assign to divine wisdom in the life of the believer.[3] This tradition differs from the Kantian and post-Kantian views on the role of "pure reason" in moral theory. These positions generally affirm that the categories of practical reason intervene at each discrete moment of moral choice, but their normative character derives from sources which remain *a priori* and, therefore, independent of cumulative human experience and inclinations.

212 / Romanus Cessario

Christian wisdom, on the other hand, develops in an individual, at least in part, as a result of both inclination and experience. Thus, Aquinas insists that the moral virtues and prudence operate according to a kind of synergy, that is, they exercise a causal influence on each other. As a result of this synergy of prudence and the virtues, Christian wisdom, in accord with *lex aeterna*, really enters into and shapes the appetitive life of the individual. In turn, the rectified appetitive powers enable prudence to grasp intellectually the will's bent toward the good. As J. O. Urmson observes, "How different this is from Kant's view that an action in accordance with one's inclination, *Neigung*, has no moral worth!"[4]

Virtuous activity means human activity at its best. "Every virtue," wrote Aristotle, "causes its possessors to be in good state and to perform their functions well."[5] Virtue requires that the whole person participate in the perfection of virtue. There exists a difference between actions that arise out of authentic virtue and those that result when a person exercises self-control at a particular moment. For example, on occasion an individual who lacks the right conformity that temperance establishes in the concupiscible appetite can actually choose to perform a particular temperate act. In order to distinguish this kind of action from that of authentic virtue, theologians refer to such discrete acts as the result of certain dispositions. For example, the decision to act temperately in a given situation produces a continent action, that is, a simple exercise of self-control. Or, when it is the case of simply commanding the irascible appetites to act or to refrain from action, the individual shows a disposition toward perseverance. In both cases, the actions unquestionably do not represent authentic virtue, nor do they require prudence.

As we have already observed, virtue implies more than the will to commit a virtuous action. Authentic virtue exists only when the human person possesses a certain interior conformity of both the cognitive and the appetitive powers to the purposes or goals of a virtuous life. The medieval theologians referred to these purposes as "ends." Consequently, to take a familiar example, in order for a husband and wife to fulfill virtuously the purpose or end of conjugal chastity, their embrace of married love must amount to more than the simple act of coitus. Although continent spouses could fulfill the marriage obligation in precisely that way, genuinely virtuous wedlock means more than a shared bed. The partners in a Christian marriage should love one another as a result of an authentic conformity to all that the married state encompasses as its purpose or end, including mutual love for each other.[6] Once this virtuous conformity takes root in the married couple, conjugal chastity no longer remains a matter of simply performing the marriage act or, for that matter, refraining from it. Rather, virtue now makes the manifold expressions of married love and communication easy, prompt, and joyful within the context of a complete and satisfactory married life.

The development of this conformity to the ends or purposes of the moral virtues does not happen accidentally. The principal means for such a development remains the moral virtue of prudence. Although prudence perfects our *intellectual* powers, moralists traditionally include it among the four cardinal *moral* virtues. St. Augustine wrote that prudence is love choosing wisely between the helpful and the harmful.[7] But Aquinas, recognizing the importance of the Aristotelian doctrine on practical reasoning, qualified this definition of prudence. "The initial activity of the appetitive power is loving," he wrote, "and it is in this sense that prudence is said to be love, not that of its nature it is a kind of love, but because its activity is caused by love."[8]

THE ROLE OF PRUDENCE

The moral virtue of prudence plays an essential role in the Christian moral life. Historically, the excessive preoccupation of the casuists with the formation and states of conscience reduced prudence to a subsidiary place in Christian moral theory. They treated prudence as the equivalent of discretion or caution, as if only certain people needed to practice it under specific circumstances. Popular usage, moreover, confirmed this erroneous impression. The current renewal of moral theology affords the opportunity for retrieving a correct understanding of this cardinal virtue in moral decision making.

Realist moral theology assigns prudence a large and ambitious role, for prudence must assure that each human action embody both the complete form of moral goodness and, at the same time, the truth claims of moral science. Christian prudence, then, combines both the intellectual emphasis of classical philosophy, for example, Aristotle's doctrine of *phronesis*, with the quest of the Christian tradition—*"amor meus, pondus meum*," my love, my inclination. Each of these features of prudence reveals distinctive elements of New Law morality. Aquinas, especially, recognized this fact when he inquired about the burdensomeness of the New Law. Observing that the New Law prohibited certain interior mental acts not expressly prohibited in all cases in the Old Law, he wrote:

> But this is extremely difficult for someone without the virtue; as Aristotle himself says, it is easy to do what the just man does, but to do it in the way in which the just man does it, that is, with pleasure and promptly, is difficult for someone who does not have the virtue of justice. The same point is made in I John, that "his commandments are not burdensome," on which Augustine comments that "they are not burdensome to someone who loves, but they are burdensome to someone who does not love."[9]

Prudence, then, transforms knowledge of moral truth into specific virtuous actions which are not burdensome, that is, which do not include friction, internal strife, forcing oneself.[10]

Generally speaking, the developed virtue of prudence represents the achievement of a complete moral culture in the human person whose intelligence and appetites function harmoniously toward good human activity. Likewise imprudence, the vice opposed to prudence, results from the influence of disordered passions or vicious habits as well as from some deficiency in moral learning. First, prudence shapes the discursive development of practical reason toward the making of a moral judgment. Although prudence is a virtue of the mind, it nonetheless ensures conformity between the several stages of moral knowledge and the appetite's bent toward good ends, especially, the basic goods of human fulfillment. Secondly, prudence is imperative. It regulates the finalization of a moral action insofar as its principal act, command, terminates in the enjoyment of human flourishing. To sum up, to imperate a virtuous action remains an act of the intellect, but, in order to effect this, prudence requires that the commanded action conform to the inclinations of rectified appetites.

One may easily distinguish this meaning of prudence from the intellectualist conception of the virtue, such as proposed by Duns

Scotus. In an opinion similar to that of Kant, Scotus alleged that prudence remains a kind of pure knowing. Though he held that the virtue perfects human intelligence, Scotus also averred that prudence can operate independent of the influence of right appetite.[11] According to this conception, prudence, defined as a simple intellectual virtue, can provide direction for the moral life, but it can contribute nothing toward shaping the appetites to follow that direction.[12] Contemporary controversies about the purpose and role of conscience indicate the perennial allure this kind of proposal holds in theological ethics. Such a construal of how virtue operates effectively eliminates what we will describe as the "unitive function" of prudence in the moral life. Any theory that supposes that the actual shape of one's appetites does not affect the principal cognitive moral faculty—whether it be called conscience or not—advances an asymmetric view of the moral life.

The truth of this assertion may be seen if one considers the potential for inevitable conflicts between what conscience dictates and what appetite inclines or strives for. Given a sovereign view of conscience, only two alternatives are possible. On the one hand, conscience can assume the role of a dictator and judge, employing psychological guilt as the principal instrument for enforcing its commands. Or, on the other hand, conscience, especially when confronted with strong but disordered appetite, can issue an exemption from the observance of any moral norm that otherwise would conflict with the untoward craving of appetite. To implement the second alternative supposes a kind of autonomy alien to New Testament liberty. Since the first alternative can result in much psychic and spiritual distress, the option for "freedom" through exemption naturally holds a much broader appeal. Not a few contemporary moral theologians stand ready to allow a complete range of erratic behavior, especially in the area of sexual morality, on the basis that strong, felt dispositions justify conscientious exceptions in a given case or in an entire class of cases.[13] To put it differently, whenever conscience plays an autonomous role in the moral life, even with due insistence on the obligation to inform it, the importance of a rational measure harmoniously directing and shaping the movement of appetite toward the authentic ends of human nature vanishes.

For the most part, modern moral philosophy chooses disjunctively between emotion or reason as the principal justification for moral norms.[14] Neither of these partial methods, however, can affirm the synergy between intellect and appetite in the way realist moral theology describes the working of the virtue of prudence. First, rational principles, no matter how well worked out, can only partially assure that a particular human action actually instantiates a full measure of moral goodness. Secondly, human appetites lack in themselves the ability to develop a correct moral measure, even if, as Aquinas claims,[15] they contain the seeds of virtue. Only the virtue of prudence shapes practical reason in accordance with authentic moral knowledge and, therefore, renders it capable of conforming human behavior toward the achievement of virtuous ends already in a sense possessed by rectified appetites.[16]

THE UNITIVE FUNCTION OF PRUDENCE

Drawing on a tradition first formulated by the classical philosopher Boethius, Christian theology generally understands the human person, at least materially, as "the individual substance of a rational nature."[17] On the assumption that no contingent being can offer an adequate explanation for its own existence, human nature requires God both for its coming-to-be and its preservation in being. As a result of the relationship that exists between God and the rational creature, each human person possesses natural law inclinations and receives moral instruction. Aquinas defines the natural law as the participation of the rational creature in the Eternal Law.[18] Recall that the Eternal Law is nothing else than God's wise plan for directing every movement and action in creation.

Creation in the image of God means that the moral life derives from the *lex aeterna*, which trinitarian theology usually attributes to the *Logos*, the eternal Son. All that God communicates to us by way of instruction, broadly construed, includes whatever moral reason alone can discover along with the entirety of moral truth revealed in Christ. Although some authors question this thesis, it is a reasonable assumption that the teaching of all moral truth, including the principles of natural law, fulfills an essential part of the church's prophetic role.[19] Christian moral teaching remains a faith-knowledge even when certain elements of the teaching, for example, the common precepts of the natural law, do not necessarily require faith for their full comprehension. Aquinas suggested that moral precepts fall into three categories: the most general precepts of the natural law; natural law precepts that require an elucidation by those advanced in moral wisdom; and precepts revealed by God.[20]

In using *imago Dei* as a theological category to describe human nature, theologians consciously make a statement about the origins and the destiny of the human person. In order to discover where the created representation of the Blessed Trinity principally manifests itself in us, St. Augustine pointed theology toward the chief psychological activities in human nature. Hence, knowing and loving serve as the focal points both for the doctrine of the *imago Dei* and for natural law theory. The *imago*, at least aptitudinally, images the Blessed Trinity when, in accord with natural law inclinations, it performs the basic operations of the cognitive and appetitive capacities. In particular, this image of representation, as the Scholastics called it, seeks perfection: first, in loving certain ends but, especially, in conforming to the Supreme Good; second, in knowing certain truths but, especially, in adhering to the Highest Truth.

Aquinas clearly recognizes the twofold activity of the divine image in us when he affirms that "the commandments of natural law sometimes are actually adverted to by the reason and sometimes just settled convictions there" in human nature.[21] *Synderesis* is a *quasi-habitus* that offers the first principles of the practical reason. This *habitus* forms a companion with *intellectus*, or understanding, which serves a similar purpose for the speculative intellect. Some authors, lacking such precisions, even call *synderesis* the law of our understanding, to the extent that it amounts to the *habitus* of keeping the precepts of the natural law. These precepts, of course, constitute the first principles of human activity, so that *synderesis* actually starts the process of transforming the inclinations of the *imago* into working principles for concrete moral activity.[22] Of course, the practical principle that good is to be sought and done and evil is to be avoided forms only the basis or starting point for the development of right conduct.

Acquired moral learning plays an important role in this development. At the level of the appetitive, the common principles of natural law remain settled convictions ordered toward the basic goods of human flourishing.[23] However, at the rational level of properly discursive human knowledge, *synderesis* contributes by offering the first principles to the development of practical moral knowledge through the work of prudence and its integral parts.[24] Prudence, then, integrates moral knowledge and rectified appetites to provide concrete, particular norms for human behavior. All of the moral virtues require prudence because this virtue alone guarantees the actual production of virtuous behavior, not simply the knowledge of what to do. Prudence promises that when correct moral reasoning combines with rectified appetite for good ends, a virtuous action inevitably results.

The Scholastics called these good ends the "thing" or *res* of nature.[25] So that detraction, for example, destroys the *res* of human social life and communication in the same way that a contagious disease harms the *res* of public health. On the other hand, prudential conformity with a *res* of human flourishing produces a virtuous person who easily and surely achieves that perfection of human life. Unlike the good musician who, in order to instruct a student, may deliberately play a false note, the prudent person cannot voluntarily act imprudently. One cannot hypothetically set aside what prudence teaches. For the cardinal virtue of prudence ultimately shapes the person in such a way that acting properly, as St. Paul reminds the Corinthians, results from a new or second nature. "Therefore, if any one is in Christ, he is a new creation; the old has passed away, behold, the new has come" (2 Cor 5:17).

PRUDENCE AND MORAL KNOWLEDGE

Yet, even as it shares in the perfection of the moral virtues in commanding a virtuous mean and, therefore, the realization of a moral action, prudence remains an intellectual virtue. Thus, the first principles of practical reason, held by *synderesis*, develop into a large body of specific moral knowledge. Recall that prudence particularizes moral truth for application to concrete cases. Although the precision of moral learning varies in different people, the ethicist can isolate at least three discrete moments in the development of moral consciousness. These moments occur in each mature individual no matter what stage of intellectual advancement the person has attained.

1. Basic moral reflection. This amounts to the prescientific grasp of general moral principles that results from ordinary human

experience: for example, the principle that each one receives a just share of common goods.

2. Moral science. The reasoned, organized development of this reflection into a coherent body of truths: for example, Rawls's theory of justice. In fact, any ethical theory attempts to formulate moral science.

3. Conscience. The application of general or developed moral principles to an individual's singular action either about to be done or already accomplished: for example, here and now I should pay (or should have paid) $1,000 to the federal government for income tax.

It should be emphasized, however, that moral knowledge, which differs from speculative knowledge because of the practical end it pursues, belongs to the order of action. Since the contingency of human events impairs a fully accurate prediction of outcomes, a practical science produces scientific results only in the broad sense.

Three distinct acts embody prudence's principal working. These are counsel, judgment, and command. Counsel, shaped by the special virtue of *eubulia*, supplies a rational deliberation about means that ensures that the prudent person solicits whatever established moral wisdom provides for a certain matter. Judgment makes a decision about what one is going to do now; it follows the settling onto concrete means. The practical judgment of conscience applies this particularized wisdom to the actual circumstances of a given case. If a poorly informed conscience makes a faulty judgment about particulars, no virtue can develop; the question of culpability, however, raises other questions. Because of the importance the act of judgment holds in the moral life, two special virtues aid its formation: *synesis* ensures sound judgment in ordinary matters and *gnome* provides the wit to judge the exceptional cases. Finally, command supplies the efficacious imperative note in the act of prudence. To command remains the principal act of prudence that gives to the judgment of conscience its imperative value. By this, prudence enters into the formal act of the moral virtues, that is, the choosing of the good as such.

The goal of seeking conformity between the human person and the good moral ends of human flourishing requires the *dictamen* or "saying" of conscience. For conscience, the act of the intellect that most immediately affects free choice serves as the final instance of applied moral truth. Although it brings the full weight of formed moral truth to bear on decision, conscience does not constitute choice. Moral theories that rely exclusively on conscience restrict the parameters within which moral decision making occurs. Such theories exhibit a mistrust of nature and experience as an authentic source of moral wisdom. The cardinal virtue of prudence, however, both provides the ability for making concrete moral decisions and, at the same time, ensures that these decisions actually satisfy human nature created after the *imago Dei*. Practical moral knowledge, then, easily leads to theological reflection. In fact, theology—being a certain impression in us of the knowledge that God shares with the blessed in heaven—qualifies as a practical science. "St. John of the Cross and St. Alphonsus," observes Jacques Maritain, "were able to produce absolutely sure practical doctrine not only because they were learned but also prudent and experienced."[26]

PRUDENCE AND ACTION

Prudence, even though a virtue of the mind, operates differently than the virtues of the speculative intellect, wisdom, science, and understanding. Aquinas emphasizes that the perfect correctness of reason in speculative matters depends upon the principles from which it argues. For example, speculative science depends on and presupposes understanding, which is the *habitus* of its principles. "In human acts, however, ends are what principles are in speculative matters, as stated in the *Ethics* (7, 1151a16). Consequently, prudence, which is right reason about things to be done, requires that a man be rightly disposed with regard to ends; and this depends on rightness of appetite."[27] Prudence operates only in connection with the inclinations of the human person to achieve a well-defined moral end. In this, moral realism differs from ethical rationalism that begins with wholly abstract principles or "rules" of reasoning and regards the objectives of particular virtues as secondary and relative.

Although prudence is a virtue of the practical intellect, it also differs from art. The distinction between art and prudence offers the most helpful insight into its uniqueness. Philosophers consider art a virtue of the practical intellect since it produces the capacity, by means of a *habitus*, for the artist to make something properly. Art, according to a realist aesthetics, finds its norm or measure in an object that exists outside of the virtue's own principles. For example, the person who sits for a portrait is the measure of the work of the artist who produces it. Art, then, seeks to represent that which exists outside itself, even if, as happens with abstract forms, the measure exists principally in the imagination of the artist. Prudence, on the other hand, works differently for it must discover the measure for a moral act within its own structure, as this measure depends on the actual state of one's appetites. In other words, prudence incorporates personal experience into its own *habitus* formation. Thus, in order to function as a directive truth for moral action, acquired prudence presupposes that a person has learned from human experience something about right dispositions.[28]

The term *human experience* has been made to carry considerable theological weight in recent decades. Theologians influenced by Marxist thought find the category fruitful for theological analysis and critique, as did authors involved in the Modernist crisis at the turn of the twentieth century.[29] It would be unfortunate if reaction to these schools of thought resulted in a wholesale rejection of such an important element in Christian moral theology. For the moral theologian, human experience entails the proper interaction between the human subject and a world of created realities, that is, specific objects of experience. In turn, these objects make up the particular configuration of one's moral universe for weal or woe.[30]

The congruity that exists between human nature and the objects capable of satisfying its needs is called the order of intention. An end-in-intention (*finis in intentione*) develops precisely because human nature seeks to complete itself by moving toward and embracing those good objects that comprise its well-being.[31] The obvious examples include such things as food, truth, sexual gratification, but other goods such as friendship, personal accomplishment, integrity, play, and so forth also constitute objects that become ends-in-intention for us.[32] Again, realist moral theology trusts both nature and experience as contributing to the development of moral wisdom. For example, everyone recognizes that materials that the human body cannot assimilate fail to qualify as foodstuffs. Rocks simply do not fit nature's digestive system in the way an authentic moral object, such as Peking duck, must do in order to serve as an end-in-intention for humans. Of course, good instruction can spare one the chagrin of having to learn by experience about such inappropriate objects.

The moral virtues ensure in principle that we are disposed to pursue only honorable ends-in-intention. Consider the futility of seeking sound moral judgment about sobriety from one who habitually drinks too much. Why is this so? The answer lies in the way such a person has made bourbon or beer an end. In this sense, each one acts in accord with the way he or she intends, that is, regards, a given end of human life. For the drunkard, this is a disordered attachment to drink. A Scholastic adage summarizes this truth: *qualis sum secundum appetitum meum, talis mihi videtur finis.*[33] In other words, the shape of one's emotional life actually dictates how an individual will discriminate among a range of options, and consequently, if asked, will give advice to others. Disordered desires obviously affect the practical judgment an individual makes about the use of certain goods, about how he or she approaches an intended end. Accordingly, the miser wants only more money; the profligate seeks more sexual gratification; the glutton more food, and so forth. These are the carnal sinners, as Dante calls them in the *Inferno*, "who subject reason to desire."[34]

Still, disordered appetite can affect prudence only in an indirect way. For command, the proper act of prudence itself, originates in the intellect. Aquinas expresses this truth with utmost clarity: "A commander orders a subordinate to do something, and his order is conveyed by way of imitation or declaration. This is a function of reason."[35] Although moral theologians of a voluntarist bent raise questions such as whether God could change his will about divine commands, this kind of speculation holds no interest for the moral realist. For in the final analysis, moral realism measures moral truth according to the likeness of divine wisdom that exists in the created order. In other terms, prudence looks to introduce the *veritas vitae*, the truth about life, into the world. Within this context, we can appreciate the important role which the church's magisterium plays in giving proper direction to moral conduct. Recent instructions on matters as diverse as prayer and bioethics indicate the range of moral topics that require clarification from a competent "lawmaker" in light of revealed truth.

Notes

1. Charles Curran insists that "from a more philosophical anthropological perspective the relationality-responsibility model fits in better with the emphasis on historicity." Hence Curran argues for what he calls a more adequate conscience theory. See *Directions in Fundamental Moral Theology* (Notre Dame, IN: University of Notre Dame Press, 1986), 230ff.

2. Brian V. Johnstone examines the way moral theologians discuss practical reason in "The Structures of Practical Reason: Traditional Theories and Contemporary Challenges," *Thomist* 50 (1986): 417–46. J. O. Urmson, "Aristotle's Doctrine of the Mean," *American Philosophical Quarterly* 10 (1973): 223–30, critiques the intellectualist bias that sees emotion's role in virtue as either peripheral or beguiling. All in all, contemporary discussions of practical reason mostly reflect the parameters established by Kantian and other forms of purely rationalist moral philosophy. On the other hand, since *recta ratio* depends on the Eternal Law, the Scholastic notion of right reason transcends the impartial character of Kantian ethics with respect to the appetites.

3. Ceslaus Spicq, OP, *Charity and Liberty in the New Testament*, trans. F. V. Manning (New York: Alba House, 1965), provides one of the few essays on the subject of freedom in the New Testament that takes knowledge of moral truth seriously into consideration. See also his more recent work, *Connaissance et Morale dans la Bible* (Fribourg: Editions Universitaires, 1985), which points out the general importance of cognition in the New Testament's account of morality.

4. Urmson, "Excellence of Character," 35.

5. *Nicomachean Ethics*, Bk. 2, chap. 6 (1106a16, 17).

6. See *Gaudium et spes*, no. 48: "Husband and wife, by the covenant of marriage, are no longer two, but one flesh. By their intimate union of persons and of actions they give mutual help and service to each other, experience the meaning of their unity, and gain an ever deeper understanding of it day by day. This intimate union in the mutual self-giving of two persons, as well as the good of the children, demands full fidelity from both, and an indissoluble unity between them."

7. See his *De moribus ecclesiae catholicae*, Bk. 1, chap. 15: "prudentia, amor ea quibus adjuvatur ab eis quibus impeditur, sagaciter seligens" (*PL* 32, col. 1322).

8. IIa IIae, q. 47, a. 1, ad 1.

9. Ia IIae, q. 107, a. 4.

10. For a classic analysis of this important point, see R. Garrigou-Lagrange, OP, "La prudence. Sa place dans l'organisme des vertus," *Revue*

théologique 9 (1926): 411–26. But for a more recent study, see Charles O'Neill, "Is Prudence Love?" *Monist* 58 (1974): 119–39.

11. For an accurate appraisal of the status of contemporary research on this point, see Stephen D. Dumont, "The Necessary Connection of Moral Virtue to Prudence According to John Duns Scotus—Revisited," *Recherches de Théologie ancienne et médiévale* 55 (1988): 184–206.

12. Although, as Dumont's study indicates, we do not possess a critical edition of *In Libros Sententiarum*, Bk. 3, d. 36, a. 2, the actual textual evidence supports the view that Duns Scotus denied that prudence necessarily requires moral virtue. For further information, see Allan Wolter, *Duns Scotus on the Will and Morality* (Washington, DC: Catholic University of America Press, 1986). In addition, the position of Scotus certainly prejudiced subsequent German Nominalism, so that the influential Gabriel Biel, for example, adopted much of the Scotistic view on prudence. See John L. Farthing, *Thomas Aquinas and Gabriel Biel: Interpretations of St. Thomas Aquinas in German Nominalism on the Eve of the Reformation* (Durham, NC: Duke University Press, 1988), esp. chap. 5, "Ethics."

13. Thus, Richard M. Gula, SS, mistakenly identifies the following situation as "a prudential judgment" concerning artificial contraception: "A Catholic married couple, who give presumptive authority to the church's teaching on marriage and want to live by it, know that for now they can best preserve their marriage and family life by using artificial means of birth control. Given their limited moral capacity, and the limiting factors of their marital and familial situation, they are unable to live by what the church prescribes in its official teaching for marriage. Their choice to use artificial contraception is a prudential judgment. It should not be confused with dissent." See his *Reason Informed by Faith: Foundations of Catholic Morality* (New York: Paulist Press, 1989), 160.

14. Alasdair MacIntyre, *A Short History of Ethics* (New York: Macmillan, 1966), provides a readable survey of these various schools of rational ethics.

15. For example, see his *De virtutibus in communi*, a. 8.

16. See Yves R. Simon, "Introduction to the Study of Practical Wisdom," *New Scholasticism* 35 (1961): 1–40, for a full presentation of these pivotal points in realist morals. Also, Michel Labourdette, "Conscience practique et savoir moral," *Revue Thomiste* 48 (1948): 142–79.

17. Aquinas discusses this definition taken from Boethius's *De duabus naturis* (*PL* 64, col. 1343) in Ia, q. 29, a. 1. For an excellent treatment of how the Thomist tradition accounted for the uniqueness of the created person, see T. U. Mullaney, "Created Personality: The Unity of Thomistic Tradition," *New Scholasticism* 29 (1955): 369–402.

18. See Ia IIae, q. 91, a. 2.

19. Lucien Richard, OMI, provides a survey of opinion on the question of a specifically Christian morality in *Is There a Christian Ethics?* (New York: Paulist Press, 1988).

20. Aquinas probes the question of the relationship of positive morality to the law of nature in Ia–IIae q. 100, a. 1, where he inquires whether all the moral precepts of the Old Law come under the law of nature. There he distinguishes between natural law precepts, precepts perceived only by the morally wise, and precepts that require divine instruction.

21. Ia IIae, q. 94, a. 1.

22. Ia IIae, q. 94, a. 2, ad 2. Also see Ia IIae, q. 94, a. 1, where Aquinas describes *synderesis* as "habitus continens praecepta legis naturalis, quae sunt prima principia operum humanorum." Timothy C. Potts, *Conscience in Medieval Philosophy* (Cambridge: Cambridge University Press, 1980), 45–60, gives a good historical study of Aquinas's use of *synderesis*. For a complete discussion of its role according to an authoritative Thomist point of view, see Labourdette, "Connaisance practique et savoir moral," esp. pp. 149ff., and Luc-Thomas Somme, "The Infallibility, Impeccability and Indestructibility of Synderesis," *Studies in Christian Ethics* 19 (2006): 403–16.

23. At present there exists considerable discussion, even among Thomists, concerning the place basic goods hold in theories of natural law. Russell Hittinger provides a useful summary of the different schools of thought in his *A Critique of the New Natural Law Theory* (Notre Dame, IN: University of Notre Dame Press, 1987), especially chaps. 1–2.

24. Aquinas in IIa IIae, q. 49 treats eight component parts of prudence: memory, insight, teachableness, acumen, reasoned judgment, foresight, circumspection, and caution.

25. The Scholastics used the term *res* in a broad and analogical sense. For instance, since he proceeds from the mutual love of the Father and Son, they even called the Holy Spirit the *res amoris*, that is, the "Thing of Love." But as *res* points chiefly to the complete constitution of any physical or moral entity, theological ethics uses the term to refer to the particular, concrete goals or ends of the different virtues. These ends, in turn, illustrate a moral order that accords with how Divine Providence ordains that creatures, including the free actions of men and women, should reach their perfection.

26. See *The Degrees of Knowledge*, translated from the 4th French edition under the supervision of Gerald B. Phelan (New York: Charles Scribner's Sons, 1959), 463. For an important discussion by a French Dominican of the last century, see Leonard Lehu, OP, *La Raison: Règle de la Moralité d'après Saint Thomas* (Paris: J. Gabalda et Fils, 1930).

27. See Ia IIae, q. 57, a. 4. The attention of specialists should be drawn to the treatise of Cajetan on this material, especially *In Iam–IIae* q. 57, a. 5.

28. Ralph McInerny offers a brief but lucid description of this point in *Ethica Thomistica: The Moral Philosophy of Thomas Aquinas* (Washington, DC: Catholic University of America Press, 1982), 38ff. (revised edition, 1997, 40–59).

29. See Leo Scheffczyk, "Christology in the Context of Experience: On the Interpretation of Christ by E. Schillebeeckx," *Thomist* 48 (1984): 383–408, for some pertinent observations on the subject. Similarly, one can consult the works of Baron von Hügel (1852–1924) on the question of experience in Christian theology.

30. See William van der Marck, "Ethics as a Key to Aquinas's Theology: The Significance of Specification by Object," *Thomist* 40 (1976): 535–54.

31. Admittedly certain later Scholastics overworked the term with the result that human persons became conflated with infrapersonal objects. However, to state that a person can be a moral object for another person simply affirms that the person-as-object stands in some kind of interpersonal relationship to the other. See the excellent treatment of this matter by T. C. O'Brien, *Faith* (2a2ae. 1–7), vol. 31 (New York: McGraw-Hill, 1966), esp. "Objects and Virtues." Also L. Dewan, "'Objectum': Notes on the Invention of a Word," *Archives d'histoire doctrinale et littéraire du moyen age* 48 (1981): 37–96, esp. 64–78, 91, 93–94.

32. See John Finnis, *Natural Law and Natural Rights* (Oxford: Oxford University Press, 1980), esp. chap. 4, for an exposition of the various ways thinkers have enumerated lists of basic or fundamental goods.

33. The literal translation runs: "how I am according to my appetites, in such a way I view the end of human existence."

34. *Inferno*, Canto V, 37–39: "Intesi ch'a cosi fatto tormento enno dannati i peccator carnali, che la ragion sommettono al talento."

35. Ia IIae, q. 17, a. 1.

11. Courage

Stanley Hauerwas and Charles Pinches

This chapter first appeared in Stanley Hauerwas and Charles Pinches, *Christians Among the Virtues: Theological Conversations with Ancient and Modern Ethics* (Notre Dame, IN: University of Notre Dame Press, 1997).

The newfound enthusiasm for a recovery of an ethic of virtue that has concerned us in this book might be thought to be a "good thing" for religious communities in the United States. Widespread enthusiasm for virtue may provide churches, who have become increasingly irrelevant to the public discussion of the issues before the American polity, a way to contribute to that polity by producing people of virtue. Or so some hope. In this chapter we want to suggest that, even if enticing, this is a false hope, one Christians must eschew.

To be clear, we do not mean to deny that issues concerning virtue are important for political practice and/or theory. Indeed we have argued against the predominant forms of moral theory produced by liberal society precisely because they have been based on a lawlike paradigm that ignores the significance of the virtues. In short, it has been the project of liberal political and ethical theory to create just societies without just people, primarily by attempting to set in place social institutions and/or discover moral principles that ensure cooperation between people who share common goods or virtues. Examples of this project are legion, although none is better than John Rawls's *A Theory of Justice*,[1] where the art of argument is elegantly displayed. Mind you, Rawls does not exclude considerations of virtue, but he follows the standard theories we have already investigated in assuming that any account of virtue is secondary to "principles of justice" and institutions based upon them.

Without systematically engaging Rawls at this point,[2] we hope it is sufficiently plain that we think the liberal project he represents has failed, as it was bound to. But now, one might interject, with this failure behind us, isn't the public recovery of virtue all the more pressing? And isn't it irresponsible not to work to further it? For if liberalism cannot create a just society without just people, must we not return with renewed vigor to creating just people so a just society can remain within our sights?

While not unfamiliar in the more distant past, this is a new and interesting challenge for our age, one we must take seriously. To begin to respond, we would like to draw attention to a series of comments made by Jean Bethke Elshtain written in answer to the call for a return to civic virtue made by the authors of *Habits of the Heart*. As she notes, "the problem with the tradition of civic virtue can be stated succinctly: that virtue is *armed*."[3] "Virtue" is of Greek origin, and not accidentally so. As Elshtain observes, for the Greeks war was a natural state of affairs and the basis of society. Moreover, the presumption of war was continued by the great civil republicans such as Machiavelli and Rousseau. Thus the first duty of Machiavelli's prince is to be a soldier and create an army of citizens, that is, not simply to create an army to protect citizens, but to make citizens an army. Napoleon in this respect is but the full realization of Machiavelli, and democratic order itself is based on the idea that all citizens should be armed.[4]

In fact, according to Elshtain, Rousseau is the great prophet of armed civic virtue, because he saw most clearly that for modern societies a vision of total civic virtue is required. The chief process that draws people out of their provincial loyalties and makes them conscious of belonging to a wider community—a national community—is military conscription. Elshtain comments, "[the] *national* identity that we assume, or yearn for, is historically inseparable from war. The nation-state, including our own, rests on mounds of bodies."[5] Indeed, the United States is a society that is especially constituted by war. As Elshtain observes, a nation-state can exist on paper long before it exists in fact. Accordingly "a *united* United States is a historical construction that most visibly comes into being as cause and consequence of

American involvement in the Great War. Prior to the nationalistic enthusiasm of that era, America was a loosely united federation with strong and regional identities."[6]

Within this context the virtue of courage assumes great importance, for at root courage is a virtue of war that is best exemplified by soldiers facing death in battle. This fits well with the common notion that courage involves a disposition toward death that pervades many aspects of our life, but for all of these aspects the courage of soldiers in battle is the paradigm. However, we want to suggest that for Christians "courage" cannot start with these assumptions nor this paradigm. In fact, from a Christian point of view such "courage" is not courage at all but only its semblance, which when wrongly used can turn demonic.[7]

If, then, the trumpeted return to civic virtue involves the arming of virtue with the courage of the soldier (as Elshtain has suggested) and if Christians are committed to another sort of courage not formed on war, there is good reason to think that the Christian churches cannot nor should not underwrite a program of return to civic virtue, at least not in all of its aspects.

ARISTOTLE ON COURAGE

To see how accounts of courage might differ, we propose to look, once again, to the two great proponents of virtue: Aristotle and Aquinas. The latter, of course, depends significantly on the former, yet with great insight deviates on an especially important point: for Aquinas it is the martyr and not the soldier who exemplifies true courage.

To see the significance of this difference, we must begin with Aristotle's account of courage. It is offered in Book III of the *Nicomachean Ethics*,[8] where it is coupled with an analysis of temperance. Although Aristotle says little about this explicitly, we may suppose that he followed others in believing that this pair of virtues, courage and temperance, controls our desires, rendering us capable of the habits that make possible the lifelong process of formation of our characters to the good.

For Aristotle, and Aquinas as well, any account of the virtues requires that they be exemplified in concrete lives; after all, we become virtuous people by copying the deeds of virtuous people. Here to "copy" is not to imitate mechanically, though that may not be a bad way to start, but it involves having the same feelings, emotions, desires, and so on that the virtuous person has when she acts. As Aristotle observes, it is a hard task to be good, and it requires growth in knowledge: "not everyone can find the middle of a circle, but only a man who has the proper knowledge. Similarly, anyone can get angry—that is easy—or can give away money or spend it; but to do all this to the right person, to the right extent, at the right time, for the right reason, and in the right way is no longer something easy that anyone can do. It is for this reason that good conduct is rare, praiseworthy, and noble" (1109a25).

The point, then, is that being virtuous involves not only having dispositions for appropriate action, but also a right "attitude" that includes having the appropriate emotions and desires. This is one of the reasons virtue requires such training, for we become what we are only through the gradual buildup of the appropriate characteristics. It also helps us see why and how courage needs to be carefully distinguished from its counterfeit: recklessness.

Courage and temperance are the virtues that form what Aristotle assumed were our most basic appetites—fear and pleasure. Their purpose is not to repress these appetites but to form them to function rightly. Hence courage does not eliminate fear—that would be recklessness. Rather, courage forms us to have fear in the right amount, at the right time, about the right things, and so on. Granted, a reckless person may appear to do just what a courageous person does but he is not acting courageously as he does, for he is not being properly affected by fear.[9]

It follows that courage is not only difficult to practice, it is difficult to recognize. To decipher it we must consider the various possible objects of fear, and which of these is most fearful. So Aristotle comments:

> [I]t is true that we fear all evils, e.g., disrepute, poverty, disease, friendlessness, death. But it does not seem that a courageous man is concerned with all of these. There are some evils, such as disrepute, which are proper and right for him to fear and wrong not to fear: a man who fears disrepute is decent and has a sense of shame, a man who does not fear it is shameless. Still, some people describe a man who fears no disrepute as courageous in a metaphorical sense, for he

resembles a courageous man in that a courageous man, too, is fearless. Perhaps one should not fear poverty or disease or generally any evil that does not spring from vice or is not due to oneself. However, it is not the man who has no fear of these things who is courageous. But we call him so because of his resemblance to the courageous man. For some people who are cowards on the battlefield are generous and face the loss of money cheerfully. On the other hand, a man is not a coward if he fears insult to his wife and children, or if he fears envy or the like; nor is he courageous if he is of good cheer when he is about to be flogged. (1115a10)

The great variety of circumstances in which we are faced with fear calls for a paradigm case. What fears put courage to the test? What circumstances plainly distinguish the truly courageous person from those who display its counterfeits like recklessness, or even from those who display courage, but only now and then? The paradigm must involve death, for it is the most fearful thing. Yet not all deaths allow for the display of courage.

For example, death by drowning or by disease does not. What kind of death, then, does bring out courage? Doubtless the noblest kind, and that is death in battle, for in battle a man is faced by the greatest and most noble of dangers. This is corroborated by the honors which states as well as monarchs bestow upon courage. Properly speaking, therefore, we might define as courageous a man who fearlessly faces a noble death and in situations that bring a sudden death. Such eventualities are usually brought about by war. But of course a courageous man is also fearless at sea and in illness, though not in the same way as sailors are. Because of their experience, the sailors are optimistic, while the courageous man has given up hope of saving his life but finds the thought of such an (inglorious) death revolting. Furthermore, circumstances which bring out courage are those in which a man can show his prowess or where he can die a noble death, neither of which is true of death by drowning or illness. (1115a28–1115b5)

It should not surprise us that the paradigm for courage for Aristotle is facing death in battle, for we know that his ethics is but the preface to his politics.[10] All virtues are in a sense political virtues, since they reflect the common good as well as provide it with specific content. They are, therefore, inescapably conventional, as they depend on practices that are generally agreed to be good. To call them conventional is not to call them into question but rather to indicate that any account of the virtues for any community requires the display of behavior that is commonly held to be good.

It is important to see that this behavior is more than an example of virtue in the way chess is an example of a board game, for the virtues have no sense unless there are practices that hold them in place in the arena of everyday human exchange. To take an example from another culture than our own, Lee Yearley has noted that propriety was a virtue central to Chinese culture in the time of Mencius. It covered such activities as solemn religious activities, like funerals, as well as what we call etiquette, including not just which fork to use when but also common rituals such as saying "excuse me" after a sneeze. Mencius links the solemn activities with the more mundane because he assumes they both foster a behavior that manifests distinctly human activities rather than instinctive reactions. As Yearley comments:

> Mencius believes these emotional reactions require conventional rules for their expression; they can find expression only through the ritual forms a society possesses. The rules or forms, in fact, are what allow people to achieve the good found in expressing and cultivating these reactions. For example, I cannot easily, or even adequately, show my respect for a cook, a host, or an elderly person unless social forms exist that allow me to express such attitudes. Furthermore, both I and others must know what those forms are and what they express. I need to know, for instance, that a slight bow and somewhat servile smile express respect, not irony or rancor. The attitude of respect toward others, Mencius thinks, must

express itself in a disposition to follow the conventional rules of propriety. A person observes these rules as an expression of reverence for people, their roles, and even the social-organism that they embody and help preserve.[11]

The point we can derive from this is that virtues such as "respect" or "courage" are more than the attitudes a person might hold within himself, bringing them to expression now and then in some activity. No doubt respect or courage includes certain attitudes, as we have noted, but they require display as well. Indeed, we cannot know their shape unless we see them in particular behaviors that we together identify as good. As the central paradigm of courage, facing death in battle is like this for Aristotle. It not merely an example of courage, it is rather the rightful *exemplification* of what true courage entails. It follows that without war courage could not be fully known.

All this is not to say that Aristotle thinks the courageous person is by necessity warlike. Courage cannot stand on its own; at the very least it requires the guidance of prudence regarding how much fear to have, about what, and so on. Soldiers may lack fear in battle, but that does not by itself mean they are courageous. For example, Aquinas notes that some soldiers "through skill and practice in the use of arms, think little of the dangers of battle, as they reckon themselves capable of defending themselves against them; thus Vegetius says 'no man fears to do what he is confident of having learned to do well.'"[12]

Likely this is true of a certain General Skobeleff, whose comments are reproduced by Yearley, although there is something more than mere familiarity with danger or with arms at work in his self-appraisal. Says he:

> I believe that my bravery is simply the passion for and at the same time the contempt of danger. The risk of life fills me with an exaggerated rapture. The fewer there are to share it, the more I like it. The participation of my body in the event is required to furnish me an adequate excitement. Everything intellectual appears to me to be reflex; but a meeting of man to man, a duel, a danger into which I can throw myself head-foremost, attracts me, moves me, intoxicates me. I am crazy

for it, I love it, I adore it. I run after danger as one runs after women; I wish it never to stop.[13]

From Aristotle's perspective, General Skobeleff is not a courageous man, not only because he is untouched by appropriate fear, but also because he lacks the wisdom to subject his daring to the appropriate purposes. Nevertheless, who would doubt that Skobeleff is in one sense an excellent soldier, perhaps even better because he lacks true courage? Indeed, at one point Aristotle muses that the very best soldiers are not courageous but rather those who are ready to face danger because "they have no other good" (1117b).

The General Skobeleffs of the world notwithstanding, the battlefield is still the true test of courage for Aristotle. As opposed to men like Skobeleff, the courageous person, because he has the other virtues (he is "happy"), knows that his life is a true good, rightly prized, and its loss is rightly feared. Nevertheless, this man stands and fights knowing full well what this might bring.

> Death and wounds will be painful for a courageous man, and he will suffer them unwillingly, but he will endure them because it is noble to do so or base to do otherwise. And the closer a man is to having virtue or excellence in its entirety and the happier he is, the more pain will death bring to him. Life is more worth living for such a man than for anyone else, and he stands to lose the greatest goods, and realizes that fact, and it is painful. But he is no less courageous for that and perhaps rather more so, since he chooses noble deeds in war in return for suffering pain. Accordingly, only insofar as it attains its end is it true to say of every virtue that it is pleasant when practiced. (1117b15)

Death on the battlefield, therefore, stands as the paradigm of courage for Aristotle precisely because it gives the genuinely courageous person the chance to offer the one great good that unifies all other particular goods, that is, his life, for an even higher good, namely, the common good of the state. Moreover, he can do this in a noble manner—in what Aristotle calls the "noble deeds of war"—with full knowledge of what is at stake. This is the height of courage, by which all other acts of courage take their bearing.

AQUINAS ON COURAGE

Many of us are prone to a certain suspicion of Aquinas's intellectual originality when we discover how frequently he borrows from Aristotle.[14] This suspicion can arise particularly when Aquinas moves from the natural to the theological virtues, for at first glance the latter appear as no more than a fluffy topping spread over the natural virtues— which virtues depend substantially on Aristotle for their clearest articulation. Yet this perspective cannot jibe with the role Aquinas ascribes to the theological virtues, and particularly to charity. As he says,

> In morals the form of an act is taken chiefly from the end. The reason for this is that the principle of moral acts is the will, whose object and form, so to speak, are the end. Now the form of an act always follows from a form of the agent. Now it is evident that it is charity which directs the acts of all other virtues to the last end, and which, consequently, also gives the form to all other acts of virtue; and it is precisely in this sense that charity is called the form of the virtues, for these are called virtues in relation to "formed" acts. (IIa IIae, q. 23, a. 8)

If we take Aquinas at his word, no true virtue is possible without charity. Yet, as he specifies, apart from the true virtues formed by charity, there exist semblances of the virtues that have their particular orderings, generally corresponding to the ordering of the true virtues. Indeed, as Yearley points out, these semblances themselves have semblances according as we move closer or further from a given true virtue.

> For instance, acquired virtues are semblances of virtue if we use infused virtues as the standard of measurement. But any specific, acquired virtue will resemble more or less closely the integral form of that virtue. Acquired courage always is a semblance of infused courage and yet a particular instance of

acquired courage will be only a semblance of real acquired courage. Indeed, he [Aquinas] can identify the "same" phenomenon (e.g., giving up one's life for one's country) both as a semblance and as a standard. That identification depends on which criteria of value or sort of explanation he uses and thus on which hierarchies he employs.[15]

This complex pattern helps us begin to see how Aquinas's account of courage can be at once very similar to and yet significantly different from Aristotle's. Like Aristotle, Aquinas assumes that courage (or fortitude) is a mean between inordinate fear and daring.

> It belongs to the virtue of fortitude to remove any obstacle that withdraws the will from following the reason. Now to be withdrawn from something difficult belongs to the notion of fear, which denotes withdrawal from an evil that entails difficulty. Hence fortitude is chiefly about fear of difficult things, which can withdraw the will from following the reason. And it behooves one not only firmly to bear the assault of these difficulties by restraining fear, but also moderately to withstand them, when, to wit, it is necessary to dispel them altogether in order to free oneself therefrom for the future, which seems under the notion of daring. Therefore fortitude is about fear and daring, as curbing fear and moderating daring. (IIa IIae, q. 123, a. 3)

Having already considered the complexities of Aristotle's account of courage, we should not be surprised by this structural similarity. For the meaning of daring and of excessive fear cannot be clear until the practices that correspond to each—or to fortitude itself—have been specified. If Aquinas is good to his word, we should expect that what we should fear and in what we should place our confidence will depend in some way upon charity, which ultimately determines the mean of courage. This turns out to be the case. For according to Aquinas, it is spiritual goods that are truly virtuous people's first concern. Thus hope in God, who promises these goods, cannot but modify our fears about loss of temporal goods. So Yearley comments,

Aquinas never claims that Christ teaches that temporal goods will appear if spiritual goods are sought. He does claim, however, that spiritual goods should be people's major concern, and they should hope (not presume) that temporal goods will appear. The higher perspective of "a view to the final good for the whole of life" allows people to understand the crucial issue of what really ought to be feared. The major fear courage ultimately should deal with is the fear of not possessing fully the spiritual goods virtuous people pursue and manifest, as Christ's teachings on providence both underline and illuminate.[16]

Of course the pursuit of spiritual goods as well as the pursuit of temporal goods depends upon our having life. Hence death is rightly to be feared as well as avoided.

It belongs to the notion of virtue that it should regard something extreme: and the most fearful of all bodily evils is death, since it does away with all bodily goods. Wherefore Augustine says (De Morib. Eccl. XXII) that "the soul is shaken by its fellow body, with fear of toil and pain, lest the body be stricken and harassed with fear of death lest it be done away and destroyed." Therefore the virtue of fortitude is about the fear of dangers of death. (IIa IIae, q. 123, a. 4)

So Aristotle and Aquinas are in agreement that a key locus of courage is our fear of death. Yet we must go on to ask what *kind* of death each thinks we should fear if we are to draw nearer to the thing Aquinas calls fortitude. We might recall, for instance, that Aristotle thought certain deaths, for example, by drowning, could not be undertaken courageously.[17] And of course, for him it is death on the battlefield while fighting for a noble end that best displays courage.

What does Aquinas think? He follows Aristotle's assumption that fortitude has something to do with death in battle, but adds that "a brave man behaves well in face of danger of any other kind of death; especially since man may be in danger of any kind of death on account of virtue: thus may a man not fail to attend on a sick friend through fear of deadly infection, or not refuse to undertake a journey with some godly object in view through fear of shipwreck or robbers" (IIa IIae, q. 123, a. 5).

Quite simply, with these additions and in the texts surrounding them, Aquinas treats fortitude in such a way that its ends are transformed by charity, so that death in battle no longer stands as its paradigm. In this particular text, Aquinas considers death in battle, but he then adds *as equivalents* death while tending to the sick or while undertaking a journey with some godly object. To consider the first, one might ask, what is the noble end of this? And why is it noble? But plainly charity tells us, for charity demands care for the sick and dying, and the risk of one's life in it is courageous, no less than the risk for the common good in battle.

With regard to the second, a "journey with a godly end," where we might face "shipwreck or robbers," Aquinas appears to mean this literally; no doubt the missionary journeys of Paul or the man who journeys from Jerusalem to Jericho in the parable of the good Samaritan echo in the back of his mind as he writes. Yet it is possible to take the notion of journey in a more metaphorical way such that it connects to the journey of the Christian life, which is not only difficult but extended through time. In any case, in a journey (as well as in the tending of the sick) the immediacy and excitement of a pitched battle disappears, and the courage required is quieted. Indeed, Aquinas's "fortitude," while used synonymously with "courage," suggests that what is demanded is a kind of endurance in the face of difficulty, danger, or oppression, a steadfastness of purpose and vision that will not be swayed even by threat of death. Hence, for Aquinas, patience and perseverance are integral to the very meaning of courage. To return to the metaphor, this emphasis connects to Aquinas's settled view that the moral life is a journey to God during which we must learn to endure much.[18] In this, patience and perseverance are key. Again Yearley provides a concise account of Aquinas's position: "Perseverance, with its opposed vices of obstinacy and softness (a too easy yielding to pleasure), concerns the need to adhere to the good sought. Patience concerns the need to overcome the sorrow brought by the inevitable loss of some goods."[19]

Wittgenstein was right, the world of the courageous person is different from that of the coward. This is borne out in Aristotle's account when one considers the vision of the soldier who faces death with indifference since he sees no other good. But it is also true that the world of the courageous Christian is different from the world of the courageous pagan. This is so because of their differing visions of the good that exceeds the good of life itself. These differing visions come to bear, ultimately, on the differing paradigms for courage. For Aristotle, as we have seen, this is death in battle. Yet Aquinas has already introduced additional cases as equivalents, which serves to demote death in battle to one of a number of possible ways to die courageously. As for a new paradigm for Aquinas, it is *martyrdom*. He speaks of it, still, as a kind of death in battle, but of course the battle has been transformed, and the persons fighting it, as is shown by the weapons required in it, such as patience and faith.[20] So Christians are required patiently to persevere in the face of persecution, since they have the confidence that enduring wrong is a gift of charity.

> Now it is evident that in martyrdom man is firmly strengthened in the good of virtue, since he cleaves to faith and justice notwithstanding the threatening danger of death, the imminence of which is moreover due to a kind of particular contest with his persecutors. Hence Cyprian says in a sermon: "The crowd of onlookers wondered to see an unearthly battle, and Christ's servants fighting erect, undaunted in speech, with souls unmoved, and strength divine." Wherefore it is evident that martyrdom is an act of fortitude; for which reason the Church reads in the office of Martyrs: They "became valiant in battle." (IIa IIae, q. 124, a. 2)

The prominence of martyrdom in Aquinas's account of courage confirms that true courage, as opposed to its semblances, is a gift of the Holy Spirit. Thus the patience of Christians is that which displays the joy of being of service to God (IIa IIae, q. 136, a. 3). Such joy is possible because patience is formed by charity. In like manner, courage as a gift of the Spirit protects the martyr from the "dread of dangers" in a distinctive manner:

> The Holy Spirit moves the human mind further (than the steadfastness of normal courage), in order that one may reach the end of any work begun and avoid threatening dan-

gers of any kind. This transcends human nature, for sometimes it does not lie within human power to attain the end of one's work, or to escape evils or dangers, since these sometimes press in upon us to the point of death. But the Holy Spirit achieves this in us when he leads us to eternal life, which is the end of all good works and the escape from all dangers. And he pours into our mind a certain confidence that this will be, refusing to admit the opposing fear.[21]

Put another way, the work of our lives transcends our capacities since it demands that we love and serve God. Yet we receive of the Spirit the strength and courage to persevere in it precisely because we have been given confidence that God will complete God's work in us even if our lives are taken by our enemies.

It follows that the fear of death, around which both Aristotle's and Aquinas's courage takes shape, will actually be a different sort of fear for Christians and pagans. Both fear the loss of the possibility of the various goods that give our lives form and texture. Yet the good that life is for, and therefore the good for which it can be courageously sacrificed, is not for Aquinas the common good of the nation but rather friendship with God. This good, interestingly, is beyond the power of human beings to effect; they must learn to accept it as a gift. Yet this is also the source of their strength, for they trust that God will bring to completion the work he has begun in them even in the face of death itself.

It follows that Christians are freed from the anxiety of having to secure the meaning of their lives in the mode of their death. Indeed, there is considerable anxiety in death in the battlefield, since the courageous warrior must see himself as carrying the life of his nation on his shoulders. He dies for its continued life, but if all die like him, all die in vain. The martyr dies with the hope that her death will strengthen the church, but it is not quite right to say she dies for the church. Rather in her death, she imitates Christ.

This is why the martyr can *receive* her death in a way a warrior cannot. As the warrior dies in the midst of the frenzied whir of battle, he is active as he dies; as Aristotle would have it, he dies displaying his prowess in the "noble deeds of war." The martyr dies precisely because she refuses to act as others have specified. Moreover, precisely as she is able to receive death as a consequence of her life's commitments, her martyrdom, while extraordinary, is not different in kind from the other things she has done or suffered throughout her life. In fact, this is an important final difference between the two paradigms of courage. Courage based on martyrdom is no easier than courage based on heroics in battle; it is, however, more accessible. Heroics in battle require not only extraordinary talents but also extraordinary luck at death; indeed, most of those even who serve in war will die, not in this service, but at home or in hospitals, like most of us. For Aristotle such deaths cannot be courageous, since, as he implies (1115a37), like the water that surrounds the drowning man, their illness has made a mockery of their prowess and they cannot display it at death.

By contrast, the martyr's acceptance of her death as a continuing part of her service to God demonstrates how fortitude can infuse our lives and remain even as we die in our weakness. Martyrs, in effect, have to be ready to lose to their persecutors, dying ingloriously. They can do so only because they recognize that neither their life nor their death carries its own (or anyone else's) weight of meaning; rather, that is carried by the God who supplies it. Unlike the great heroes of war, martyrs can be followed in daily life, for their courage is none other than an extension of the daily courage we need to carry on as faithful servants of God, which courage we receive as a daily gift of the Spirit. Yearley rightly notes that courageous Christians have confidence that God will secure their ultimate future. But, as he goes on to say, this "confidence includes more than just an assurance about what will happen in the future. They [the courageous] also feel assurance about the meaning of those signs that ensure them that the Holy Spirit moves them and that they are participating in the relationship of friendship with God that characterizes charity."[23]

COURAGE: CHRISTIAN OR AMERICAN?

One matter remains unresolved. Earlier in this chapter we noted, with the help of Jean Bethke Elshtain, that civic virtue comes armed. For those of us living in America this is especially true, since we have little common history that is not also a history of war. Moreover, as we in our daily lives become ever more distant from the spiritual goods for which we might live, we begin to hunger for the meaning war can bestow or perhaps even for a shot at dying courageously in battle rather than wasting away in an aging body as we lose control over the physical pleasures that have heretofore diverted us from facing our mortality.

But some will say that is just the point. We in America have lost our moral vision precisely as we have lost our courage to fight for what is right and good. A return to virtue may indeed require a new call to arms, but there is no other way to save the soul of our nation. Moreover, as some Christians might add, not only Aristotle but Aquinas (and many other thoughtful Christians) recognized the duty we all have to fight for the common good. Enthusiastic pacifists may wish to gloss it over, but the fact remains that although Aquinas added to Aristotle's list of courageous deaths some of those that occur elsewhere than on the battlefield, he yet retained it as a genuinely courageous act.

It is no part of our purpose to turn Aquinas into a pacifist. Aquinas was not a pacifist, he was a just warrior.[24] Yet Aristotle was not a just warrior. The relevant consideration, then, is not that both Aristotle and Aquinas thought war was permissible, but rather what sort of view each carried about war and therefore about what kind of behavior within it could be called courageous. In this way we would suggest that for Aquinas the transformation of courage worked by charity cannot but change the meaning of a death on the battlefield.

To return briefly to the relevant passage in Aquinas, he remarks that "the dangers of death which occur in battle come to man directly on account of some good, because, to wit, he is defending the common good *by a just fight*" (IIa IIae, q. 123, a. 5, emphasis added). This is the first important qualification. The noble good that courage necessarily serves (else it is not courage) is not made noble by the fight itself or by the party involved in the fight (that is, my city or my country), but rather by the justice of the fight. There is, for Aquinas, no such freestanding category as the "noble acts of war," even though this evidently figures strongly in Aristotle's articulation of the paradigm of courage. For Aquinas, the nobility of the cause in war must be judged independently of our allegiance to one of the parties; consequently, glamorous deaths in battle fighting for an unjust cause cannot be for him acts of courage. There is no hint of this in Aristotle.

Furthermore, Aquinas goes on in this same passage to speak of a "just fight" as falling into two types, each with an illustration. First, there is courage as displayed in battle within a just war, and second, there is the courage displayed in "private combat," as when a judge rules justly even when this places his life or person in considerable peril. By supposing that both of these "just fights" are equally capable of displaying courage, Aquinas places the violent combat of war in relation to other sorts of (nonviolent) combat. In so doing he effectively reorients the courage displayed in war on the new paradigm, namely martyrdom. Courage in war is not courage because it is particularly glamorous or valiant, nor because it involves the "noble acts of war," nor because it is highly honored in city-states, nor because it provides the warrior a unique chance to display his prowess as he dies—all possible reasons suggested by Aristotle's account, which assumes its paradigmatic status. Rather, courage in battle is courage because in the face of great peril the soldier has persevered in doing what is just—according to a justice now formed by charity.

To sum up the point in a different light, Aquinas offers Christians a courage that will make us patient enough to fight a just war. Indeed, Aristotle's remark that it is unlikely that the truly courageous man will make the very best soldier applies all the more to Aquinas's just warrior, for not only will he know what is at stake in his own death, he will be dogged by the concern that he not kill unjustly. He will not follow the command of his superiors or his country without giving this thought— which means, we think, that precisely as he is courageous according to the courage formed by charity he will be the more likely to subvert the political order as he seeks to serve it by fighting for it.[25] Put ironically, Christian courage will subvert any political order based on courage, that is, upon the courage that derives its intelligibility from the practice of war. That is why Rousseau was right to think that the Christians should be suppressed. Their "acts of courage," even when allegedly in service of the social order, do not sustain it but rather threaten its very foundations.

In reply to his line of argument, it might be suggested that the subversion has already occurred and we are now reaping its benefits with the coming of age of modern representative democracy. The great difference with democracy is that it is a social order that thrives on difference and dissent, and so the peculiar courage of Christians can be tolerated, or even welcomed. Yet this response will not work, for inherent in such an account of the church's relation to democracy is the distinction between the public and private, which cannot but marginalize courage of any sort. Indeed, that distinction is itself the principal agent of the destruction of any coherent account of civic virtue in liberal societies.

Here we return once again to Elshtain's armed civic virtue and so to a form of the earlier suggestion that any virtue is better than none, even if it arms us. For a nonliberal Christian (like Richard John Neuhaus), while the revival of civic virtue may bring only a semblance of courage (and of the other virtues) to social orders like America, a semblance of virtue, as Aquinas himself saw, can teach true virtue. Hence, those formed by the courage necessary to face death well will be more easily led to the fuller account of courage offered by Christians.

This is a powerful suggestion and one reason why we are initially disposed to take those who have fought in war with great seriousness. However, there is no reason—in fact, there is reason to the contrary—to think that it is the job of the Christian churches to shore up virtue's semblances for the sake of the wider society in which they live.[26] They may articulate the connections, but this will remain possible only as they speak clearly of, and clearly live, the true virtues that are formed by charity. This is not just a matter of the division of labor, but of truth, for without true courage the semblance of courage cannot be known as it truly is, namely, a semblance. Moreover, at no time can Christians assume that their articulation of true courage will be received as such in the wider society. Besides showing us the shape of true courage, this is another thing the martyrs have taught us. The martyrs must yet stand as a reminder to us all, and particularly to those American Christians who would revive it, that the spirit of civic virtue can and has killed many Christians, and more Jews, all in the name of the common good.

Notes

1. John Rawls, *A Theory of Justice* (Cambridge, MA: Harvard University Press, 1971).

2. For a more thorough critique of Rawls's project see Michael Sandel, *Liberalism and the Limits of Justice* (Cambridge: Cambridge University Press,

1982) and George Parkin Grant, *English-Speaking Justice* (Notre Dame, IN: University of Notre Dame Press, 1985).

    3. Jean Bethke Elshtain, "Citizenship and Armed Civic Virtue: Some Questions on the Commitment to Public Life," in *Community in America: The Challenge of Habits of the Heart*, ed. Charles H. Reynolds and Ralph Norman (Berkeley: University of California Press, 1988), 50.

    4. Hegel perhaps best understood this as he saw that without war bourgeois life would be a "bog" in which the citizens of the liberal state would lack the means to rise above their own self-interest. For Hegel, without war the state cannot become the embodiment of the universal. For a good exposition of Hegel's views see Michael Gillespie, "Death and Desire: War and Bourgeoisification in the Thought of Hegel," in *Understanding the Political Spirit: Philosophical Investigations from Socrates to Nietzsche* (New Haven: Yale University Press, 1988), 153–79.

    5. Elshtain, "Citizenship and Armed Civic Virtue," 51.

    6. Ibid.

    7. By placing "courage" in quotation marks we mean to suggest that all "courages" are not created equal, nor, for that matter, are any of the virtues. Investigation of the full implications of such a claim is complex, and we have not treated the question with the rigor it deserves. At the least such an investigation would require inquiry concerning how the virtues are individuated or if and how they are unified. As usual, MacIntyre makes some fascinating suggestions about these matters in *After Virtue*. He criticizes Aquinas for trying to provide an exhaustive and consistent classificatory scheme of the virtues because such a scheme betrays the empirical character of much of the knowledge of the virtues. "[We] learn what kind of quality truthfulness or courage is, what its practice amounts to, what obstacles it creates and what it avoids and so on, only in key part by observing its practice in others and in ourselves. And since we have to be educated into the virtues and most of us are incompletely and unevenly educated in them for a good part of our lives, there is necessarily a kind of empirical untidiness in the way that our knowledge of the virtues is ordered, more particularly in respect of how the practice of each relates to the practice of all the others" (178). This problem bedevils not only Aquinas, but also Aristotle, who continued the Platonic assumption of the unity of the virtues, thus committing himself to the corollary that the virtuous person must have all the virtues at once. There certainly seems something right about the insistence on the interrelation of the virtues, since, for example, courage depends to some degree on temperance. Yet as MacIntyre suggests, strong accounts of the unity of the virtues have difficulty accounting for their acquisition over time.

    MacIntyre notes that, because of his insistence on the unity of the virtues, P. T. Geach is led to deny that a devoted Nazi can possess the virtue of courage. MacIntyre resists this because the moral reeducation of the Nazi would not require relearning everything, since he already knows what cowardice in the face of harm amounts to, even if his notion of what harm or danger might involve, and why it should be borne, would need to be transformed by humility and charity.

MacIntyre also rightly notes, however, that an account of the virtues cannot be generated from practices alone. The virtues, for both their identification and their relation, require a narrative that displays what a concrete human life looks like in a community of such lives. Thus we can see the importance of the paradigms through which courage is exemplified.

8. We are using the translation of the *Nicomachean Ethics* by Martin Ostwald (Indianapolis: Bobbs-Merrill, 1962). All references will appear in the text.

9. It is important to see how Aristotle, and later Aquinas, assumes the descriptions of actions are separable from the character of the agent. That certain actions are always wrong is but a way of saying that no virtuous person could ever envision so acting. Accounts of the virtues do not exclude rules of prohibited actions, but they may very well insist as well that rules (laws) against such actions injure the practices of the community necessary for sustaining virtuous people. (See MacIntyre's comments in *After Virtue*, 149–52.) For an important discussion of the relation of these matters to Roman Catholic moral disputes see Martin Rhonheimer, "'Intrinsically Evil Acts' and the Moral Viewpoint: Clarifying a Central Teaching of *Veritatis Splendor*," *Thomist* 58, 1 (1994): 1–39.

10. Aristotle's reflections on Sparta are especially interesting, given his account of courage and its relation to war in the *Ethics*. He observed that the Spartans, because of their skill and training for war, "remained secure as long as they were at war; but they collapsed as soon as they acquired an empire. They did not know how to use the leisure which peace brought; and they had never accustomed themselves to any discipline other and better than that of war." *The Politics of Aristotle*, trans. Ernest Barker (New York: Oxford University Press, 1958), 29 [1271b2–61]. See also Steven White's *Sovereign Virtue: Aristotle on the Relation between Happiness and Prosperity* (Stanford: Stanford University Press, 1992), 219–46. We are indebted to White for helping us see the significance of Aristotle's criticism of Sparta for understanding courage. Had Aristotle pressed these criticisms systematically, letting them inform his account more deeply, we suspect he could have escaped many of the criticisms we attempt to articulate in this chapter.

11. Lee Yearley, *Mencius and Aquinas: Theories of Virtue and Conceptions of Courage* (Albany: State University of New York Press, 1990), 37.

12. Thomas Aquinas, *Summa Theologiae*, IIa IIae, q. 123, aa. 1 and 2. From this point all references to the *Summa* will be included in the text.

13. Yearley, *Mencius and Aquinas*, 18.

14. MacIntyre rightly observes that Aquinas's appropriation of Aristotle involves fitting together the inheritance from heroic cultures with a Christianized culture but also with specifically biblical virtues. "Aquinas in his treatise on the virtues treats them in terms of what had become the conventional scheme of the cardinal virtues (prudence, justice, temperance, courage) and the trio of theological virtues. But what then of, for example, patience? Aquinas quotes the Epistle of St. James: 'Patience has its perfect work' *(S. Th.*, qu. LXI art. 3) and considers whether patience should not therefore be listed as a principal virtue. But then Cicero is quoted against St. James, and it is argued that all the other virtues are contained within the four cardinal virtues. Yet if this is so Aquinas cannot of course mean by the Latin names of the cardinal virtues entirely what Aristotle meant by their Greek equivalents, since one or more of the cardinal virtues must contain within itself both patience and another biblical virtue which Aquinas explicitly acknowledges, namely humility. Yet in the only place in Aristotle's account of the virtues where anything resembling humility is mentioned, it is a vice, and patience is not mentioned at all by Aristotle" *(After Virtue*, 77).

15. Yearley, *Mencius and Aquinas*, 33.

16. Ibid., 129.

17. That Aristotle uses the example of drowning is in itself interesting. One can easily imagine a case in which the courageous person dies in battle by drowning. For example, he is storming the deck of an enemy's ship, slips, and falls to his watery grave. Is this a courageous death? Aristotle provides no analysis, but we could imagine it. In such a death the cause is not the battle itself but rather the water; it is not the thrust of the opponent's sword that finishes the man off but rather the vast and indifferent sea. He therefore does not die fighting but is swallowed by a sea against which his struggling is petty and hopeless. Of course with some imagination we can construct a case where a man drowns while fighting, perhaps with his rival in a choke-hold. If there is a casuistry of the "noble acts of war," it would be interestingly applied here. (For example, how did the two of them happen to get into the water?) If a problem arose it would likely center on the question of whether the man died while displaying his prowess, for, again, who can display prowess against the sea?

18. MacIntyre argues that medieval thinkers did not have the modern conception of history as discontinuous discovery and rediscovery of what history is, but that is in part because medieval thinkers took the basic historical scheme of the Bible to be one within which they could rest assured. On this kind of medieval view the virtues are therefore those qualities that enable human beings to survive evils on their historical journey. See *After Virtue*, 176.

19. Yearley, *Mencius and Aquinas*, 130.

20. The use of the military imagery to apply within the arena of the Christian life is, of course, hardly of Aquinas's invention; it infuses the Bible.

Unfortunately this has been frequently narrowed to refer to "the defense of the faith," which allows for a transference of militarism rather than its transformation. This is plainly refuted in Ephesians 6, where Christians are urged to "take up the whole armor of God," which includes the shoes that "will make you ready to proclaim the gospel of peace." Moreover, Isaiah's oft-repeated hope for a day when the nations "shall beat their swords into plowshares, their spears into pruning hooks" (Isa 2:4) suggests not so much the utter ceasing of a certain kind of activity, but rather its transformation, as evidenced by its changed weaponry, and so too the purposes of those who wield it.

21. Aquinas, IIa IIae, q. 139, a. 1 as quoted in Yearley, *Mencius and Aquinas*, 141.

22. Peter Geach resists R. M. Hare's view that courage is largely a thing of the past on the ground that Hare has assumed, with Plato and Aristotle, that courage had mainly to do with conduct on the battlefield. Quite to the contrary, as Geach asserts, the "ordinary course of the world, even in times of peace, is so ordered that men regularly need some courage; courage to endure, courage to face the worst." As we are alleging in the text, Geach takes the courage of the martyrs to be accessible to us all, and castigates those who would use the term "heroic virtue" as applied traditionally by the church to the martyrs as a reason to suppose "it is not to be expected of ordinary folk." (Understanding "heroic virtue" in this way is, he thinks, a "cunning snare of Hell's Philological Arm.") Accordingly, in an ironic twist, he urges that the answer "to the plea 'I'm no hero' the reply may be made: 'You are a hero, in the Greek sense of the word: a son not just of mortal parents, but of God.'" See *The Virtues* (New York: Cambridge University Press, 1977), 153–54. Yearley, *Mencius and Aquinas*, 141.

23. While we think just warriors are wrong, they might not be—another way of saying that we think the just-war position as articulated by an Augustine or a Paul Ramsey is a significant challenge to our own Christian pacifism and is theological to its core. Just warriors and pacifists within the Christian church must be committed to continued engagements that teach them not only to recognize their differences but also their similarities, similarities that make them far more like one another than the standard realists' accounts of war that rule our contemporary culture and that have taken a firm hold in the church. For a concrete display of how this engagement might go, see Hauerwas and Ramsey's *Speak Up for Just War or Pacifism* (University Park: Pennsylvania State University Press, 1988).

24. Tertullian counsels new believers to abandon military service, not just because of the bloodshed or idolatry that so frequently accompanied it but also because staying in the service as a Christian will mean that "all sorts of quibbling will have to be resorted to in order to avoid offending God, and this

is not allowed [for Christians] even outside of military service" (*On the Crown*, XI).

25. MacIntyre explores how the semblance of virtue can distort and even render impossible living virtuously in his "How to Seem Virtuous without Actually Being So," *Committee of the Centre for the Study of Cultural Values, Occasional Papers* (Lancaster University, England, 1991), 1–20.

12. Humility and Its Moral Epistemological Implications

Lisa A. Fullam

This chapter first appeared in Lisa A. Fullam, *The Virtue of Humility: A Thomistic Apologetic* (New York: Mellen Press, 2009).

What is moral truth, and how is it attained? In this essay, I want to consider moral epistemology in light of the virtue of humility: what effect does humility have on moral knowing? I will address two related questions: first, what does humility do—how does humility work in moral cognition? I will suggest that humility works at the basic, ground level of moral life and also that humility is required for the process of the acquisition of virtue itself. It is a virtue of the acquisition of virtue, a "metavirtue."

Second, I will look at moral knowledge in light of the virtue of humility: once we posit humility as a virtue, how does that influence our conception of moral truth? Because virtues are, at heart, truth claims about human nature, declaring traits of character to be virtues also implicitly redefines our understanding of human nature and also the nature of moral truth, at least as we can comprehend it. I will argue that the virtue of humility implies that moral truth is a personal, communal process of discovery. Each of these aspects will be considered in turn.

HUMILITY: A TWO-TIER VIRTUE

So what is humility? Humility calls us to be people of moral inquisitiveness, which then is played out in particular circumstances. Most basically, humility is the virtue that helps us achieve accurate self-understanding in context. Humility has often been mistaken for self-abasement, especially in Christian tradition. Instead humility should be understood in terms of its general mode of other-centeredness. Humility calls us to look outside ourselves to appreciate the gifts of others, not to denigrate our own gifts.[1] In Thomas's schema, humility brings under the aegis of reason the human passion of hope. Humility generally calls us to minimize our self-focus, contrary to the usual human drive for self-celebration. This is humility simply, or first-order humility, in which the virtue acts on the data of self-knowledge.

But humility works in another way as well. Augustine suggests that an aspect of humility that makes it different from other virtues is the extent to which humility reflects the degree of humility we already possess.[2] In the case of chastity, for example, at least where Thomas's strict division of intellect from appetite is granted, the intellect may feel itself powerfully influenced by the sexual appetite, but the intellect can still recognize unchastity as unchastity, even though one's adherence to the reasonable mean may be imperfect. Since the intellect is distinct from the sex drive, it can direct it to its reasonable end. But humility is different: the appetite for self-aggrandizement affects the intellect in a more direct way than the other appetites.[3] If sexual passion affects the intellect's vision like steamed-up glasses, the appetite that humility regulates affects the intellect's vision like cataracts: it is a problem in the sensory apparatus itself. The data for humility, our self-assessment in particular or in general, reflects our degree of humility to start with, as Augustine knew.

The close connection of the appetite to the intellect calls into question the role of the intellect in moral discernment. It challenges the way we can speak about moral truth, not because of any abstract formulations about the nature of truth, but more simply, because our intellect's grasp of truth is affected by the appetite perfected by humility.

Because humility invites us to recognize and appreciate the gifts of others, including their moral excellences, humility acts as a kind of "metavirtue," a virtue that affects the acquisition of virtue. This function is distinct from first-order, direct humility, because it concerns our perception, not of a particular gift or capacity we possess, but our perception of moral goals in general. This is the level at which humility influences moral knowledge in a personal sense, at the level of the agent pursuing virtue. It's important to keep in mind that humility is not the primary drive that urges us to virtue—that is more mysterious, concerning human goodness rather than the rightness that is the proper turf of moral virtues. Still, without humility, the acquisition of virtue in general is impaired. This seems like a very unhumble claim for humility.

Interestingly, Thomas's consideration of the vice and sin of pride, the vice that opposes humility, also examines that sin at two different levels. These two levels reflect his twofold understanding of sin in general. Venial sin reflects disorder in a particular matter that doesn't affect the supernatural status of the agent, while mortal sin imperils the soul in a more holistic sense. Pride can destroy humility, a specific human capacity, or it can lead to the destruction of the human person in supernatural totality, as a mortal sin. When Thomas bifurcates pride, he divides humility into two roles as well—one being a matter of humility protecting us from disordered attraction to our own perfection, which is pride in its venial form, and one at which humility protects us from pride in the sense of turning away from God, in which form pride can be a venial or a mortal sin:

> Two things are to be observed in sin, conversion to a mutable good, and this is the material part of sin; and aversion from the immutable good, and this gives sin its formal aspect and complement. Now on the part of conversion, there is no reason for pride being the greatest of sins, because uplifting, which pride covets inordinately, is not essentially most incompatible with the good of virtue. But on the part of the aversion, pride has extreme gravity, because in other sins man turns away from God, either through ignorance or through weakness, or through desire for any other good whatever; whereas pride denotes aversion from God simply through being unwilling to be subject to God and His rule....Wherefore aversion from God and His commandments, which is a consequence as it were in other sins,

belongs to pride by its very nature, for its act is the contempt of God. And since that which belongs to a thing by its nature is always of greater weight than that which belongs to it through something else, it follows that pride is the most grievous of sins by its genus, because it exceeds in aversion which is the formal complement of sin. (q. 162, a. 6c)[4]

In its conversive sense, pride entails inordinate attachment to our own aggrandizement specifically, while pride in its aversive sense destroys all virtues. Pride in the sense of tempting us to turn away from God is a more general category than turning toward a specific lesser good: turning away from God is an effect of all sin, because all sin implies disordered attachment to a good other than God. "A sin may destroy a virtue in two ways. In one way by direct contrariety to a virtue, and thus pride does not corrupt every virtue, but only humility….In another way sin destroys a virtue, by making ill use of that virtue: and thus pride destroys every virtue…" (q. 162, a. 2, ad 3). There are two kinds of pride here: pride generically and the specific form of pride. Pride in its specific sense of turning inordinately to our own uplifting is generally a matter of venial sin.[5] Pride in the generic sense of aversion from God can be a matter of mortal or venial sin, and is, in general, mortal.[6]

One virtue, though, defends against pride in both its venial and mortal senses: humility. The opposition of venial pride to humility is evident from the role of humility in calling us to be reasonable in our attachment to our own excellence, but Thomas cites humility in opposition to mortal pride as well, by defining pride in a way that clearly indicates mortal sin.

Pride is opposed to humility. Now humility properly regards the subjection of man to God, as stated above…(q. 161, a. 1, ad 5). The root of pride is found to consist in man not being, in some way, subject to God and his rule. Now it is evident that not to be subject to God is of its very nature a mortal sin, for this consists in turning away from God: and consequently pride is, of its genus, a mortal sin. (q. 162, a. 5c)

One point of clarification: we are saved by grace, not works—how is it that a moral virtue, acquired by practice, is connected to grace, which saves? Pride in its mortal form destroys all infused virtues, and also is a form of block to the infusion of grace, a "thanks but no thanks" to the infusion of the theological virtues that are salvific. The offer of grace is God's initiative, is saving, and cannot be achieved by human effort. However, the cultivation of humility is the preparation of the soul to receive grace, as one would plow and harrow a field before planting.

In summary, when he discusses pride, Thomas sketches one vice in two forms, one that reflects a disordered appetite for our own excellence, which is rectified by the moral virtue of humility, and one form that can lead to the derailing of the agent from the supernatural *telos*, against which destruction the agent has two weapons, grace and a moral virtue: humility. The first form of pride entails a turning to a lesser good, our own excellence, and, while sinful, it does not jeopardize our souls in any fundamental sense—it is a venial sin. The second form of pride is pride as aversion, in which pride serves to cause us to turn away from God. Here pride can be a venial sin, or a mortal sin, depending on the degree of consent of the intellect. Where pride is a mortal sin, it is the greatest sin and root of all sins. Mortal sin, though, is mortal in that it kills the soul: it is the destiny of the agent as a whole that is jeopardized, not the perfection of a particular capacity only.

Thomas had no category at hand to describe what I refer to here as a metavirtue—a virtue that conditions the way we become virtuous. But I would like to suggest that humility works as a metavirtue—a virtue that influences the acquisition of virtue itself, as well as functioning in a direct or first-order sense. Without humility, the impetus by which we acquire virtue at all is stunted—the whole agent's growth in virtue is affected. Thomas's distinction between the destruction of the whole human soul by mortal sin and the imperfection of a particular capacity is analogous (though not identical) to this distinction, and is coherent with Thomas's basic impulse to assert a fundamental ground of a single truth accessible, at least potentially, to diligent reason. Again, according to Thomas, there is no truth that is separable from the ultimate truth in the mind of God, and the human person finds perfection as a whole person only in union with God, which union is the product only of God's grace. But human pride, which, as sin, is human in origin, not divine, blocks that process. Our access to the ultimate truth, and the only truth that saves, is impeded by the vice that is fended off by humility.

Thomas's double vice of pride works at two levels also, two levels that he framed in the language of Christian orthodoxy—indeed, the complexity of Thomas's presentation is due entirely to the Christian theological understanding that grace is pure gift, while sin is ultimately human in origin. Only God can fix mortal sin, but only we can get ourselves into it. Thomas has no other language available to him that encompasses the entire human person—if this level of understanding did not comprise nature and supernature, it would be incomplete.[7]

What happens when we posit humility as a virtue that affects the acquisition of virtue? Most basically, this constitutes the basis of an epistemology with a "hermeneutic of humility." Virtues are anthropological truth claims[8]—the goal is not to perfect our acts, but to become virtuous people, as Aristotle said. Epistemology concerns arguments about truth and justification. Claims regarding justification in an ethics of virtue will be agent-based, not so much questions like "how can I justify this or that moral truth?" but, in line with Aristotle, "by what process(es) may I become a person who recognizes, pursues, and lives in accordance with moral truth?" An epistemological hermeneutic of humility asserts that we see moral truth—moral claims are justified—via the practice of the virtue of humility that calls us to look outside ourselves, to turn our moral attention to the virtues at work in the world—to, as Thomas would say, the gifts of God in others.

MORAL TRUTH WITH A HERMENEUTIC OF HUMILITY

The second question of this discussion concerns the traits of moral truth when the virtue of humility is put into practice. If declaring a trait to be a virtue is a kind of truth claim, then the opposite process is at work as well: accepting a trait as a virtue means that we accept it as a reflection of moral truth—our notion of moral truth itself is revealed and constructed by accepting a virtue as a moral truth claim. This is a familiar process: if I make the unexceptionable claim that Eric Clapton is a great guitarist then I am not just making a statement about Clapton, but also about the parameters for being a great guitarist—that, for example, it is not necessary to limit oneself to a classical repertoire to be considered great, nor is it true that only acoustic guitar counts.

I defined humility as accurate self-assessment in context, emphasizing other-centeredness as mode. But if other-centeredness is the path to this virtue, the path to moral truth, then clearly humility implies that moral truth is pursued in community with others. If virtues are qualities of persons, not acts, then we look for humility as a quality of a whole life, not an isolated incident in a person's life: moral truth thus becomes personal. If humility is a continual interplay of the appetite for self-aggrandizement and the intellect's self-assessment, an interplay in which the two factors are interdetermining in a closer way than is the case with other virtues, then moral truth becomes intrinsically a process, not a static target. And if virtues are a reflection of human nature, rather than an externally imposed code, we do not create virtues out of whole cloth; rather, we discover them in the process of our moral development. In sum, moral truth with a "hermeneutic of humility" is a personal, communal process of discovery.

Personal

In virtue ethics generally, moral truth is conceived as personal. When I say that moral truth is personal, I do not mean by this that truth is relative to and answerable only to individual whim, but rather that virtues are not qualities of acts, they are qualities of persons. At the same time, what human beings see of each other is our acts: we cannot see the depth of a particular individual's degree of any given virtue. Acts, in a sense, may be symptoms of virtues: a pattern of acts consistent with a given virtue raises the index of suspicion that a certain virtue is at work, but no act, nor even a collection of acts, is adequate to establish that "so-and-so is humble." One corollary of a hermeneutic of humility is to recognize the limitations on our ability to see through the act to the person.

Thomas held that the moral value of the act is that of the actor's intention, which may or may not coincide with the external act. If I intend to tell a lie, and, because I am misinformed, I accidentally tell the truth, then, morally speaking, I am a liar.

> Now, in a voluntary action, there is a twofold action, viz.,
> the interior action of the will, and the external action: and
> each of these actions has its object. The end is properly the

object of the interior act of the will: while the object of the external action, is that on which the action is brought to bear. Therefore just as the external action takes its species from the object on which it bears: so the interior act of the will takes its species [i.e., it is good or evil] from the end, as from its own proper object. (I IIae, q. 18, a. 6c)

We are morally responsible for external acts only to the extent that we have willed them: "nor have external actions any measure of morality, save insofar as they are voluntary" (loc. cit.). If the morality of the act is not necessarily revealed in the structure of the observed act, then acts alone cannot be described in terms of virtue.[9]

Consider, for example, a virtuous act done for base motives. Ordinarily, almsgiving is morally praiseworthy. But a person giving alms out of a sense of noblesse oblige, or in order to impress onlookers, is not acting out of the virtue of justice, but out of the vice of pride. What appears to be virtuous is not. This is true not only where base motives may be at work, but also in the ordinary course of acquisition of virtues. The relationship between act and person for Thomas is reciprocal: we act out of virtues that we possess, and also we acquire virtues by acting in ways that are consistent with virtue. This also makes observation of acts ambiguous: is a gesture of humility a reflection of the true indwelling of the virtue in the actor, or an attempt to acquire humility by struggling, for this one time at least, to keep pride in check?[10]

Virtue already possessed and virtue desired, then, both lead to virtuous-looking acts. For most people, for most virtues, there is a balance of what is possessed and what is striven for—even a fairly courageous person still feels the tug of fear that tempts to cowardice. But should we be strict about virtue? Should we only consider as truly virtuous the person whose virtue is absolute, where virtue has become "second nature"? Thomas approaches this question in a quantitative way: can we be said to have more or less of a given virtue? His answer is that virtue can be greater or less in two ways, one an objective assessment, one subjective. A virtue is greater if it extends further—if I return a wallet I found on the street containing $100,000, my virtue is greater than when I return a wallet with $10.00 in it. The second way virtues can be greater or lesser, though, is rooted in the agent:

> If however we consider virtue on the part of the subject, it
> may then be greater or less, either in relation to different
> times, or in different men. Because one man is better dis-
> posed than another to attain to the mean of virtue which is
> defined by right reason; and this, on account of either
> greater habituation, or a better natural disposition, or a more
> discerning judgment of reason, or again a greater gift of
> grace, which is given to each one "according to the measure
> of the giving of Christ," as stated in Ephes. iv. 9—And here
> the Stoics erred, for they held that no man should be deemed
> virtuous, unless he were, in the highest degree, disposed to
> virtue. (I IIae, q. 66, a. 1c)

What we see of each other is external acts.[11] We cannot evaluate
from the outside whether an act reflects a virtue possessed, or if it comes
from base motives, or if it is an attempt to cultivate virtue, or some mixture of these. But Thomas tells us here that each person will have a different threshold of virtue, based on circumstance, personality, judgment,
and grace. So while justice is giving to each their due, and this definition of justice fits for all acts that can be described in terms of justice,
the complex interplay of virtue attained and striving-for-virtue-by-
reasonable-act will be different for each person, and for the same person in different circumstances and different times in life.

This is true of virtues in general. But where does humility come
in? First, we need to recognize that our view of others is limited and
imperfect. One direct corollary of humility is a measure of leniency in
evaluating the acts of others. A second contribution of humility is
equally obvious: humility is a virtue, therefore the standard of humility
will be different for each person, and the way that humility is manifested
will also show the distinctive marks of that individual's character. The
flip side of this is also true: those aspects of moral life where each of us
struggles to be virtuous do not necessarily mark us as hopeless
wretches—humility forbids the moral despair that can result from seeing only the excellences of others.

Virtues can manifest themselves in unexpected and nonobvious
ways in different people. But we can go a step further, and see virtues at
work in a paradoxical way in those who appear to be without them.

Consider for example the "whiskey priest" in Graham Greene's *The Power and the Glory*. The man is easy to condemn. He's a drunk, he's a coward. He shows none of the usual traits of proper religious heroism. Martyrs are supposed to sing on the way to the scaffold, not take refuge in alcohol. But where we see in him a measure of courage, a measure of fidelity, in the light of—perhaps because of—the very fear that haunted him, there we have expanded our understanding of what courage and fidelity mean. If we allow ourselves to be surprised by virtues that inhere in the obviously vicious, we learn something about the virtues. And if we see the nidus of true virtue in the acts of those who strive with some small imperfect success against fear, or greed, or whatever vice, we learn something about virtue in its humblest form.

This is achieved by the kind of other-centeredness that humility cultivates. If I see justice only as I know it from my own particular struggles with justice, I don't see other possible opportunities for justice: I have established my own experience as the referent for justice, which limits my capacity to see different ways in which I might be just. My progress in justice is stultified. By the practice of humility, we gain a better knowledge of virtue, and thus can pursue it ourselves in more and varied ways and circumstances. We come to know virtue better.

So do we discount as irrelevant the tales of heroic acts of virtue when we embrace humility? Not at all—but it is important to recognize what those acts mean. Spectacular or heroic acts of virtue are such because they are less ambiguous than ordinary acts: they are less liable to alternative interpretations. Spectacular acts of virtue are gnomonic of the virtues they exemplify, and as such are challenges to each of us to embrace the virtue as well—this is the purpose of tales of moral heroism. For the same reason, humility is most clearly seen in those of great capacities rather than those of modest achievements.[12] Commenting on Jesus' humility, Buthelezi captures this paradox of humility: "Only strong people and those of high moral fiber are capable of humility. Humility involves voluntarily lowering yourself....There is no contradiction between greatness and humility; humility is an attribute of greatness."[13] Virtue is not an act, even a heroic act—it is a quality of character. Virtue, truly, in its most basic and universal form, is ordinary and everyday. Virtue is personal.

Communal

On the face of it, to say that moral truth where humility is a virtue is understood to be communal is an obvious statement: if humility is acquired by the practice of other-centeredness, there must be others involved. Above I argued that the understanding of moral truth as personal was a two-directional phenomenon: it is personal because the locus of virtue is in persons, not acts, but also looking at persons shows us with greater depth and complexity the scope of what the particular virtues could mean. The same thing happens when we look at moral truth as communal because humility demands it. That obvious dimension in which there must be others in our moral communities leads us inevitably to ask: Well, who?

In *Humility: Solidarity of the Humiliated*, Klaus Wengst has traced a history of the virtue of humility in terms of social solidarity. He argues for an understanding of humility as basically a stance of solidarity with the humiliated, an interpretation he finds to be in keeping with Jewish and early Christian sources. In following humility from its classical to its Jewish-to-early-Christian settings, Wengst finds not just a shift in the valuation of humility, but a shift in its meaning.

In the Greco-Roman world, the "humble" included not only slaves, but the vast majority of the population, and represented more or less simple lowliness. In the Hebrew sources, though, we see a change. The history of Israel is hardly a journey "from strength to strength." The humiliations suffered by Israel are not understood as final estrangement from God, but rather are seen in light of God's faithfulness to the downtrodden. The hoped-for messiah will not merely judge impartially, but will be an advocate for the poor. Humility is a social stance of solidarity in light of oppression, which will be recognized and ultimately rewarded by God. The Wisdom literature goes a step further: humility isn't just the condition of the socially or economically humiliated, but is a virtue for those seeking wisdom. "The fear of [the Lord] is instruction in wisdom, and humility (*anawa*) goes before honor" (Prov 15:33).

The Christian Testament continues the Jewish approbation of humility, especially in Jesus' recommendation of the virtue, and in James's paradoxical-sounding assurance to the rich that they, too, can achieve lowliness if they are in solidarity with the poor. Paul, as well, exemplifies the solidarity with the lowly that marks the followers of Jesus.

In the text of I Clement, though, Wengst sees another shift in the understanding of humility:

> The substantive and social dimension of the concept which corresponds to a perception "from below" has completely disappeared. "Humility" is no longer, as in Paul, a condition of the possibility of a community in solidarity, but is made to serve the development and establishment of hierarchical structures. In view of the situation in Corinth Clement adopts a standpoint "from above," namely within the leadership of the community. Over against that, humility becomes an attitude of subservience.[14]

Wengst notes that the cross of Christ, with its powerful message of ultimate solidarity with all humankind but particularly with those who suffer, plays no role in I Clement. Humility has become a virtue that the powerful recommend to the powerless, which keeps them powerless.

Wengst's book provides an important corrective for both those who from power recommend humility to the oppressed (a fundamental abuse of the virtue), and those who would privatize the virtue (a fundamental risk of virtue ethics). Just as you can't be virtuous alone, since an isolated individual would have neither models nor companions with whom to grow in virtue, you can't be humble alone. The central dynamic of humility itself leads to the development of moral communities by challenging us to widen the circles of those who we see as "us," to extend our solidarity not just to those who can give us social standing in return, but to join with those to whom Jesus promised the kingdom of God.

Process of Discovery

The idea that moral truth where humility is a virtue is communal can be understood in a very straightforward way—if we're to be other-centered, there must be others. Similarly, there's a first-order, facile way to understand that moral truth with a hermeneutic of humility is a process of discovery. The obvious way in which this is true is this: agent-centered ethical theories will reflect in their epistemology the qualities of moral agents. Since each of us in our moral development acquires knowledge of moral truth, then coming to know that truth is a process, just as learning mathematics is a process. Since an account of the full array of human virtues constitutes a moral anthropology, the moral truth we come to is not something we create, but something we discover: in other words, in becoming virtuous, we live out the virtues in new and personal ways, but we do not create new virtues.[15] So at the most basic level, moral truth where humility is a virtue is a process of discovery because we ourselves are in process, discovering the virtues as we go. But there's more to say than that.

Virtue ethics is inductive, agent-centered ethics. Therefore, the starting point for all ethical deliberation, and the level at which the truth or falsehood of an ethical point is claimed, is at the level of the agent. Because of this, abstract formulations of ethical norms are true only and only insofar as they are accurate representations of moral rightness lived. The criterion for moral rightness is not conformity with a moral norm, but congruence[16] with virtuous persons. This is from Aristotle: the aim is not merely to do virtuous acts, and not to theorize about virtue, but to become the sort of person who acts virtuously by a kind of second nature.

> Actions, then, are called just and temperate when they are such as the just or temperate man would do; but it is not the man who does these that is just and temperate, but the man who also does them *as* just and temperate men do them....But most people do not do these, but take refuge in theory and think they are becoming philosophers and will become good in this way, behaving somewhat like patients who listen attentively to their doctors, but do none of the things they are ordered to do. As the latter will not be made well in body by such a course of treatment, the former will not be made well in soul by such a course of philosophy. (1105b4–18)

Aristotle does not recommend that we abandon moral theory—the book of the *Nicomachean Ethics* itself belies that interpretation. And abstract formulations do have a function: for one thing they serve to prevent moral atomism, in which every agent or even every act is a law unto itself. Norms, even though they arise from practice, do serve as a guide of our behavior in similar circumstances. But the starting point and the criterion and the goal of virtue is the virtuous person.

So what's a norm? A moral norm is essentially linguistic shorthand for a clade of moral wisdom or experience. In general, we can regard moral norms as either induced from experience, or deduced from undemonstrable general moral principles such as "do good and avoid evil." On the inductive side, moral experience—life lived—yields habits: intellectual reflection on experience yields norms of virtue. But in thinking about moral norms, we cross an important line. In constructing moral norms, we shift, in Thomistic terms, into the realm of the speculative intellect, the part of the intellect with which we ponder truth in itself.

The business of the practical intellect, like the speculative intellect, is truth, but truth ordered to action; the speculative intellect is not ordered to acts. For the speculative intellect to influence action requires that the practical intellect be engaged:

> [I]f a man possess a habit of speculative science, it does not follow that he is inclined to make use of it, but he is made able to consider the truth in those matters of which he has scientific knowledge—that he make use of the knowledge which he has, is due to the motion of his will. Consequently, a virtue which perfects the will, as charity or justice, confers the right use of these speculative habits. (I IIae, q. 57, a. 1c)

Charity is a formal virtue that acts through the other virtues. Justice and the other moral virtues are directed to their ends by the practical intellect's virtue of prudence. Moral virtue requires prudence, but the speculative intellect does not. In essence, the speculative intellect alone—our grasp of the truth alone—does not suffice for us to act in accord with it. The will must also be engaged, and thus the moral virtues under the guidance of the practical intellect.[17]

So when we engage in speculation about moral matters, we are, as Aristotle warned, already a step away from moral life lived. This is where the concept of epistemological humility comes in. Humility concerns accurate self-understanding in context. As we approach our understanding of moral norms with humility, we need to keep in mind exactly what conception of truth is influencing our idea of norms—if we interpret moral norms outside their epistemological context, we violate humility as applied to moral norms. The root of that kind of epistemological hubris can be seen already in Aristotle and Thomas, and it comes from their understanding of the nature of the speculative intellect itself.

According to Aristotle, "the states by virtue of which the soul possesses truth by way of affirmation or denial are five in number, i.e. art, scientific knowledge, practical wisdom, philosophic wisdom and intuitive reason…" (1139b14–17). Intuitive reason is the basic grasp of first principles that cannot be demonstrated; philosophic wisdom is the scientific knowledge of the highest objects: philosophic wisdom ponders the things known by intuitive reason. Scientific knowledge deals with what is necessary and eternal. Art is right reason about things made, that is, its activity affects objects outside the agent. Practical wisdom (which Thomas calls prudence) is "a true and reasoned state of capacity to act with regard to the things that are good or bad for man" (1140b5), or, in Thomas's terms, right reason about things to be done. Practical wisdom affects the actor as a whole because of the effects of acts on the actor— we acquire virtues by our acts, so our reasoned choosing of our acts is a reflexive self-construction in acts. Where art shapes the object formed, prudence shapes the actor. Art and practical wisdom deal with things that are variable, contingent, and particular, not invariable, necessary, and eternal: for example, prudence renders one capable of deliberating well, and "no one deliberates about things that are invariable…" (1140a32).

Thomas draws a stronger distinction than Aristotle between intellectual virtues that concern the variable and those that concern the invariable: in the sed contra of I IIae, q. 57, a. 2, he cites Aristotle: "The Philosopher reckons these three alone as being intellectual virtues, viz., wisdom, science and understanding" (I IIae, q. 57, a. 2).[18] While Aristotle mixes art and practical wisdom with the other intellectual virtues, Thomas separates these two out for special consideration. But the point is similar: art and practical wisdom concern variable things, while the others are concerned with eternal and necessary things. Thomas's shift is to underscore the distinction between the two. Variable and invariable are parallel in Thomas with the particular and the universal, for obvious reasons: what is variable cannot be universal, except insofar as it may be expressed in terms that are themselves universal—that is, by ridding the case of its particulars. Addressing whether prudence is a necessary virtue, an objection is raised that intellectual virtues always tell the truth, while prudence can err.[19] Thomas replies by distinguishing the variable from the invariable, at the level of truth itself:

> As stated in *Ethic.* vi.2, truth is not the same for the practical as for the speculative intellect. Because the truth of the speculative intellect depends on conformity between the intellect and the thing. [sic] And since the intellect cannot be infallibly in conformity with things in contingent matters, but only in necessary matters, therefore no speculative habit about contingent things is an intellectual virtue, but only such as is about necessary things. On the other hand, the truth of the practical intellect depends on conformity with right appetite. This conformity has no place in necessary matters, which are not affected by the human will; but only in contingent matters which can be effected by us, whether they be matters of interior action, or the products of external work. Hence it is only about contingent matters that an intellectual virtue is assigned to the practical intellect, viz., art, as regards things to be made, and prudence, as regards things to be done. (I IIae, q. 57, a. 5, ad 3)

Speculation cannot handle the contingent and particular, because of its requirement of infallible conformity with the thing considered. But we can speculate about the virtues. Justice, for example, as a virtue of human beings, may be an object of contemplation by the speculative intellect exactly because it transcends the particularity of virtues in practice. The virtue of intuitive reason (which Thomas calls understanding) is the virtue of the speculative intellect that would concern itself with morals abstractly conceived. "For it is by the virtue of understanding that we know self-evident principles both in speculative and in practical matters" (I IIae, q. 58, a. 4c).

On the other hand, prudence and art are practical virtues: they are concerned with directing acts, not with the intellectual abstraction about morals. Prudence sets the mean for the moral virtues; prudence navigates the waters between the vices that flank the virtues, but that navigation is geared to act, not to abstraction. For example, prudence does not ponder justice in itself, because justice is not an action. The task of prudence would be to discern what justice requires in a given set of circumstances. In Thomas's terms, prudence goes beyond speculation to command:

> Prudence is *right reason applied to action*, as stated above (a. 2). Hence that which is the chief act of reason in regard to action must needs be the chief act of prudence. Now there are three such acts. The first is *to take counsel*, which belongs to discovery, for counsel is an act of inquiry, as stated above (I IIae, q. 14, a. 1). The second act is *to judge of what one has discovered*, and this is an act of the speculative reason. But the practical reason, which is directed to action, goes further, and its third act is *to command*, which act consists in applying to action the things counseled and judged. (II IIae, q. 47, a. 8c)

Clearly, then, this is not a stance of some kind of polar opposition between the speculative and the practical intellect. This is really a parallel intellectual move to Thomas's distinction between the concupiscible and irascible: the object of the concupiscible is the perceived good itself, while the irascible overcomes obstacles to the attainment of those goods desired. Here, the speculative grasps invariant truth, while the practical intellect is needed in addition to overcome the obstacle posed by the sometimes-disobedient appetite in order that truth become embodied in action.

It is precisely when we move from the abstract to the particular that the complications of the passions arise. We encounter opposition within ourselves, which the practical intellect addresses by ordering the will and the appetites. For Aristotle, on the other hand, the distinction was not that of overcoming opposition, but one of activity versus unmoving invariability: "[i]ntellect itself...moves nothing, but only the intellect which aims at an end and is practical" (1139a36). For Thomas, as for Augustine, there is conflict in the human soul:[20]

Other intellectual virtues can, but prudence cannot, be without moral virtue. The reason for this is that prudence is the right reason about things to be done (and this, not merely in general, but also in particular); about which things actions are. Now right reason demands principles from which reason proceeds to argue. And when reason argues about particular cases, it needs not only universal but also particular principles. As to universal principles of action, man is rightly disposed by the natural understanding of principles, whereby he understands that he should do no evil; or again by some practical science. But this is not enough in order that man may reason aright about particular cases. For it happens sometimes that the aforesaid universal principle, known by means of understanding or science, is destroyed in a particular case by a passion….Consequently, as by the habit of natural understanding or of science, man is made to be rightly disposed in regard to the universal principles of action; so, in order that he be rightly disposed with regard to the particular principles of action, viz., the ends, he needs to be perfected by certain habits, whereby it becomes connatural, as it were, to man to judge aright to the end. This is done by moral virtue. (I IIae, q. 58, a. 5c)

The question of epistemological humility regarding moral norms is a question of keeping straight which context of truth we are working in when we engage in speculation about moral matters. Intellectual moral speculation may claim an epistemological invariance that the acts of virtuous persons, precisely because they are particular and contingent, cannot. But that eternal flavor of the fruit of moral speculation is illusory when dealing with what is innately temporal. Moral life consists in the fruits of deliberation, where the answers aren't necessary, but contingent. The business of morals is at the level of moral life lived, with the complexities of circumstances (including the complications of not-yet-orderly appetites), that speculation cannot grasp. As Thomas understood it, human life has one end, human happiness. But "the means to the end, in human concerns, far from being fixed, are of manifold variety according to the variety of persons and affairs" (II IIae, q. 47, a. 15c).

The speculative and the practical are not in conflict, as Aristotle and Thomas made clear. Again, Thomas's fundamental hermeneutic is an assertion of the unity of all truth: there can be no opposition between truths, or God, the source and locus of all truth according to Thomas, would be divided. We need not discard moral norms—in fact, we cannot, because of the structure of the relationship between speculative and practical that Thomas delineated. But we fail in epistemological humility when we don't know the proper place of moral norms. Moral norms are abstractions from a living truth: valuable in communicating part of that truth, but not the sum of that truth themselves. Epistemological humility calls us to beware of the temptation to consider moral norms as completely constituting the center of moral life, or the contrary error of seeing them as meaningless. We come, instead, to see them as part of an interpretative process of insight, characterizing the moral growth of human beings. Moral truth itself is not a static—eternal, invariant— state. It is intrinsically a process.

And there is another step to take, when we bring to bear on this process an awareness of the situatedness not just of moral norms, but of human reason itself. Moral norms are a linguistically mediated phenomenon, as is all conscious human apprehension of the world. Humility is about knowing one's place. When we apply humility to our concept of moral norms, we see moral norms in their place in the hermeneutical circle of practice and linguistic abstraction. The vicious extremes around humility in this sense are, on the one hand, to assert moral norms as absolute and possessed of an absolute clarity that transcends interpretation—in other words, we make cognitive idols of them—or, on the other hand, to practice a self-abnegating rejection of any moral norms in favor of complete moral relativism—in other words, cognitive iconoclasm.

An example of an appropriately humble understanding of moral norms may be seen in the work of Thomas Kopfensteiner. He begins by underscoring the linguistic nature of human cognition. Reporting Kuhn's understanding of scientific knowledge, Kopfensteiner writes:

> Our perceptions of the world are not pure and immediate; we
> do not just gaze upon the world, we see it *as* something and not
> another. Our access to the world, then is through language.[21]

Language is a historical and developing phenomenon: to say that moral norms are linguistic is to recognize them as developing and changing through time.

> [A] language is a living reality; words receive new and different meanings, and old meanings are discarded; new contexts arise and give the same word new content. In other terms, with the experience of distanciation we learn that a norm's propositional formulation is always accompanied by a certain cognitive content. Though a norm may be read prescriptively the same, its propositional univocalness is no guarantee for an agreement in the norm's cognitive content. From this perspective, the norm assumes a hypothetical character or an openness to assume new meanings from the effective history of human self-understanding.[22]

But human history is human moral praxis; norms and praxis form, for Kopfensteiner, a hermeneutical spiral: "not only is praxis the goal of the norm, praxis is the foundation for the understanding of the norm. It is the interpretive explication of the norm."[23] In understanding norms, then, Kopfensteiner draws us away from the realm of pure idealized speculation back into the messier and complex history of human moral praxis—life lived. This is not a reversion to act-centered ethics—this is agent-centered ethics.

In his 1997 paper "The Metaphorical Structure of Normativity," Kopfensteiner conceives moral norms in terms of a metaphorical relationship between person and nature, using a semantic interaction theory of metaphor. Nature is not mere facticity; rather, it is "the vehicle of normativity. Nature is a dynamic potential that requires interpretation."[24] So reflection on nature becomes understood in hermeneutical terms: nature itself is ambiguous, and like a reader engaging a text to disclose its meaning, person interprets nature. Moral reasoning, then, "has an active, imaginative and creative role in fashioning human goods in the service of the ideology of human fulfillment."[25] Just as hermeneutics takes the focus away from the text as the source of meaning and shifts it to the interaction between text and reader, so a metaphorical understanding of norms shifts attention away from the norms to the interaction between person and

270 / Lisa A. Fullam

nature: to moral life lived. The "ideology of human fulfillment" that Kopfensteiner mentions may be spoken of in Thomistic terms as happiness—the end of human moral life, and that to which we are drawn most fundamentally by virtue of our nature. This shift in emphasis also changes the nature of the pursuit of moral life: moral reasoning is fundamentally phronetic—we become people of moral deliberation.

How is this humble? First, in the process model of moral epistemology I outlined above, this approach is humble because it keeps norms in their place with respect to the agent: the end of human moral life is human happiness, not the rigid fulfilling of norms. The error of the rich young man in the Synoptic Gospels, after all, wasn't his failure to grasp or fulfill the norms of the Law; his mistake was to fail to recognize that the locus of human happiness was to be found in a person, Jesus, and in his relationship to him, or discipleship. So he held on to his possessions and lost his soul. Second, Kopfensteiner's approach is humble in that it fulfills other characteristics of humility: it builds communities, and cultivates a morally attentive other-centeredness. Where moral norms are understood as absolute or uninterpreted, those who break the rules are wrong, benighted, sinful, or whatever dismissive term might be chosen. With a hermeneutic of humility, we are invited to try to discern human rightness in ways that escaped us before, due to our own circumstances of personality, culture, or situation. We develop a broader notion of the scope of human moral striving, and are taken beyond our own moral horizons in a process of moral inculturation.

Feminist and other liberation theologies hold as axiomatic the inadequacy of the understanding of one group to represent the entirety of humanity. Carol Gilligan's critique of Kohlberg's stages of moral development works along the same lines: Kohlberg's work took a particular group's mode of moral growth as universally true—and universally ideal—for all human beings. On a more individual level, an approach like this helps us avoid one kind of moral blindness: the possibility for moral hubris arises from the mistaken notion that, even though we might not always obey the letter of the law, at least we know all the rules. Just like the rich young man.

Summary

This chapter was intended to explore the ramifications of humility in the context of moral epistemology. First, I explored the virtue of humility as functioning at two discrete levels of moral knowing: first, the first-order or basic level at which we strive for self-understanding in context in any realm of human living; but also in a broader, indirect, second-order way that influences the acquisition of virtue in general. Second, I addressed the ramifications for moral epistemology of the virtue of humility. If humility is a virtue, and we approach morals not just as humble persons, but as persons who conceive moral norms humbly, a basic shift in moral epistemology ensues. Moral truth becomes not a collection of abstract a priori axioms, but rather a personal, communal process of discovery. When we approach morals with a hermeneutic of humility, we strive to become people of discernment and moral creativity. Because of this, we look for virtues in the proper context of human beings living in the world—our moral teachers are people of wisdom who lived virtuous lives, not a set of proscriptions or prescriptions. Moral norms are not empty or meaningless, by any means. They are, however, only correctly understood in the larger context of the ends of the human moral agent wholly. This humbler construction of moral norms also coheres with the contemporary concept of moral norms as the product of human cognition that is theory laden: we aim for a broader scope of our moral vision, but we know that objectivity is impossible for us. We are finite, culturally situated beings. At the same time, we are invited to a moral vision that continually calls us beyond our own limitations of time and place: humility itself, by cultivating other-centeredness, brings us to reject any notion that our own experience is the final word. Humility, calling us to recognize our limits, also calls us beyond them into an ever-widening moral community without limits. To see, as Thomas put it, that which is of God in others.

Notes

1. Thomas Aquinas, *Summa Theologiae*, II IIae, trans. English Dominican Province (Westminster, MD: Christian Classics, 1981). All citations from Thomas are from the II IIae, unless otherwise noted.

2. The distinction of humility from magnanimity is a tricky point in many assessments of humility. I argue in my longer work that humility is distinguished from magnanimity by its mode of other-centeredness. In Thomistic language, mode indicates the general "direction" of a virtue. Temperance, for example, generally requires that we restrain ourselves from overindulgence in some perceived good: its mode is restraint. Courage, on the other hand, is a virtue that encourages us onward against the usual pullback of fear. While some have to restrain their foolish tendency to rush into danger, for most of us the mode of courage is to push us forward, in line with reason. Magnanimity, as I construct it, calls us to strive to achieve great things by appreciating and using well our own gifts, while humility turns our attention outward, to perceive and appreciate the gifts of others. For a more complete explanation, see Lisa A. Fullam, *The Virtue of Humility: A Thomistic Apologetic* (New York: Mellen Press, 2009), chaps. 2, 3.

3. Fullam, *The Virtue of Humility*, 87ff.

4. To recap: as I mentioned before, Thomas does warn against drunkenness in a special way exactly because it disarms the intellect. Even here there is another step interposed: we want to drink, using reason (well or badly), we choose to drink, we become drunk, and the intellect is affected as a result. The impairment of the intellect by alcohol is not caused by lack of rational control over the appetite in the first place, but is its result.

5. Of course, according to Thomas any sin is potentially mortal, as he indicated when he said that even an idle word (which is usually a matter of venial sin) can have mortal consequences.

6. Thomas's distinction between mortal and venial aversive pride concerns the degree to which the will consents to the desire for inordinate exaltation. In speaking of venial pride, Thomas seems to refer more to the temptation to pride than to pride itself. See q. 162, a. 5c.

7. The role of prudence in setting the mean of moral virtues and that of charity in forming the agent as a whole are different phenomena.

8. Because we are social animals, virtues, in perfecting human beings, are conducive to the perfection of human societies. It is arguable, though I will not pursue the concept here, that virtues function in the lives of individuals in a way that is analogous to the function of rights in societies. An articulated doctrine of rights defines a concept of the conditions required for the flourishing of human societies: similarly, an articulated doctrine of virtues is at heart a moral anthropology.

9. The same is true with vice, in Thomas's understanding, but there's a difference. According to Thomas, for an act to be good, every aspect of the act must be in order: we must will a good end, we must act rightly (that is, reasonably), circumstances must not thwart the achievement of the end. If any part of

the act is bad or wrong, then the entire act is, at best, morally excusable (those who, for example, will a good end and reason wrongly are morally excused, but that does not justify the act). But even here, since the intention is unclear even though the act is wrong, the vice of the actor is inaccessible by observation alone.

10. Here the concept of *akrasia*, or incontinence, may also be helpful. The akratic person, while not vicious, is unable consistently to exercise rational control over the appetites, so exhibits behavior that's not in keeping with virtue. Ultimately this reflects a weakness in prudence vis-à-vis the strength of the appetite. See Aristotle, *Nicomachean Ethics*, trans. D. Ross (New York: Oxford University Press, 1980), Book VII, chaps. 1–10. For Thomas's interpretation, see *S.T.* II IIae, q. 156. See also Bonnie Kent, "Aquinas and Weakness of Will," *Philosophy and Phenomenological Research* 75 (July 2007): 70–91.

11. This includes speech-acts, even those in which the agent tries to reveal the motivation for the act.

12. Like the Mac Davis song: "Oh Lord, it's hard to be humble when you're perfect in every way. I can't wait to look in the mirror, 'cause I get better-looking each day. To know me is to love me, I must be a hell of a man. Oh Lord, it's hard to be humble, but I'm doing the best that I can…" (Mac Davis, 1980).

13. Manas Buthelezi, Untitled Meditation, *One World* 110 (1985): 10.

14. Klaus Wengst, *Humility: Solidarity of the Humiliated: The Transformation of an Attitude and Its Social Relevance in Graeco-Roman, Old Testament-Jewish, and Early Christian Tradition* (Philadelphia: Fortress Press, 1988), 57.

15. A new virtue would require a new human capacity that can be perfected. New virtues on a small scale are easily imagined: to be a courteous driver requires the development of roads and vehicles, for example. But the basic act of being considerate, a fundamental virtue of communities, is as old as those communities themselves. Where new cardinal virtues are posited they represent a different moral anthropology: as it were, a different slicing of the cake of human capacity, rather than a claim that a wholly new human capacity was discovered. See, for example, Keenan, "Proposing Cardinal Virtues," *Theological Studies* 56 (Dec. 1995): 709–29; he suggests virtues based on scales or levels of human relationships. A whole set of virtues is intended to represent a complete moral anthropology: suggesting a new cardinal virtue (in an extant system) implies that a basic human capacity has been missed or underrepresented in older models of human nature, not that human nature itself has changed.

16. "Congruence" is used both in its general sense of being agreeable or suitable (Latin *congruo*, agree) and in its geometrical sense of figures that coincide when superimposed: virtue ethics is often critiqued as an inadequate action-guide, though in fact virtuous persons will behave similarly in similar circumstances. Given that human beings are unique, there are no identical cir-

cumstances in agent-centered understandings of ethics. Literary critic William F. Lynch and fundamental theologian David Tracy have explored the concept of the analogical imagination in unpacking this dynamism. William Spohn, in *Go and Do Likewise: Jesus and Virtue Ethics*, explains ongoing growth in discipleship as Christians beginning to "'spot the rhyme' between present experience and the sayings and stories of Jesus....Jesus Christ is the Rosetta Stone that helps them decode experience to recognize whom God is calling them to become" (63).

17. To be precise, the will and the appetites as well must be ordered to reason by prudence in order that the agent act in accord with truth. Strictly, the will is perfected by justice and charity, while temperance and fortitude perfect the concupiscible and irascible faculties.

18. The citation in the English Dominicans' translation of the *Summa* is incorrect: they cite *Ethics* vi.1, in which Aristotle offers reasons for studying the intellectual virtues, and divides the intellect into contemplative and calculative, that is, that which handles the eternal, unchanging, and necessary, and that which handles the contingent and variable. Neither Thomas's statement nor the Dominicans' citation is accurate.

19. The objection concludes, "Therefore it seems that prudence should not be reckoned an intellectual virtue" (I IIae, q. 57, a. 5, obj. 3). This objection and its response seem out of place in a question on the necessity of prudence.

20. Viz,. Paul's Letter to the Romans: "I delight in the law of God in my inmost self, but I see in my members another law at war with the law of my mind, making me captive to the law of sin that dwells in my members. Wretched man that I am!" (Rom 7:22ff.).

21. Thomas Kopfensteiner, "Historical Epistemology and Moral Progress," *Heythrop Journal* 23 (1992): 48.

22. Ibid., 49.

23. Ibid., 50.

24. Thomas Kopfensteiner, "The Metaphorical Structure of Normativity," *Theological Studies* 58 (1997): 337.

25. Ibid., 339.

List of Contributors

Romanus Cessario is professor of systematic theology at St. John's Seminary of the Archdiocese of Boston.

Charles E. Curran is the Elizabeth Scurlock University Professor of Human Values at Southern Methodist University.

Lisa A. Fullam is associate professor of moral theology at the Jesuit School of Theology of Santa Clara University.

Stanley Hauerwas is Gilbert T. Rowe Professor of Theological Ethics at Duke University Divinity School.

Brad J. Kallenberg is associate professor of religious studies at the University of Dayton.

James F. Keenan holds the Founders Professorship in Theology at Boston College.

William F. May is the Cary M. Maguire University Professor of Ethics Emeritus at Southern Methodist University.

Anne Patrick is the William H. Laird Professor of Religion Emerita at Carleton College.

Charles R. Pinches is chair and professor in the department of theology/religious studies at the University of Scranton.

Stephen J. Pope is professor of theology at Boston College.

Jean Porter is the John A. O'Brien Professor of Theology at the University of Notre Dame.

Louke van Wensveen is an independent scholar and ethics consultant in the Netherlands who formerly taught at Loyola Marymount University.

Paul J. Wadell is professor of religious studies at St. Norbert College.